WESTERING

Footways and folkways from Norfolk to the Welsh Coast

LAURENCE MITCHELL

Saraband

Published by Saraband
Digital World Centre, 1 Lowry Plaza
The Quays, Salford, M50 3UB

www.saraband.net

ISBN: 9781913393069
ebook: 9781913393076

Printed and bound in Great Britain by Clays Ltd, Elcograf S.p.A.

1 3 5 7 9 10 8 6 4 2

The author does not imply that any of the places visited during his travels as described in this book are suitable to visit, either on safety or right-of-access grounds. Please check before departing if you decide to investigate for yourself. Neither the author nor the publisher can be held responsible for anyone attempting to recreate all or part of the journeys described here.

For my mother, Joyce

The best line! say cabbage planters – is the shortest line, says Archimedes, which can be drawn from one given point to another.

Laurence Sterne, *The Life and Opinions of Tristram Shandy, Gentleman*

caminante, no hay camino,
se hace camino al andar

wanderer, there is no path
the path is made by walking

Antonio Machado

Contents

Map of the Western segment *(middle to end of the route)*

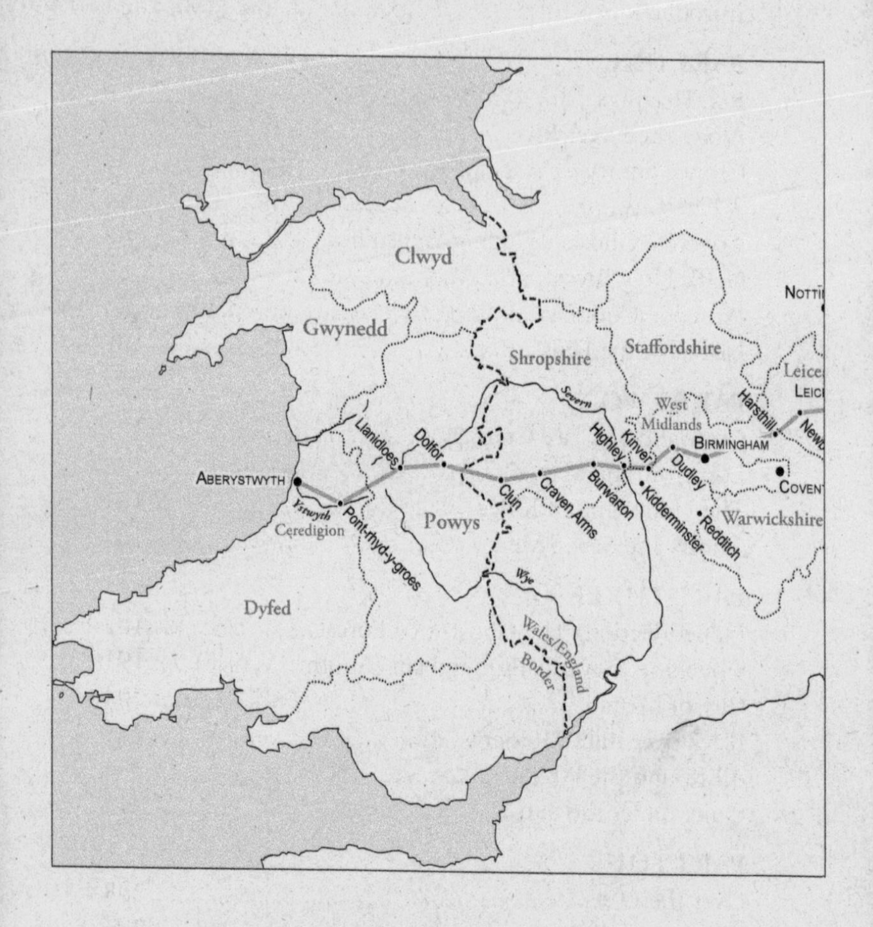

Map of the Eastern segment *(beginning to middle of the route)*

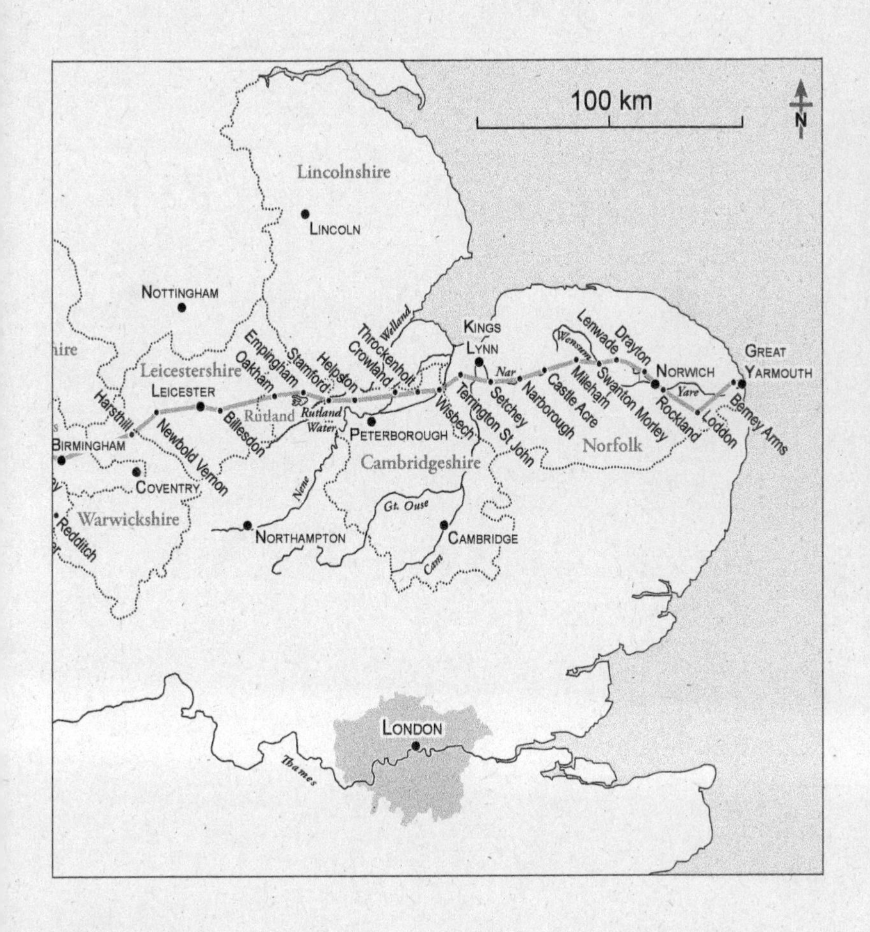

Introduction

Drift

The idea was to drift west, to etch a furrow in the map of England and Wales. My plan was to walk coast to coast across the country with some sort of agenda, to follow a dreamed-up route that started in East Anglia and headed west until it reached the Welsh coast. All of the best walks begin or end at the sea – mine would do both.

I wanted to devise a route that passed through some of the places that held personal resonance for me. Norfolk and the West Midlands were familiar territory, but those regions between and beyond – the Fens, East Midlands, Welsh Marches and Wales itself – I knew less well, although their unfamiliarity gave them their own sort of appeal. For much of the way there was no obvious route to follow so, as in the Machado poem, my path would be made by my walking of it.

As a simple matter of physical geography, most of the nation's major corridors of movement, whether for motor traffic, railways or even long-distance walkers, tend to be oriented north–south. Apart from the well-trodden Coast to Coast Walk in the north of England, there are no long-distance walking routes that run east to west across the centre of the country. Differences in geology, land use, industry, climate and even culture are as pronounced along an east–west axis as they are from south to north. Consequently, this meant that any cross-country walk would be going against the grain of the land and would require an oblique approach to the country's topography. In hindsight, I was fortunate that there were no further barriers to consider – this was a journey that was completed in pre-Covid times, when public transport, accommodation and the close proximity of strangers had yet to become things to worry about.

Across the country: against the grain. Quite literally to begin with – East Anglia, a low-lying region that was largely bypassed by the Industrial Revolution, remains, for the most part, a land of barley, wheat and sugar beet. To the west is the more elevated landscape of the East Midlands – rolling country with a largely pastoral tradition. Next, the West Midlands, the cradle of the Industrial Revolution, the place where the ticking clock of the Anthropocene was first set into motion. Then, after the industrial conurbation of Birmingham and the Black Country, the Midlands gives way to the bucolic borderland of the Welsh Marches before, finally, the rain-soaked hills of Wales itself.

The route was one thing – the walking of it, another. The Scottish-born conservationist John Muir is often credited with saying, 'Of all the paths you take in life, make sure a few of them are dirt.' According to the Sierra Club, who are understandably indignant about any misrepresentation of their founder, the great man never said anything remotely like this and it was merely a misattributed T-shirt slogan that somehow managed to gain credence. Falsely attributed or not, it was nevertheless a dictum that held great appeal. Not only did I want to walk but I wanted to avoid roads as much as possible and instead follow footpaths, bridleways, farm tracks, green lanes and canal tow-paths, whichever led in roughly the right direction.

But footpaths wherever possible: the human imprints of purposeful walking – before the coming of the toll roads, footpaths and lanes barely wide enough for a horse and cart – were the only routes that most country folk ever experienced in their largely geographically constrained lives. Footpaths have a close relationship with human settlement: made for human feet, they were also created and maintained by their movement – between villages, from cottage to church, from village to market town.

Drift

The repeated footfall of hundreds of years' transit has etched thoroughfares into the landscape that still remain in place today: the desire paths of local geography. Every step along an ancient footpath is to make a connection with the past and the people who forged the landscape. Our modern landscape is, after all, as much the result of human impact as it is of colliding continents, the earth-gouging power of ice or the shifting course of rivers.

Today, there are those who almost never use footpaths, who rarely touch ground other than through the medium of concrete or tarmac. In fact, there are also people who rarely walk anywhere. Given the wide availability of the all-you-can-eat buffet that is cut-price foreign travel, it is easier just to lie back and be transported – air miles by plane, road miles by taxi or hire car, cities navigated by e-scooter and Segway. It is probably no coincidence that since the development of mechanised transport our language has become peppered with pejoratives that describe the simple act of putting one foot in front of another: trudge, slog, traipse, tramp, yomp, plod – all words that imply an inherent weariness to the act of walking. Even those words that suggest pleasure come with a hint of laziness – dawdle, amble, saunter, mosey, ramble – and seem to suggest that the time might be better spent doing something else.

I was in no great hurry. The walk I had in mind was not intended to be any sort of severe physical challenge, nor did I feel any compulsion to complete it all in one go. It would be less of a route march, more of a slow westwards drift.

All I needed was a starting point, so I plumped for the coast closest to where I lived. Great Yarmouth, Norfolk's principal coastal town at the mouth of the county's greatest river, seemed to be the natural choice. A one-time fishing port built on a spit of land created by the gradual accretion of shifting sand, Yarmouth itself was a place of drift.

Part One

East Anglia

Chapter 1

Red Herrings

Great Yarmouth, Norfolk

The strangest place in the wide world.
Charles Dickens

The Taoist philosopher Lao Tzu is attributed with saying that 'a journey of a thousand miles begins with a single step'. My own journey, less than half that distance, began with 217 of them: the narrow stone steps that twist up the spiral staircase of Great Yarmouth's Britannia Monument.

I had long wanted to get a gull's-eye view of the Norfolk coast from the top of the tall monument that commemorates Admiral Horatio Nelson, the county's go-to hero. With this in mind, my wife Jackie and I took advantage of the town's annual heritage weekend, when doors that are ordinarily locked are flung open for members of the public. The Britannia Monument was among those offering a rare opportunity for anyone with sufficient lung capacity to climb its vertiginous internal staircase.

We waited at the entrance while a few other visitors made their way in twos and threes up to the viewing platform that sits immediately below the statue of Britannia on her plinth. When our turn came we ascended in the company of a local biker, a man in early middle age who, despite a fierce demeanour prompted by an almost neckless shaved head, Gothic-lettered tattoos and head-to-toe black leather, seemed amicable enough as we climbed the steps together.

By the time we reached the top of the staircase our calf muscles were complaining and our hearts, unaccustomed to steep ascents in normally horizontal Norfolk, were thumping hard. The view, whilst panoramic, was just a little disappointing: a window on a world sub-divided into small squares by the protective wire cage installed to prevent seabirds roosting.

We already knew that Britannia and the caryatids that support her are fibreglass replacements of the Coade stone originals. The Roman goddess's original head now resides at the town's Time and Tide Museum, while the six caryatids have somehow found their way as architectural salvage to the grounds of Ketteringham Hall twenty miles to the west, a country seat that, like many others of its kind, has latterly been repurposed as a wedding venue. But we had underestimated the disheartening effect that the all-encompassing mesh would have on our appreciation of the view, which was akin to that seen by a chicken in a coop, albeit one perched aloft a forty-metre-high Doric column.

From our high viewpoint it was clear that Yarmouth developed on a sand spit, a narrow finger of land squeezed between the North Sea and the River Yare that points accusingly southwards in the direction of Lowestoft. Modern housing and light industry have long filled in the space between the river and the sea, and an industrial estate now surrounds the base of the column, but when the monument was first erected in the second decade of the 19th century, to commemorate Nelson's maritime victories, it stood alone on a fishing beach, isolated from the town to the north.

Looking south, we could see the mouth of the River Yare at Gorleston. Just beyond were the Suffolk border and a cluster of holiday villages before the sprawl of Yarmouth's historic rival, Lowestoft, Britain's most easterly town. Further south still was the prim resort of Southwold, which, like its neighbours Dunwich and Walberswick, was once a mighty port before silting and coastal erosion took their toll. To the east lay the taut curve of the North Sea – a wave-flecked, grey-green expanse that diminished to a hazy vanishing point. A cluster of wind turbines, their blades almost immobile on this calm late-summer day, stood someway offshore at Scroby Sands. Across the water, far beyond the horizon, unseen even from our elevated viewpoint, were the polders and dykes of the Netherlands, a country that once had close economic ties with this easternmost part of England.

Some impulse had me imagining a time before the rising sea levels that followed the last glacial period, a time when a land bridge still connected Britain to Europe. Doggerland, as the territory has become known, now lies beneath the waves but it was a land of plenty just a few thousand years ago, roamed by mammoths, bison and small bands of Mesolithic hunters.

Our biker companion chatted amiably, pointing out landmarks that were familiar to him from his childhood on Cobholm Island, an outlying Yarmouth district that is no longer an island but part of Southtown on the west bank of the River Yare. Gesturing towards the water tower in Caister-on-Sea to the north, he showed us where his uncle used to keep watch during World War II. Great Yarmouth was bombed sporadically by the Luftwaffe throughout the war, its east-coast location making it a convenient dumping ground for surplus bombs on the fuel-short leg back to Germany. The town, he opined, was nothing like it used to be during its heyday. Anyone from Yarmouth over the age of forty-five would probably say much the same. The town's decline over the past few decades has been multi-faceted: the once-thriving fishing industry has collapsed, summer visitors to the town's beaches have decreased dramatically since cheap package holidays in the Mediterranean became available to all and, more recently, the lucrative service industry for the North Sea oil rigs has largely relocated to Aberdeen.

Rotating awkwardly in the confined space of the viewing deck, we turned to gaze inland at the wide silver snake of Breydon Water, the gleaming, bird-rich estuary that the Yare and Bure rivers flow into before the channel narrows past Yarmouth's South Quay on its way to the sea. On a clear day, you might just about make out the spire of Norwich Cathedral twenty miles to the west. Today though, a blue haze limited the view beyond the glimmering mud of the estuary.

Viewed from the ground, the caryatids, suitably draped in classical togas, had appeared to be playing quoits with unseen partners, but a closer look revealed that the circular objects held in their right hands are laurel wreaths. Standing above these fibreglass figures is an aloof Britannia, hedging her bets by offering an olive branch of peace in one hand and a war trident in the other. The Sphinx-like mystery that surrounds this monument is, as any local might tell you, the question of why Britannia faces inland rather than out to sea. The standard explanation is that she looks towards Nelson's birthplace at Burnham Thorpe across the county to the northwest, but a less generous interpretation suggests that her orientation was simply a mistake and that the architect, William Wilkins, horrified by his error, took his own life by throwing himself from the top of the column. This is untrue: Wilkins went on to design many more illustrious monuments in the years that followed – although a careless acrobat really did fall from the top in 1863 after slipping from Britannia's shoulders during a foolhardy display of what now might be called extreme parkour. There was also an earlier casualty when the superintendent of works (and Yarmouth's first librarian), Thomas Sutton, suffered a fatal heart attack whilst inspecting the top of the monument shortly before its completion in 1819. Clearly, the ascent was too much for him. As casual visitors we had been duly warned: the steps were only to be ascended by those without 'heart, lung or mobility problems'.

*

Yarmouth was at its peak as a successful port during the Nelson glory years, although the town was already thriving well before the wars with France and Spain that made the Norfolk-born admiral a household name. Daniel Defoe visited the town almost a century earlier, when the herring industry was at its zenith, and had only words of praise for it. Writing in his 1724 odyssey *A tour thro' the whole island of Great Britain, divided into circuits or journies*, he noted:

> *Yarmouth is an ancient town, much older than Norwich; and at present, tho' not standing on so much ground, yet better built; much more compleat; for number of inhabitants, not much inferior; and for wealth, trade, and advantage of its situation, infinitely superior to Norwich.*

Defoe's contemporary, William Cobbett, was similarly impressed with what he found, writing, 'in all my life I never saw a set of men more worthy of my respect and gratitude'. On his departure from the town he left his 'best wishes for the happiness of all its inhabitants, even the parsons not excepted'. For the fervently anti-cleric Cobbett to include men of the cloth was praise indeed. Charles Dickens, too, who stayed for a short time at Yarmouth's Royal Hotel during 1849 whilst writing his semi-autobiographical and 'favourite child' *David Copperfield*, had sufficient affection for the town for his character Peggotty to declare it as the 'finest place in the universe'. The fictional setting for the Peggotty household, a ramshackle but welcoming upturned boat-hut on the beach, was clearly inspired by what the author witnessed here. Nowadays, there are no fishing boats on the sand, upturned or otherwise, only deckchair merchants, although Peggotty's name has since been immortalised in a road name and a pub on King Street. Peggotty's enthusiasm aside, the long journey from the capital and Yarmouth's relative isolation may have influenced Dickens' own perception of the town, describing it as 'the strangest place in the wide world, one hundred and forty-six miles of hill-less marsh between it and London'.

For centuries the herring was king here, and these 'silver darlings' were the main source of the town's prosperity. Vast quantities were caught offshore and salted, smoked and barrelled on Yarmouth's quays; and every year gangs of Scottish fisher girls would migrate down the coast for the work, their fingers perpetually raw and reeking as they skilfully gutted herrings and tossed them into barrels filled with salt. We had already seen fuzzy black and white photographs of these doughty women in the town's Time and Tide Museum – pale, bonneted faces blurred by movement and slow shutter speeds – and perused the display boards that told of Yarmouth's seafaring past. The museum also has a room devoted to the town's halcyon days as a holiday resort: there are photomontages of happy day-trippers strolling along Marine Parade, children in knitted swimwear with Mister Whippy ice-creams on the beach; collections of saucy McGill postcards, the essential post-war iconography of the English seaside holiday. (Red-faced man to curvaceous young woman in newsagent: 'Do you keep stationery, Miss?' 'No Love – I wriggle a bit.')

But it was herrings – in particular 'red herrings' kippered by salting and smoking – that were the key to the town and, although the bottom has long since dropped out of the fishing industry, there is still the tang of honest commerce about the place. A trace of red herrings, too: the bare brick interior of the Time and Tide Museum, housed in what was once a smokehouse, is still strongly redolent of kippers, an olfactory ghost that serves as an oddly appetising reminder of a prosperous past.

The Scottish herring girls were fishing port nomads who stayed for just a matter of weeks on their migratory route up and down the North Sea coast. In more recent decades, migrants have come to stay for much longer periods, settling down to live, work and raise children. A small Greek community has lived in Yarmouth since the 1940s, but in recent years other European migrants have outnumbered them: citizens of EU member states obliged to tick the 'Other White' box on government census forms – Poles, Romanians, Bulgarians and, most especially, Portuguese.

Their arrival coincided with the downturn in the town's fortunes that accompanied the global recession of 2008–09. Recruited by international human resource agencies that promised much but delivered little, many of the new migrants came to labour in the area's food processing plants – hard, unpleasant, poorly paid work that many of the 'indigenous' locals would not go near. Away from the seafront, the Portuguese presence is now quite visible, the sizeable community having set up its own food supermarkets and cafés in premises otherwise destined to become charity shops or pound stores.

*

After spiralling down the Britannia Monument's staircase, we headed for the seafront. Flitting about in the dunes behind the Pleasure Beach amusement park was a small party of wheatears, freshly landed from breeding grounds to the north. Bulging out into the North Sea like an eight-pint-a-night beer belly, the Norfolk coast is first landfall for many migratory birds fleeing harsher climes to the north and east. Periodically, one of the elegant grey and black birds perched fleetingly on a concrete fence posts to get its bearings, brilliant white rump flashing like a beacon as it eyed the herring gulls that swaggered around like mobsters protecting their patch. Across the road on the wall of Lacons Brewery, a large sign depicting the firm's emblem, a pouncing falcon, talons outstretched for the kill, gave the exhausted new arrivals further cause for anxiety.

This was good timing on our part as the wheatears would not be here for long, just for time enough to refuel before the next leg on their long migration south. These birds had probably spent the summer somewhere in Scandinavia but were now intent on escaping the impending winter that would soon freeze the territory where they raised their young. It was remarkable to think that every single one of their species – wheatears from Greenland, Europe and Siberia, or even those that had bred in Canada and Alaska – were all heading for the same destination: sub-Saharan Africa. For birds from northern Europe, it is a long and dangerous journey; for those flying from Alaska or eastern Siberia, it is one of the longest migrations in the avian world.

A familiar sight on moorland in the north and west of the UK, we could claim wheatears as one of our own: a native breeding species. But where was home to the birds? The wide belt of suitable breeding habitat that stretched across the northern hemisphere from one side of the world map to the other, or their commonly shared African wintering ground? As humans in this modern, mobile age, many of us accustomed to regular movement or, less fortunate, forced to migrate by political or economic circumstances, we might well ask the same question.

We took a short walk down to the beach. Whatever your taste in seaside towns, it is undeniable that Great Yarmouth possesses an outstanding stretch of shoreline – an extensive beach of fine golden sand that might be the envy of many an upmarket resort. The perfect place to build a sandcastle, slump in a deckchair, swim or paddle, Yarmouth is, after all, a town that has risen from a depositional spit; it is a place built *on* sand.

The tide had recently turned and the sand was still moist, darkened to the colour of Demerara sugar. We walked to the tide's edge, a gentle soughing of rippled water that shimmered in the bright September sunshine. I picked up a stone that took my eye – a sea-smoothed brown pebble the size and shape of a half-used bar of soap. The pebble's reassuring mass sat comfortably in my palm. I slipped it into my pocket – a talisman, a marker of place.

Further along South Parade, we passed a line of horse-towed carriages waiting patiently for customers, although trade seemed sluggish. A fortune teller's hut, wedged in the barbed-wire protected wall of Merrivale Model Village, Railway & Gardens, bore the legend: *LENA PETULENGRO, ROMANY PALMIST – Lena has read the hands of many Stars and Celebrities of Radio and T.V. All Have Had The Benefit Of Her Advice. VISIT HER NOW.* But Lena's door and fly-screen curtain were uninvitingly closed; the palmist had gone for lunch.

A little way beyond the entrance to Wellington Pier stands the intricate Victorian wrought-iron framework of the Winter Gardens, the last remaining building of its type in the country. Impressive but now empty and neglected, the structure resembles a giant multi-storey conservatory in need of a paint job: a potential future Eden Project in waiting (this is still one council member's dream), if only the necessary funding could be raised. Although it looks perfectly at home here on the North Sea coast, the building was a blow-in from the southwest. Originally constructed in Torquay, it stood in that resort for twenty-four years before being carefully dismantled and barged around the coast in 1903 to take up residence here alongside Yarmouth's then brand-new Wellington Pier.

Across the road from the Winter Gardens, the Windmill Theatre has a facsimile set of sails attached to its façade in impersonation of the Moulin Rouge in Paris, although it is doubtful if the floor show here was ever quite as racy as its French equivalent. Back in the 1950s, this building – which started life as The Gem, the country's first electric picture house – hosted George Formby summer residencies. The Norfolk coast and the nearby Broads had become a second home for Formby in his twilight years when, rather than old-fashioned variety, public taste was starting to demand a more exciting, rock n' roll flavour for its entertainment. But the entertainer and his ukulele always had a loyal following here on the Norfolk coast, where tastes were more down to earth. It did not take much imagination to turn the clock back to Yarmouth's heyday and picture a grinning, Brylcreemed Formby strolling along this very same seafront in pullover and baggy flannels as he dreamed up double-entendres in the briny air.

Much of the Yarmouth that would have been familiar to Formby is still evident: the beach, the town's 'Golden Mile' of amusement arcades, the miniature golf courses and pleasure gardens, the fast food outlets that gift the seafront a pungent cocktail of chip fat and fried onions (with notes of biodegraded phytoplankton from the beach and horse shit from the pony-drawn landaus). Such attributes are not as popular as they once were, but the town's latter-day decline is the familiar story of many English seaside resorts in the late 20th century. The beach is still as pristine as ever, but a number of the town's once-flourishing entertainment palaces now lie empty and abandoned. The Empire was one such place, a former theatre that lacked both audience and, until recently, a full complement of letters above its art nouveau doorway, its former terracotta cladding stripped and once-proud colonial name reduced by weathering and gravity to read 'EMPI'. Although touted by some as an ideal venue for a future art gallery, it still stands empty and unloved.

Away from the seafront, opposite the marketplace, another of the town's institutions was open to the public for the heritage weekend. The Great Yarmouth Fishermen's Hospital, a cosy quadrangle of terraced cottages arranged around a gravelled courtyard, is not a hospital in the modern sense but an historic set of almshouses. Standing above the cottages' central entrance is a cupola with a statue of St Peter, the patron saint of fishermen.

The saint, naked but for a fisherman's hat and a fold of robe, gazes towards the market place, stroking his beard absent-mindedly as if contemplating the day's catch on sale at the fish stalls. An eroded stone plaque above the doorway announces in lapidary copper script: *An Hospital For Decayed Fishermen founded by The Corporation 1702*. The plaster of the pediment above the doorway bears a sailing vessel on the waves. A later consultation with the appropriate Pevsner guide spoke of a detail that had gone unnoticed: the billowing sails of the ship indicate it to be sailing backwards, an unkind symbol for what such an institution represented – old salts all heading in the wrong direction, sailing slowly towards old age, decrepitude and death.

It was a short walk from the hospital to the Church – Minster, no less – of St Nicholas. Along the way we passed the birthplace of Anna Sewell, author of *Black Beauty*, a neat cottage sequestered away from the hoi polloi and suitably blue-plaqued. Close by, another more run-down looking residence displayed a protest from its window that made up for spelling imprecision with revolutionary zeal: *POLITITIANS ARE CORPORATE SLAGS, INJUSTICE IS NOT AN OPTION ITS A CHOICE*. A smaller, more instructional, sticker with a *V for Vendetta* mask simply urged *DO NOT OBEY*.

St Nicholas' is a post-war Gothic facsimile, albeit a convincing one: a comprehensive 1961 rebuild of the original medieval structure that was bombed and burned out in 1942 to leave only its outer walls and tower. Propped up in the rose beds in front of the entrance was an art installation that required visitors to pass beneath an arch of glittering silver fish – an aluminium foil shoal of herrings, the town's latter-day totem.

The interior of the building shimmered with light, modern stained glass panels filtering beams of sunlight to dapple the pews blue and yellow. In keeping with the church's modernist style, the Stations of the Cross were depicted by quasi-cubist paintings in a Yarmouth setting: Christ on the seafront with a backdrop of trawlers out to sea; a tortured Christ dragging his cross past the NatWest bank; blue-uniformed policemen holding back the crowd in front of Dave's Diner as Christ processed to his fate; a safety-helmeted workman hammering in the nails; Christ on Golgotha attended by herring gulls. It was an engaging juxtaposition of place and time, of ancient and modern, of sacred and profane. If, as claimed, Norfolk's pilgrimage shrine village of Little Walsingham represents 'England's Nazareth' then is there any chance that Great Yarmouth might be similarly repackaged as some sort of east-coast Jerusalem?

We wandered back to the bus station at Market Gates to catch the X1 back to Norwich. Today was just a preamble: all of Norfolk lay ahead to be walked. Not only Norfolk, either, but the entire breadth of the country, all the way west until I reached another coast in Wales.

It seemed a good place to start out from. Great Yarmouth is more or less the most easterly point of Norfolk, a flat, watery county of rivers, marshes and seashore. Bound by the North Sea to the north and east, and to the northwest by the wide bay of The Wash, the county's southern frontier is also liquid – a natural boundary marked by the Waveney and Ouse rivers that delineate the border with Suffolk. The two rivers emerge from the same south Norfolk bog to flow east and west respectively. A chance flood on the road that divides the two sources and the county would effectively become an island. Shape shifting has always been one of Norfolk's characteristics.

It may have been fanciful but the notion of 'island' rang true. There is something of an island mentality to the county where I have spent most of my adult life: a defiant attitude, an inherent stubbornness, an insistence on being a bit different even from its closest neighbours. It is the part of the country that I know best, but there is still a mystery to it. But if Yarmouth, as Dickens asserted, is 'the strangest of places', what can you say about the rest of the county? Norwich, where I live, is, as its road sign suggests, 'a fine city' but before I reached it there were miles of open country to be traversed. Marshes and broads, rivers and reed beds; cornfields and cattle, flat terrain and big skies – here was the Norfolk that kept to the approved script. Was this the Norfolk that would meet expectations?

Chapter 2

Along the Eager River

River Yare, Norfolk

Yare! Yare! Take in the topsail.
William Shakespeare, *The Tempest*

Yare (adj)*:*
1. *(archaic or dialect)* ready; brisk; eager
2. (of a vessel) answering swiftly to the helm; easily handled
Collins English Dictionary

Jackie and I returned to Great Yarmouth by train a few days later. A footpath tucked away behind the railway station and the hangar-like edifice of an Asda supermarket led the way out of town. Passing under a road bridge – the first few metres of the A12, which rumbles south towards Lowestoft and the Suffolk coast – was akin to slipping through some sort of underworld portal, a door that opened out onto the foreshore of Breydon Water and the salt-tang freedom of open water and marshes.

This was the start of the Wherryman's Way, a long-distance footpath that shadows the River Yare all the way to Norwich, thirty-five meandering miles to the west. The name is, of course, a ruse – a fragment of local history hijacked for promotional purposes. It refers to the men who used to crew the flat-bottomed, black-sailed cargo boats that dominated Norfolk's navigable waterways from the late 18th to the early 20th century. The Norfolk wherrymen who passed this way were probably reluctant walkers on the whole, happier to catch the wind and guide their vessels along the water without the need to muddy their boots on the riverbank.

At least the route's name is geographically correct. It is less of a credibility stretch than other long-distance paths in Norfolk, like Boudica's Way, named after the Queen of the Iceni who ventured considerably further than the villages of the Tas Valley south of Norwich, preferring the convenience and speed of a chariot whenever she went on a revenge-raiding tour of Romano-British settlements. Or the Weavers' Way, which stretches between Cromer and Yarmouth, and whose constituent footpaths, cobbled together from none-too-ancient rights of way, create a fictional thoroughfare that never saw much in the way of cloth trade or exchange of loom-weaving gossip. The River Yare, on the other hand, had long been an important trade route that took full advantage of the navigable waterway that connected medieval England's second city with the sea. The long-distance path traces the course of the river closely, following the north shore of the Yare as far as Reedham, where a ferry carries walkers across to the southern bank to loop around the tributary of the River Chet before returning to the Yare for the final stretch into Norwich.

Perhaps it is my landlocked Midlands roots but I have always preferred rivers to the sea. It might be something to do with their perpetual state of flux, their constant mercurial motion. Ever different yet always the same, rivers possess an unerring direction of travel, a beginning and an end. The sea is different; it is always a reminder of containment, of living on an island close to the edge. A geographical prison, of sorts, the view to the horizon inevitably highlighting that which is unreachable.

We followed a raised bank next to the glistening estuary, the traffic din of the town fading rapidly as we entered a silvery world of mud, reed and wading birds. It was a territory where nature found a foothold in unlikely places. The shunting tracks of the railway parallel to the bank were colonised by large clumps of pampas grass, a plant originating in the Argentine pampas that, for some reason, seemed to thrive here. Like Norfolk reed on steroids, the thickets must have arisen from seed escaped from suburban gardens, the singularity of the local ecosystem – temperate climate, modest rainfall, salt air and an onshore breeze – managing to convince the plant's DNA that the Great Yarmouth hinterland was the next-best thing to the Argentinian lowlands.

It was a species not only out of place but out of time. Popular as an architectural garden plant in the 1960s and '70s, the exotic grass has long been out of favour with discerning gardeners, an embarrassment for *Gardeners' Question Time* discussion panels. Partly this is down to changing horticultural fashion – *Cortaderia selloana* is far too large for most city gardens – but there are other factors to consider. Sometime after the peak of its popularity it was revealed in several newspapers that the plant's presence in a garden indicated a household with a liberal sexual outlook; specifically, couples who enjoyed the company of fellow swingers. Whether or not this was anything more than urban myth hardly seemed to matter: having this species in your front garden was a good as throwing your car keys into a stranger's fruit bowl. Innocence was no excuse. These days, people mostly prefer decking and water features in their gardens rather than clumps of supersized South American grass. Besides, now there is the Internet on hand to facilitate an extra-marital dalliance, should it be required.

A wide strip of jetsam delineated the tide-line beneath the bank: fragments of reed, plastic bottles rendered opaque by saltwater, a yellow plastic safety helmet, odd shoes (never a pair); even a golf bag, its clubs and irons long claimed by the estuarine mud. Walking this multihued contour trail of non-compostable debris, a sour waft of something rotten suddenly stung the air: the mouldering carcass of a grey seal, its ribs exposed like a toast rack by scavenging gulls.

Westering

A tattered book of Bible readings sat on the ground next to the path, its pages open on the lesson for February 14th, St Valentine's Day, entitled *Love Is The Power Charge*:

> *This is my commandment. That ye love one another, as I have loved you. Greater love hath no man than this, that a man lay down his life for his friends.*

Although it was several months too late, it seemed a reasonable enough portent. Certainly, it was gentler counsel than the spluttered spray-can fiction that had been daubed on the wall of the bird hide we had just passed, an obscene graffito in which the scribe claimed carnal knowledge of the mother of someone called Dan.

Even in hazy sunshine, Breydon Water was gloomy. It seemed to be the estuary's natural state, whatever the weather was like beyond its shoreline: grey-drab, the colour of damp cardboard. Only wildfowl and waders – dapper shelducks, oystercatchers and redshanks bill-deep in the mud – could be depended upon to liven up the monochrome. And raptors – a kestrel perched on a post flew off grumpily as we approached. The bird, a female, appeared larger than normal, but so did the heron that rose sluggishly from the reed bed ahead of us. Perspective could play tricks in this treeless landscape, where distance was hard to read and near objects sometimes seemed supernaturally large.

We arrived at the tall wind-pump that had been in sight ever since we set out from Yarmouth. Four storeys high, with an aluminium cap atop its brick pepper pot frame, the Lockgate Drainage Mill is an imposing presence in this unremittingly horizontal landscape. Next to the mill, a heap of broken bricks indicated where a marshman's cottage had once stood. Demolished decades before, the rubble was yet to be removed, its value as hardcore outweighed by the inconvenience of moving anything this far from a main road. The windmill door was ajar to reveal rusted gear wheel machinery inside. The interior brickwork was fire-blackened, its floor littered with barn owl pellets jettisoned by the occupant of the wooden box that had been installed in the beams above. Although its predatory presence loomed large, the owl was missing, presumably out hunting voles in the marshes.

The estuary narrowed, then widened once more as we passed the confluence of the Yare and Waveney rivers. Across the estuary, raised on a slope above a large expanse of reeds, were the flint and brick remains of Gariannonum Roman Fort, better known locally as Burgh Castle. A small village of the same name grew up nearby in medieval times, together with the round-towered church that stands half-hidden in a copse of trees just to the north of the fort's ruined walls.

Constructed in the 3rd century AD, the fort was one of several built in southern England as a defence against the threat of Saxon invasion. Whether or not this was the actual Gariannonum of historic record is unclear as there are some historians who consider Caister-on-Sea, to the north of Yarmouth, to be the more probable site. The precise history is uncertain but Burgh Castle is also quite likely to have been the site of Cnobheresburg, where Saint Fursey founded the first Irish monastery in southern England around 630AD. If this is the case then this same strategic mound above the confluence would also have been the scene of an attack in 651AD by Penda of Mercia, a pagan king from the Midlands who did not take kindly to the Christian proselytising that was taking place in the other Anglo-Saxon kingdoms at that time. Soon after this attack, at the Battle of Bulcamp close to Blythburgh, across the county boundary in Suffolk, Penda would defeat and kill Anna, the Anglo-Saxon king, also known as Onna, who had endowed considerable wealth upon the monastery.

History – Roman, Anglo-Saxon, medieval – haunts these marshes even if most physical traces of it have vanished into the oozing mud. The landscape is a palimpsest of sequential occupation, adaption and abandon; only its ghosts could tell the story with any real accuracy. East Anglia, land of the Angles, is but part of the picture. Celtic tribes, Saxons, Vikings all settled here at one time or another – none remained pure, untainted by foreign blood or influence. Modern-day East Anglia is now a long way from the so-called 'Celtic fringe' but it was Celts – eastern Iceni tribes under the leadership of the warrior queen Boudica – who fought fiercely against Roman occupation in East Anglia in the 1st century AD. It would not be until after the Romans fully deserted British shores that Germanic Angles and Saxons would start to pitch up on England's east coast.

The nearby Norfolk coast bears traces of far more ancient occupation. A little way north of Yarmouth stands the village of Happisburgh (pronounced 'Hazeboro', with no trace of 'Happi' in its spoken form), a place best known for its red and white banded lighthouse and for bearing the brunt of ferocious coastal erosion that regularly topples some of its cliff-top properties into the sea. Although television reports of its coastal vulnerability are frequent, the village became newsworthy for a different reason in 2013 when a sediment layer on the beach, newly uncovered by scouring storm tides, exposed fossilised hominid footprints that appeared to date back to the early Pleistocene. At more than 850,000 years old these were the oldest ever to be discovered outside Africa.

The footprints revealed a group of five individuals, most likely a family, who most probably belonged to the species *Homo antecessor* ('Pioneer Man'), a long-extinct hominid hitherto only known from northern Spain. This discovery of the size-8 imprints followed in the wake of a large find of flint tools on the same foreshore that had been dated even earlier, perhaps to almost a million years ago.

At the time when the group unwittingly left their footprints to posterity they would have been walking through the soft mud of a river estuary – fishing, foraging, the children playing, perhaps. The shoreline of the sea would have been some way distant to the north. The climate then was similar to that of the current day but more continental in character, with warmer summers and colder winters; dense forest covered much of the land, and animals like rhino, hippo and mammoth roamed freely. These pioneer *antecessor* folk, who most likely withdrew south again when the weather cooled, eventually become extinct and were replaced by another human species, *Homo heidelbergensis.* These, in turn, were replaced by Neanderthals and, finally, *Homo sapiens.*

It is a challenge to imagine how the world might have looked back then – certainly markedly different from the Hammer Technicolor portrayal in *One Million Years B.C.*, which had cavewoman beauty Raquel Welch ('Loana, the Fair One') wearing full make-up and a tailored doe-skin bikini as she battled with dinosaurs that, prehistorically speaking, should have become extinct sixty-five million years earlier.

Early settlers like those at Happisburgh would have known a landscape unrecognisable on a modern map, one in which Britain was still firmly attached to the Eurasian landmass. At that time, the River Thames, rather than its present, more southerly course, would have flowed north to meet the sea at an estuary close to where modern-day Happisburgh now stands slowly crumbling into the sea. Rivers are fluid by nature, their courses ever-changing over time. Given mankind's relatively short lifespan, and a wilful urge to map his brief world in a recognisable form, it is sometimes easy to overlook this: the *EastEnders* opening credits of the river winding its way through the labyrinthine city are no more than a contemporary screen capture of a slow-shifting fluvial process.

The landmass that is now mainland Britain has been an island proper for only the swiftest of blinks in terms of geological time, a mere eight thousand years or so. A coast-to-coast walk back in the early days of the Holocene would have had to start somewhere in the region of modern-day Vladivostok. Today, the North Sea is still relentlessly chipping away at the East Anglia coastline. Coastlines are invariably difficult to map with any accuracy. In the more rugged north and west of Britain the coast is a fractal convolution of hard rock shaped into countless peninsulas and bays. Here in the east, things are different, and the landscape more fluid – a place where time and tide are continually leaving their imprint on a low, shifting coastline; a coastline that, depending on currents and long-shore drift, could be decreed to be either depositional or erosional. Great Yarmouth, having developed on a sand spit, is the former: a slowly built accretion of new land. Happisburgh though, a village that through constant erosion is slowly being depleted of the territory it once held, is the opposite. Each year, more seaside properties edge closer to their inevitable plunge into the sea. Given the worst-case scenarios of potential sea-level rise concomitant with climate change – one 2050 projection has shown Norwich to be almost on the coast – it might be considered that local coastal erosion is among the least of the environmental problems we might have to face in the coming decades.

Several measures have been taken to curtail the effects of coastal erosion but nothing seems to be wholly effective. Geomorphological processes can be understood but not fully controlled, and despite heated debate and considerable local pressure to do more to help, there seems to be no way of stopping the inexorable process of land returning to the sea. This is a doomed landscape and no place for the middle-aged to grow old or the young to linger. The future is already written; the only way ahead is to attempt to delay it.

Back in the days when I used to teach in northeast Norfolk, I once saw a large lorry lumbering past the school en route for the coast just three miles away. Strapped onto the lorry's flatbed trailer was a single huge block of what looked to be granite. This was just one of many such imported boulders – 'rock armour' in sea-defence parlance – to be deposited on Norfolk beaches in an attempt to buffer the precarious coastline from the ravages of the tide. Like a postmodern glacial erratic, the alien rock had been transported hundreds of miles to be dumped in a place of foreign geology, its movement facilitated by motor transport rather than creeping ice.

*

Six or seven miles from Yarmouth along the Yare's north bank is Berney Arms. A remote waterside pub well known for only being accessible by water or footpath, it is usually reached by first travelling to the pub's dedicated railway halt, a few hundred metres distant. Despite an enviable riverside setting it has always been difficult to make a living from the pub. Its trade is predominantly seasonal and many tenants have come and gone over the years, rarely staying for long.

This was the case today: the door was firmly locked, closed for business. It seemed a lost opportunity as half a dozen Broads cruisers were moored outside on the bank – a boat 'safari' for well-heeled landlubbers who needed the security, or perhaps just the conviviality, of sailing along the Yare in a convoy. (Sailing comes with its own perils, especially for the inexperienced. It is not unknown for inexpert sailors to experience problems in the estuary, where the commonest pitfall is to time the tides wrong and end up stuck ignominiously on a sandbank.)

The pub, like the isolated railway halt that served it, took its name from a 19th-century landowner, Thomas Trench Berney, who agreed to sell his land to the railway company only on the proviso that they would build a station here. The black-tarred windmill that stands a little way beyond the pub, next to the water, shares the landowner's name. Painstakingly restored to pristine condition, it is now in the care of English Heritage. Formerly a mill for grinding clinker, then later put to work as a drainage mill, one of many in this waterlogged landscape, the building was once the focal point for a cement works and a remote cluster of workers' cottages that had their own small chapel. All of these buildings are gone now, and there is little sense of any sort of settlement ever having existed. A solitary wooden bench now stands in front of the mill facing the water, a two-line poem – *VAST SKIES/HOW SMALL I AM* – carved into its slats for anyone who needs reminding of their place in this blunt-edged world of sky and water.

We walked up to the halt to catch the train to Norwich. We were the only passengers on the platform, a piece of raised brickwork with little more than a station sign, an information board and wholly unnecessary 'Exit' markers. Here, isolated in the middle of the marshes, the station seemed as much an architectural folly as anything else.

The train arrived on time. With estuary mud still clinging to our boots, we opened the door to enter a cosy microcosm of humanity. The carriage was three-quarters full; mostly young people speaking on their phones, making plans to meet up with friends for a night out. Our fellow passengers barely looked up as we shut the door behind us and the train slowly gained momentum to glide across the marshes back to Norwich.

*

A week later I returned to Berney Arms to continue along the riverside path. This time Jackie stayed at home and from now on I would be walking alone. The weather was brighter; the sky, swimming pool-blue and sprinkled with high wispy clouds – raw material for imagined simulacra. A marsh harrier was quartering the reed beds beyond the river's south bank as oystercatchers and redshanks raced by in pairs, heading upstream, melancholic flute notes suspended in their wake as they flew past. As I set off walking the path on top of the bank, a heron lifted slowly from a hidden dyke ahead, flapping a few lazy wing strokes before gliding down to an unseen niche somewhere in the vast forest of reeds.

Across the river where the harrier had flown out of sight is the territory known as Haddiscoe Island, although it is not really an island at all. 'The Island' constitutes a few thousand acres of marsh wedged between the Yare and Waveney rivers, the south side of its triangular outline circumscribed by the New Cut channel that links the two rivers. Almost entirely featureless, apart from a ruined windmill, the only detail the OS map could provide was a single loop of a zero-metre contour line within its boundary.

New Cut is a manmade channel that was gouged through the marshes in the 1830s in an attempt to thwart problems with goods coming through Great Yarmouth at the time. Frequent theft, difficulties with the harbour mouth and steep handling charges had all dogged the Norfolk seaport, and so the idea behind the newly created waterway was to create a shortcut for boat traffic that would allow Yarmouth's Suffolk neighbour, Lowestoft, hitherto a beach-launching fishing community, to develop as an alternative port of entry. The scheme was not wholly successful. Its failure was partly down to insufficient financing but more a consequence of the railway that arrived in the region a couple of decades later to largely replace the movement of freight by water and render the scheme a white elephant. Such attempted usurping of Yarmouth's trading crown might help explain why there seems to be no love lost between the two towns. Even today, mention Lowestoft ('Loose-toff' in local parlance) to a Yarmouth man and the chances are he will roll his eyes and change the subject.

Such regional rivalry between Norfolk and Suffolk probably extends even further back in time, to the 6th century when the two counties on either side of the River Waveney were settled by related but different Angle tribes. Civil War loyalties would later divide the two coastal towns too, with Lowestoft supporting King Charles I while Yarmouth took the side of the Parliamentarians. It came as little surprise then that plans formulated in 2008 to create three unitary authorities in Norfolk and Suffolk, with Lowestoft being transferred to the new Norfolk authority, were met with both derision and anger. The provision that Lowestoft could remain part of Suffolk for 'ceremonial purposes' did little to placate objections either, nor did the suggestion of renaming the subsequent coastal conurbation Great Lowestoft. Perhaps it was for the best that Great Lowestoft (or indeed 'Yar-toft') never came to be, given the mutual animosity that still accompanies any Norwich City vs Ipswich Town football match, the local derby a textbook example of Freud's narcissism of small differences in which the worst of enemies are frequently those found closest to hand.

*

The village of Reedham lies poised between the river and the split of the railway line, where one track leads east via Berney Arms to Great Yarmouth, the other shadowing New Cut south-east to Lowestoft. The village, now firmly inland albeit almost at sea level, had once been coastal when the Yare estuary was much longer and wider than it is today. A Roman lighthouse had stood here – fragments of which were said to be incorporated in the village's St John the Baptist Church – but the village is better known these days for its two pubs, brewery and chain ferry, which is the only means of crossing the Yare for the entire distance between Norwich and Great Yarmouth.

A ferry has operated at Reedham since the early 17th century, when it was mostly used to transport horse-drawn carriages from one bank to the other. The modern ferry, no longer hand-operated but still utilising the same chain method, can cope with up to three vehicles at a time and perhaps a dozen pedestrians, although it rarely works to capacity these days. The three-minute trip costs just 50p for a foot passenger, which is good value considering that the only alternative to this crossing is a laborious thirty-mile detour by road.

The river has always been an effective geographical barrier and remains so. It seems curious that even today no bridges span the River Yare anywhere along its entire length between Norwich and the sea, and even odder that parallel communities whose house lights twinkle at each other across the water at night might never get to visit one another.

Over on the south bank, the Wherryman's Way followed a minor road that took me away from the river to reach Nogdam End, a tiny hamlet that sounds as if it should feature in a children's picture book. To the north, further along the gently meandering course of the Yare, the huddle of industrial buildings belonging to the sugar factory at Cantley could be made out in the distance, chimneys rising high above the grazing meadows. The factory is a local landmark, a place of pilgrimage for the juddering lorries that process Norfolk's narrow country lanes for a few weeks each winter when heavy loads of beet are hauled from farm to factory for processing.

A buzzard circled overhead, its high-pitched shriek unexpectedly feeble for such a strapping bird of prey. Once scarce in the east of the country, the raptor is a rare tale of success in a sorry litany of obliterations, vanishings and near extinctions. In recent years buzzards have become common in East Anglia, and sparrowhawks, too, have somehow managed to fight their way back from the brink. It is a different story for other once plentiful species, however. Hen harriers are now rarely seen, and corncrakes – the shy secretive bird of arable fields, the skulking avian back story for the pastoral romances of Thomas Hardy and L.P. Hartley – have been driven away by intensive farming practices, to find refuge only in the furthest reaches of the Hebrides. These birds belonged to an ever-lengthening roll-call of loss in the English countryside: once-typical arable farmland species like tree sparrows, turtle doves and corn buntings are now rarely encountered and, perhaps I am just unlucky, but I can barely remember the last time I saw a little owl.

Heading southwest away from the river I passed a well-positioned bench that bore the maxim *KNOW THAT THERE IS MORE.* Then, a little further on outside St Gregory's Church at Heckingham, I came to another bench that had been chiselled with the words *ANCIENT CHURCH/MARSHES KNOW FAR OLDER SECRETS.*

Round-towered and neatly thatched, St Gregory's stands atop a low, gravestone-studded mound. A Norman-style doorway with the initials of Victorian graffitists carved into its limestone invited entry. The church seemed fully prepared for its congregation: a note in the exercise book next to the organ keyboard asserted that the instrument was tuned and fit for use. A large Bible rested firmly in place on the pulpit, pages open on the *Book of Job, XVI*:

> *The wicked man travaileth with pain all his days and the number of years is hidden to the oppressor.*

If found texts such as this and the prayer book I had chanced upon at Breydon Water were accidental auguries then their dire Old Testament warnings were unclear. Job's tormented monologue meant little to me (even though Alfred, Lord Tennyson considered the book to be 'the greatest poem of ancient and modern times'). I found the foot-polished ledger stones on the floor far more intriguing. Marked with unsentimental yet almost benign-looking skulls, they detailed the demise of various late members of the local Crowe (sometimes spelled 'Crow') family:

> *Here lyeth the body of Mary the daughter of John Crow and Elizabeth his wife. Her time was short, the longer is her rest.*

The date marked was 28th of April 1666, the same year as the last great plague epidemic and London's notable *annus horribilis.* There was an unambiguous corvid connection here: the family name tying in neatly with my entry into that part of the Yare Valley sometimes referred to as Crow Country.

I left the church and traipsed across arable fields towards the small market town of Loddon. The wind had got up by now and a fine miasma of topsoil scoured from the bare ploughed land gritted my mouth and eyes as I approached the town. I arrived to learn that a bus was due to leave for Norwich in half an hour – just enough time to swill away the dust with a pint in The Swan while I waited.

Chapter 3

Crow Country

Yare Valley, Norfolk

Norfolk is the most suspicious county in England.
H.V. Morton, *In Search of England*

I came back to Loddon a few days later, when I went to take a look at the town's parish church, an impressive Perpendicular-style flint edifice set in a leafy graveyard behind the market square. Unusually for East Anglia, Holy Trinity had managed to escape the widespread iconoclasm of the Puritans and the church still retains its painted screens. One of the panels depicts the martyrdom of St William of Norwich, which was less of a real event and more a scapegoating of an unpopular minority in post-Conquest England.

One of Norwich's least proud moments, the incident took place in the year 1144 when the city became the centre of a violent anti-Jewish pogrom, the first recorded accusation of blood libel in the country – the widespread medieval canard that Jews used virgin gentile blood in their rituals. The calamitous event followed the circulation of a rumour that accused the city's Jews of sacrificing a Christian child on the eve of Passover. The story was, of course, false – medieval fake news – but the consequences were terrifyingly all-too real. Norwich's Jews were murdered or driven out, while William, a humble Anglo-Saxon apprentice tanner who may or may not have died in suspicious circumstances, became a saint and the focus of a widespread medieval cult. The panel honours this anti-Semitic falsity by depicting unflinchingly, perhaps even gleefully, the imagined fate of the boy at the hands of the city's Jews: spread-eagled on a wooden frame, tortured, blood being drained from his chest into a bowl. Such animosity towards the Norwich Jewry came swift on the heels of their arrival in the city – the community had only become established with Norman consent nine years earlier in 1135. Further anti-Semitic actions followed and by 1290 all of England's Jews found themselves banished from the country. They remained so for nearly four centuries until Cromwell eventually allowed their return in the 1650s.

I stopped for coffee at Rosy Lee's Tearoom on the high street, a welcoming place run by Caroline, a warm-hearted woman of Indian descent who happens to speak Swahili and be married to an Irishman – Loddon is more cosmopolitan than you might imagine. The small café, gingham-clothed tables and odd chairs squeezed into a single narrow room, was busy with customers. Paintings by local artists adorned the walls, along with a large aerial photograph of the Cantley sugar factory that lay across the water a few miles distant. Having been listed alongside Claridges in a *Sunday Times* feature on the 'nation's 30 best tearooms', the Rosy Lee's is locally famous and Caroline has been interviewed several times in the local press. Yellowing cuttings clipped from local newspapers and pinned on the walls bore witness to this. Accolades or not, Rosy's – rather, Caroline's – place shouted community spirit. A familiar enough story: it sometimes took an outsider to bring a town together and connect its inhabitants. It said as much above the door: *Working for the Community.*

Thwarted by a longstanding closure of the footpath that fed back to the River Yare along the bank of the Chet tributary, I was obliged to leave Loddon by way of the minor road that leads north towards Langley. The hedgerows were heavy with blackberries, the best I had seen for years. Green scatterings of conkers lay beneath horse chestnut trees, some of which had split on impact with the tarmac to reveal their glossy treasure within. Others had been squished on the tarmac like green roadkill. At the Langley crossroads, a sign pointed along a tree-shadowed driveway towards a public school. Another sign unselfconsciously advertised a polo tournament that would soon be taking place in the school's generous grounds. A rack of second-hand books were on sale for charity outside the cottage on the corner – 50p each, honesty box. Unable to resist, I selected an early work by Joseph Conrad, *The Rover*, and clinked the change into the jam jar. The book, which I thumbed through later, was riddled with pencilled underlining and summarising marginalia, and appeared to centre upon a hard-bitten French sailor called Peyrol who 'cared little for people's stares and whispers'. A 'rover of the outer seas; he had grown into a stranger to his native country'. Now here was a found text that I could relate to.

On the approach to Carleton St Peter I passed the entrance to a farm that had four cars in the drive, each one displaying the same personalised number plate with sequential numbering. Such conspicuous affluence came with a price – the overwhelming smell of the place was the stench of pig shit. Although close now to Norwich, in human terms this was an almost deserted countryside: a sparsely inhabited territory of arable land overrun by suicidal pheasants bred for slaughter. Almost all of those who dwell in its hamlets and isolated farm cottages are city commuters – modern industrialised farming employs few farm workers.

Fumbling with refolding my OS map I came across a dog walker who seemed surprised to encounter a fellow human and greeted me with, 'Ah, a man with a map,' as if I were something rare and exotic. I explained that I was trying to work out where the footpath that branched off to the left was supposed to lead. This, he told me, with elaborate and unnecessary precision, but felt the need to add half-jokingly, 'But of course I know all this because I'm a local from the village. Where are you from?'

'Norwich,' I replied, ignoring the urge to add 'well, mainly,' or 'these days, anyway.'

'Norwich? Goodness,' he retorted with mock incredulity. 'Oh, that's far away' – he pointed west – 'in that direction.'

I felt the same sense of rural isolation at the staithe at Claxton where I picked up the route along the River Yare. The riverside path was empty and there were few boats on the water, just the odd out-of-season hire craft on its way to Surlingham Broad, a little further upstream.

Honking geese swirled up from the marshes at Buckenham Fen across the water. This part of the Yare Valley is the 'Crow Country' celebrated in Mark Cocker's eponymous book. Cocker himself resides in Claxton village, moving here with his family years ago, leaving a cosy Norwich terrace for country life in a commuter village. 'Crow country' is certainly apt: rooks and carrion crows were ubiquitous, circling and cawing gutturally overhead, pecking distractedly in the fields and perching companionably in trees like antediluvian lookouts. If another clue were needed, the next village along was called Rockland, a name that almost certainly would have derived from 'Rook-land' in this distinctly rock-less but rook-abundant terrain.

The greatest self-expression of Crow Country lay just across the river, beyond the Norwich to Yarmouth railway line at a gently sloping expanse of farmland known as Buckenham Carrs. In the winter months these fields are the setting for one of the largest rook roosts in the country, something in the order of eighty thousand birds. It is a spectacle I have witnessed several times; a slow build-up as tens of thousands of rooks and a smaller number of jackdaws assemble restlessly in the fields before an eventual, explosive denouement when the birds take off en masse to blacken the dimming sky. Minutes later they are absent, gone to ground (or rather to roost) in a small wood close to the village's redundant St Nicholas' Church. A mere 'murder' of crows seems an inadequate collective noun for such an apocalyptic gathering. Not only is it an astounding sight, it is an astonishing aural experience, too: a cacophony of caws and croaks coalescing to a wild clamour that sounds as if the sky is falling in.

The event is older than the church itself, more ancient than the field and parish boundaries drawn up after the Norman invasion. Remarkable enough to be recorded in the Domesday Book of 1086, the roost has probably been taking place in the same area since the last glacial period. The question is, why specifically here – the crows come from far and wide along the Yare Valley – why this exact spot? The woodland at Buckenham Carrs is presumably as good a location as any, but some powerful instinct has long taken hold in the collective crow-consciousness of the valley for the birds to be somehow aware that, generation after generation, *this* is their palace.

A raised path led away from the river just before Rockland Broad, the water of the broad only partially visible through a tangle of willows and alders. It emerged at a line of moored pleasure boats along a narrow staithe that ended abruptly at a road. This was familiar terrain, a place well mapped in terms of personal geography. I used to come here regularly decades before when I lived nearby. A strong mental image remains of an occasion when I witnessed an aerial battle between a barn owl and a hen harrier on a frosty winter's morning at this very same spot. The birds had tussled for minutes in the sky above the meadow, a primal act of aggression and assertion of power rather than anything merely territorial. I cannot remember which one of them came out of the conflict better – a draw, most probably – but the image of two birds of prey locked in mortal combat in broad daylight is still lodged firmly in my mind even after all these years, as is the precise location.

*

I caught a bus back to Norwich from the village and returned to Rockland a few days later. A windy day, with dark clouds filtering yellow-green sunlight, the leaves of oaks were just starting to burnish gold to signal the advent of autumn. Foraging parties of goldfinches flitted along the hedgerows uttering thin liquid calls in their wake. In the distance, beyond the indigo water of Rockland Broad, black smoke from the chimneys of the Cantley sugar works veered diagonally in the blustering wind, a wind sufficiently strong to shake still-attached, yellowing leaves on the branch – a dry rattle that could only belong to this season.

For someone afflicted with tinnitus, such natural sounds are a balm. The gentle swash of waves on a beach, or the brittle music of wind-rustled leaves, do not make the perpetual white noise in my head disappear but they do mask it in a comforting way. They provide another layer of abstract noise that takes my internal soundscape to a different, healthier place, a place that makes more sense than the incessant hiss of nerve damage. This aside, it has always been a mystery to me why anyone would want to plug themselves into headphones on days like this when the sound of nature is a joy in itself. The thrill is to walk out into the world unencumbered, to be attentive to nature's cries and whispers rather than heed the mood music of a sealed electronic universe.

A footpath along the edge of fields led to a narrow lane alongside Surlingham Wood where there was a sign for Wheatfen Nature Reserve, set up by the naturalist Ted Ellis, who back in the 1960s and '70s was a regular guest on local radio and television. A tall, avuncular figure with an encyclopaedic knowledge of the bugs, birds and plants of his adopted home, Ellis was the Broads and Yare Valley's go-to naturalist. His 1965 book *The Broads*, one of the esteemed New Naturalist series beloved of wildlife enthusiasts with book-squirrelling tendencies, is long out of print but highly collectible. Ellis had lived with his family in a cottage among the woodland and reed beds of Wheatfen, the last remaining tidal marsh in the Yare Valley. It was a Spartan existence; a life devoid of most of the usual domestic comforts that were standard for most households at that time. The cottage had no electricity supply, no central heating or television. Drinking water was drawn from a well. Family meals often included a casserole of coypu, a once-numerous South American fur farm escapee, sometimes referred to as swamp beaver, that grew up to three feet long and caused much harm to the Broads ecosystem until they were finally eradicated in the late 1980s.

I entered Surlingham at a street corner furnished with a wooden bench, a plastic road grit store and a dog-waste bin – all the essentials of modern rural life. At Surlingham Ferry I followed the riverside path, where I came across a bird hide that faced onto a small nature reserve of ponds and reed beds. Mallards dabbled contentedly on the water as a susurration of long-tailed tits fidgeted in the bushes. Above, three buzzards circled separately at different heights, each to its own slow rotating orbit.

I followed the path across a meadow up to a small ruined Norman church. St Saviour's, on a mound above the river, was a photogenic ruin. Roofless, in fact mostly wall-less, with ivy-hung Gothic arches framing fragments of flint wall. It was at the overgrown graveyard where Ted Ellis and his wife Phyllis had chosen to leave the modest plaques that marked their lives. A quiet spot with a view over the curving river, it seemed an ideal choice for a final resting place.

The church had fallen into disuse in the early 18th century when the parish's population declined to the extent that services were moved to its close neighbour of St Mary's, its subsequent ruination accelerated by the purloining of stone and other building materials by parishioners. For a number of reasons that included plague and land exhaustion, depopulation was severe at times in medieval Norfolk despite the county being one of

England's most densely populated regions in this period.

St Mary's was a short walk away, a handsome example of the round-tower churches that Norfolk has in abundance. Surrounded by tall trees, with lichen-spotted gravestones peeking out of a drift of cow parsley, the church and its pastoral setting came close to the notion of a *Midsomer Murders* idyll. Jackie and I come here to walk quite regularly, parking opposite the gate and sometimes buying jars of honey (honesty jar at the gate) from the apiarists at the house next door.

The horse chestnuts that surrounded the churchyard were in the throes of conker climax and the ground was covered with spiky green capsules, some of which had split to reveal the shiny brown nut within. In a bid to create an impromptu bit of autumnal land art, an unseen hand had placed a line of the nuts along each of the three pointers of the signpost. On the ground close to the corner of the churchyard wall sat a flattish, oblong stone of unknown provenance. Probably once used to mount horses, how it came to be here is anyone's guess: surplus masonry material from the church, perhaps, or reclaimed stone from nearby St Saviour's? Or was it one of the glacial erratics that were liberally scattered around the county – large chunks of Scottish or Scandinavian rock dragged south by ice during the last glacial period? Flint aside, any chunk of stone discovered at large in east or central Norfolk is invariably a foreigner, either a legal (surplus church masonry) or illegal (glacially transported) migrant.

I followed the river along a footpath to the next village of Bramerton, where a waterside green held benches with a choice of dedications: the Queen's Silver Jubilee 1977 or the Norfolk Wayfarer's 25th Anniversary 1988. I chose the latter and sat down to phone Jackie. As we spoke, a kingfisher bolted east along the river – a metallic flash of turquoise mere inches above the water.

The Wood's End at Bramerton has been a popular riverside pub for as long as I can remember but it has been recently rebranded and turned into a gastropub. Hitherto more of a beer and burger sort of place, it now traded in 'cask ales' and pan-fried sea bass. At five in the afternoon the pub was closed, although through the window I could make out a solitary barman looking at his mobile phone in the dark – a vignette of isolation that brought to mind an Edward Hopper painting. Standing next to the newly installed decking, adrift amongst a flotilla of pine trestle tables, was a life-size figure of local hero Billy Bluelight. This was the pseudonym of a Norwich man, William Cullum, who, dressed in shorts and cricket cap, once raced against the steam pleasure boats that plied the River Yare in the 1920s. Invariably arriving at the next landing stage just ahead of the boat, he would collect money from delighted passengers and regale them with his familiar rhyme:

'My name is Billy Bluelight. My age is forty-five. I hope to get to Carrow Bridge before the boat arrive.'

His signature rhyme never varied, even though for most of the period that he performed the trick Billy was considerably older than the forty-five years he claimed. It brought to mind something similar I once witnessed in Peru, where a local boy raced the bus that descended from the Macchu Picchu ruins to the valley town of Aguas Calientes. The boy, in league with – or more probably, related to – the driver, used to make himself known to those on board before beating a direct route steeply downhill, cutting through woodland to wave at the bus at each corner on the way to the bottom where he collected handfuls of coins from the amused passengers. Billy Bluelight probably utilised a similar technique, albeit on the Norfolk flat rather than the Andean vertical.

It was at Bramerton that I started to become aware of the dull thrum of Norwich's southern bypass – the road's acoustic shadow ranges further than might be imagined. I followed a bridleway away from the river to Whitlingham, a green woodpecker rising with a cry of alarm on the path in front of me. A green and yellow bird – Norwich City FC colours – an intimation of the city that lay ahead. Then, soon after, a less cheerful sight: the feather and bone remains of a barn owl in a hedgerow. The bird's wings were poised in the tangle of branches as if they were those of a fallen angel. The head was missing, its flesh pecked away and feathers matted, yet what remained was still not devoid of beauty. The owl's fate was hard to read but the sight evoked a visceral response, as if its carcass still held an imprint of pain and distress. Was the bird entwined and unable to escape the prison of the hedgerow? Had it been predated? The only bird powerful enough to do this that I could think of was a peregrine falcon. This was a distinct possibility – there are peregrines in Norwich, breeding to great fanfare (and with twenty-four-hour CCTV coverage) in a purpose-built box strapped to the cathedral spire, just a relatively short flight away.

I passed beneath the rumbling concrete of the city bypass to reach Whitlingham Broad. Unlike the broads of the county's northeast, which were formed by extensive peat digging in medieval times, this is a recently shaped body of water created by gravel extraction. With willows around its edge, reeds in its shallows, and ducks aplenty on its water, it was already maturing nicely.

A few late runners were out pacing the circuit track, but the sun was already starting to set. A pair of Egyptian geese lurked on the grass near the car park, tentatively hoping for scraps of bread. The city was close now, its skyline visible beyond the silhouetted electricity pylons in the distance to the west.

Chapter 4

A Fine City

Norwich

Yes, there it spreads from north to south, with its venerable houses, its numerous gardens, its thrice twelve churches, its mighty mound...

George Borrow, *Lavengro*

I returned to Whitlingham Broad the next day. Dominating the radio news that morning was talk of a UKIP by-election victory in Clacton-on-Sea. Essex is geographically close, virtually a neighbour just two counties away to the south, yet it seems another world in many ways. The consensus of opinion has always been that if UKIP has any sort of English spiritual heartland then that is probably Essex. Relatively prosperous, with a sizeable proportion of aspirational, working-class East End incomers, the county, although not geographically central is, in cultural and socio-economic terms, quintessential Middle England: a constituency that sports Union Jack underpants with pride. That, at least, is its self-image. Like Norfolk, the county is often unfairly maligned by outsiders, albeit with the casual sexism of 'Essex Girl' jokes rather than the 'Normal for Norfolk' tropes that besmirch the reputation of the county where I live.

If Essex is viewed as cavalier, mouthy and superficial, a place obsessed with money and fake tans, Norfolk is, in some eyes, insular and replete with simpletons. Although the county is often portrayed in the broadsheets as some sort of rural idyll – an old-fashioned Eden untroubled by hectic modern life, a convenient weekend getaway for up-from-Londoners – Norfolk shares with Cornwall the dubious honour of being the go-to county for jokes about incest and bumpkin ineptitude. Even the Norwich-based *Eastern Daily Press* sometimes inadvertently helps promote this stereotypical view of the county. A recent headline, without a hint of self-consciousness, read:

> *MAN DENIES SEX OFFENCES AGAINST CHICKENS AND STEALING UNDERWEAR IN HUNSTANTON*

There were decisions to be made. I knew Norwich well. Although born and brought up in the Midlands, I had lived in the city for decades, having moved there to attend university and never really managing to escape its gravity afterwards. This is nothing unusual: the city is full of what might be termed UEA refugees – one-time students, like me, who have neglected to move on and have long outstayed their welcome.

Norwich is undoubtedly the place in the world that I am now most familiar with, yet, while I had walked almost everywhere in the city at one time or another, I had never actually walked all the way *through* the city before. So, should I trace the River Wensum as it meanders through the centre? Should I follow the curve of what remains of the city walls, veering slightly south or north of the centre? Or should I, instead, beat a direct route through its heart, as straight and true as a route-marching Roman might? In the end I plumped for a compromise, forgoing the use of a map to depend on my internal satnav, which I considered, after many years in the city, reliable enough.

Jackie dropped me off at the Whitlingham Broad car park and I followed the path along the broad's southern edge. Across the water, standing proud on a leafy ridge, was the distinctive silhouette of a folly that marked one the city's highest points east of the centre. Taylor's Folly in Thorpe Hamlet is, like most follies, open to interpretation as to its original intended use. Ostensibly built as a grand Victorian chess pavilion by a successful Norwich lawyer, there were suggestions that it may also have been used as a spy tower for spotting incoming Inland Revenue boats. Jackie and I had once driven up to take a look and had been welcomed with an earful from a local woman, a vitriolic Neighbourhood Watch vigilante, who strongly objected to us parking anywhere in the vicinity of her bungalow (if we disobeyed, she threatened, photos would be taken, the police informed). Crestfallen from the unpleasantness of this encounter, we subsequently parked elsewhere and as soon as we showed our faces at the gate that led to the pavilion we chanced upon a friendly, knowledgeable man who offered to give us a tour. A plaque beside the tower entrance bore the inscription: *HM Queen Kapiolani ascended this tower 6 June 1887.* Queen Kapi'olani, who was touring England on the occasion of Queen Victoria's golden jubilee, was the Dowager Queen of Hawaii, which at the time was still an independent island monarchy, yet to become the 50th American state. The queen was a keen chess-player and so, along with its owner and builder (and author of the 1889-published *Chess Skirmishes*) John Odin Howard Taylor, she mounted the spiral staircase to view the chess room at the top of the tower. History does not record whether or not the pair played a game. Our guide suggested that as well as chess pavilion the tower may also have served as a convenient hideaway for Taylor, as his wife was too rotund to mount the narrow stairs easily. Presumably, Queen Kapi'olani was of slenderer build.

Also on the other side of the river, further to the east in Thorpe St Andrew, stood the site of St Andrew's Hospital, a former 'mental asylum' (as they used to be called) where, decades earlier, I had worked as a ward orderly. The place is now long closed, full of ghosts; part of the site converted to a business park, the rest boarded up with enough unconfirmed warnings about asbestos to keep most urban explorers at bay. An institute built in the early 19th century to provide an asylum for paupers, its treatment regime clung to an unflinching Victorian approach to mental illness right to the very end. At least that was how I remembered it: patients coshed by tranquillizers or bored mindless by vacuous routine and dull occupational therapy sessions. Many inmates should not have been there in the first place and were the victims of circumstance and unenlightened social mores in which an unwanted pregnancy or bout of depression would provide sufficient grounds for admission. The institutionalisation that ensued from long-term incarceration was almost equally as effective on the staff who worked there – an odd miscellany of eccentrics and misfits. I lasted a year.

*

It was at Whitlingham Broad that I finally left the River Yare behind. From here the upper course of the river hugged the southern edge of Norwich before passing west of the city to its source in central Norfolk. Here was a new river to trace, the tributary that is the Wensum, a winding chalk river that meanders in a broad loop through the city before it meets its confluence with the Yare just to the west of Whitlingham Broad.

I followed Whitlingham Lane to the outlying village of Trowse, where a bridge over the river led me to a roundabout on the Norwich ring road. This is a territory replete with memories. One of the exits leads into the site of Colman's, the Norwich mustard firm that also has other interests in the food industry. I recalled an early summer in the city working twelve-hour night shifts on a fruit cordial production line, a period in which real time seemed suspended as most of my waking hours were filled with repetitive tasks of such mind-numbing vacuity that it felt as if I had entered some sort of beatific Zen-like state.

Across the roundabout stands the concrete and glass cube of Norfolk County Council's headquarters, a brutalist edifice of unparalleled ugliness that brings to mind a super-sized storage heater – certainly, there are better-looking multi-storey car parks out there. I had once laboured here too, as a temporary clerk in an open-plan office. It is hard to say which of the two, the Colman's factory or the council office, was worse in terms of the mind-bruising monotony of the work involved – the office perhaps, where the much-scrutinised wall clock seemed to slow down time to a glacial beat, the minute hand appearing to be frozen motionless as I anticipated the next tea break, lunch break, the eventual release of clocking-off time. I was a smoker in those days – if I had not been then I would have probably been obliged to take up the habit purely as a means of coping with the tedium.

The location, the personal history, the genius loci of this traffic-spun city edge always makes me feel as if I am still somehow just marking time whenever I come here. Is it mere coincidence that hidden away across the river and railway tracks of Norwich's southern edgeland, only half a mile away from my time-frozen administrative cell on the fourth floor of County Hall, is the site of Arminghall woodhenge, another timepiece of sorts, which five thousand years earlier had also been diligently observed, albeit for very different and more compelling reasons? Although long reduced by ploughing and erosion to little more than a minor undulation in grazing pasture, the surviving trace of the monument is considered to be of sufficient historical importance to be marked 'henge' in gothic letters on the OS map. This earthwork of late Neolithic or Bronze Age antiquity is now little more than a set of crop marks but, in the past, deep ditches and large timbers, perhaps entire tree trunks, would have delineated its horseshoe form. Orientated on the midwinter sunset, the earthwork probably served as some sort of calendar for ritual and agricultural tasks.

The henge stands close to the confluence of two rivers, the place where the River Tas joins the Yare after gently flowing through south Norfolk. The confluence may well have been important to those who constructed the henge – a de facto sacred spot where water was fortified and shape-shifted. In a relatively flat landscape such as Norfolk, where there are few hills to serve as points of focus, flowing water may have taken on even more significance than elsewhere. It is almost certain that monuments of this kind marked locations – wet places, in particular – that were considered to be of spiritual importance. Water was especially important to the Celtic tribes that occupied the region during the Iron Age. This was once the territory of the Iceni, whose fiery-spirited leader Boudica took brutal vengeance on the Roman invaders that abused her daughters and stole her land in the first century AD. But the Arminghall henge had been here long before the Iceni arrived in the region. Even then it was ancient, a millennium older than the better-known Seahenge, which was excavated on the northwest coast of Norfolk in 1999 and dated with uncanny accuracy to the spring or early summer of 2049BC.

All that remains today of the Arminghall henge is a vague bump and dip in the turf but five millennia earlier this was a focus of power, a place of knowledge, ritual and observation. Now that power has been reduced to a ghost of landscape – a shadow of the past in a soggy field grazed by traveller horses and overlaid with the industrial hardware of an electrical substation. Most of the motorists that speed by on the southern bypass, averting their eyes from the unsightly pylons and transformers, do not give these waterlogged fields a second glance.

I headed uphill towards the city centre along Bracondale. The road traced the high escarpment of the city – the land falling away sharply to the right, down to the River Wensum, the football ground at Carrow Road and the railway station further on. The area down by the river is newly developed, with supermarkets and electronic stores mushrooming in an area that once held factories and works depots. East of Carrow Bridge, where a ruined city wall tower stands alongside the water like a broken tooth, shiny new housing developments have replaced the riverside warehouses that once lined the river here. Now there are riverside flats with balconies, even a shiny, metal-skinned apartment block that looks as if it comes from Frank Gehry's budget design collection.

West of the raise-bridge that leads to the football ground and railway station are more apartments and an elegant footbridge: the Novi Sad Friendship Bridge. Named after one of Norwich's twinned cities, it has always struck me as an ironic appellation considering that the bridge was erected just two years after NATO bombers had destroyed all three Danube bridges in the Serbian twin – hardly the friendliest of gestures.

Bracondale is lined with large Georgian town houses to the left, attractive Victorian terraces with wrought-iron verandas and long front gardens to the right. Here and there are fragments of flint walls and a couple of well-preserved towers that delineated the southern limit of the medieval city.

I passed one of the city wall towers at the top of Carrow Hill, and just beyond here, the curiously named Foulger's Opening, where a plaque next to a flinty stump marks where a former city gate had once stood at the junction with Ber Street. The pub on the junction, the Berstrete Gates, bears a mural on its gable showing how the former city portal might have once looked. The reality was not always so pretty: a fortified gate such as this served not only as a place to levy an entrance fee but also provided an opportunity *pour décourager les autres*, a shop window for displaying the heads of those who had been put to death for whatever qualified as a misdemeanour in medieval times.

Norwich became encircled by defensive walls in the first half of the 14th century. A formidable barrier protecting the city, the largely flint-built walls enclosed an area greater than the city of

London. Unlike York or Chester, where the ancient fortifications are sufficiently well preserved to attract modern-day tourists, the Norwich walls have long been neglected, although notable fragments remain in place. The Norwich walls were completed around the middle of the century – just in time for the first visitation of plague to the city in 1349 – but by the time they were finished they had already become something of a white elephant. The twelve original city gateways and most of the defensive towers are now gone. Those that survived damage in the violence of a rebellion in 1549 were finally demolished in the late 18th century to permit road widening.

The walls of medieval cities were more than mere physical obstacles to keep undesirables out at night. They were symbolic barriers, too. Anything contained within was, literally, civilised – worthy of protection, tamed of nature's more wayward forces; anything without was, in contrast, wild, unkempt, open to suspicion. Beyond the boundary of the wall, the very soil beneath one's feet was different. Walls granted an urban identity, a defensive civic pride. The zone immediately beyond the city walls was usually the place where executions took place, where plague victims were buried, where unwanted elements were swept under the extramural carpet. Beyond the safety of the walls lay danger. In Finland they describe the line that separates the capital from the rest of the country beyond as *susiraja*, the 'wolf border'. Beyond the wolf border is the imagined realm of wolves and wildness; fear, the 'other'. Living in modern times it is difficult to imagine the dread with which the medieval mind viewed that which lay immediately beyond its stone-walled control.

*

I came to Norwich as a young man. Compared to Coventry, where I had first lived as a student after leaving home, the city seemed a cultured, self-assured sort of place. It undoubtedly smelled better. Back in the 1970s, when Coventry reeked of toxic hydrocarbons, Norwich was still redolent of its traditional industries, a comforting blend of shoe leather, beer and chocolate. In those days, the city air invariably held the tang of mashed hops from its breweries, Watneys and Bullards, which in the pre-real ale era churned out indifferent keg beers that, while bland to the taste, at least smelled enticing during the production process. At the same time, an appealing aroma of chocolate usually emanated from the Rowntree's factory site where Chapelfield shopping mall now stands. I was convinced back then that I could identify the days when Kit-Kats were on the production line, as the pleasing chocolatey miasma that permeated the city centre seemed to take on a more characteristically biscuit note. More acute noses might also have been able to identify the whiff of glue and boot leather coming from one of the city's shoe factories; real bloodhounds might have even discerned the scent of illicit sex that wafted up from King Street down by the river. Now the only smell is that of other people's money – the wholesome reek of tertiary finance, insurance, banking. As well as skunk (the malodorous stimulant of choice for many of the city's younger generation) and decent coffee – independent coffee bars with gleaming chrome machinery and bewilderingly detailed menus have, in recent years, taken over from the boozers. But isn't that the case everywhere? Doesn't every city in the land now smell much the same in this age of late capitalism?

The stereotypical portrait of Norwich – old-fashioned, safe, quietly sophisticated – does not always match the reality. In tandem with the development of a more dynamic public image over the past decade – the expansion of its campus university, the construction of the glazed, horseshoe-shaped community building of The Forum next to City Hall and the Church of St Peter Mancroft, the remodelling of the Norman-era market place, the marketing of the city centre shopping streets and alleyways as

'The Lanes', and the acquisition of UNESCO City of Literature (and very nearly European City of Culture) status – there is a less appealing side. Recent years have seen a marked increase in rough sleepers in the city, and many of those tight-lipped young mothers who queue at the bus stops along St Stephen's Street clutching small children and Poundland carrier bags have seen little sign of any increased affluence – the opposite, in fact. Despite a plethora of independent coffee bars, and more degree-trained baristas than you can wave a bag of Fair Trade beans at, there are those in the city for whom even a trip to Greggs is a treat. Food banks and late-night soup kitchens have become a reality; alcohol and hard drugs, an inevitable escape route. Norwich is no different to anywhere else: the city boasts a sizeable demographic of university students, young professionals and entrepreneurs, but it also has its fair share of unemployed young, neglected elderly and zero-hours workers who are, simply, poor.

There is more violence, too, than might be imagined by any 'Let's Move To...' feature in the weekend broadsheets. Several unnecessary deaths have taken place over the past decade within a ten-minute walk of my house. One was a Saturday afternoon knife attack on a staff member in the Chapelfield shopping mall – the work of outsiders 'up from London', as the local media was quick to point out. Another was a homeless man beaten to death following some sort of petty argument. Plastic-wrapped flowers marked the spot for months afterwards, as they also did in the nearby underpass where another homeless man, an Eastern European, died of exposure. A condemnation in black marker pen – *KILLED BY THE GOVERNMENT* – screamed out from the white-tiled subway wall, until the graffito was eventually removed by the city council. Collected on the same dingy spot were the flowers and tributes of strangers touched by the event – small kindnesses, albeit too late. Such dark deeds and such sad ends, so close to home, all serve to remind that beneath the wholesome façade Norwich has a sinister side that bears little resemblance to the accepted unfashionable and slightly eccentric image personified by Delia Smith, Alan Partridge and Colman's Mustard.

*

It is said that Ber Street once had thirty-nine pubs along its length, although it is now mostly lined with car and motorbike showrooms, along with Portuguese and Chinese food supermarkets and bathroom fitting emporia. A little way along the street, past the towering flinty edifice of the Anglican-turned-Orthodox church of St John the Theologian at Finkelgate, is Jolly Butchers Yard, a courtyard that takes its name from its long-established pub. The Jolly Butchers was once the domain of Black Anna, aka Antoinette Hannant, the redoubtable bouffanted landlady turned blues and jazz singer ('the English Sophie Tucker') who also ran the last rooming house in the city in the building next door. Anna's Italian parents were rumoured to have walked all the way from Medina in northern Italy in the 1880s before finally settling in Norwich. Anna was born in 1905 and never ventured far from the street of her birth until her death in 1976. I remember the place – or rather, the former doss house that stood in the yard – for its 1980s late-night underground reggae and soul club.

Until a few years ago Ber Street was the hypotenuse of a triangle that circumscribed what remained of Norwich's red light district, a clearly defined zone that extended up a few steep streets from King Street and the river below. Historically, this part of town was the original Anglo-Saxon settlement before the arrival of the Normans. Later, it became an area where the city's French-speaking Jews settled and did business before being driven out by the pogrom that followed the discredited William of Norwich murder in 1144 (see the previous chapter). In more recent times the King Street area became an area for beer brewing and, because of its proximity to the River Wensum, the lechering ground for roaming sailors who visited the city when Norwich still served as an upriver port.

Given the zone's sometimes prurient history it seems an unlikely place to find evidence of a life that was wholly spiritual. The 14th-century Christian mystic Dame Julian of Norwich once lived in a cell attached to a tiny church tucked away on an alley-way just off King Street. St Julian's Church was one of the victims of the later Baedeker raids that visited the city in June 1942 but both cell and church have been entirely reconstructed since. The cell was where the anchoress spent most of her adult life. It was here that she experienced countless beatific visions and penned her *Revelations of Divine Love*, considered to be the first book written in English by a woman. Dame Julian lived in an era deeply troubled by endless wars, peasant revolts and the Black Death – a pre-Enlightenment, God-fearing age that must have seemed like the onset of the end of time for those who lived through it; a time when a notion such as divine love might be seen as thin gruel in the face of things. Convinced that her God was merciful and compassionate, and believing that such events were not manifestations of divine punishment as was the widely held belief at the time, Julian glowed with something that in slightly different circumstances might be seen as heresy (a worryingly serious accusation as Norwich had more than its fair share of Lollard martyrs). Ever the spiritual optimist in the face of an excepted theology in which God was seen as wrathful and punitive, her comforting words 'And all shall be well, and all manner of thing shall be well' would outlast the dim span of history in which her life was lived.

I arrived at the corner where the John Lewis department store stood. Set in the curving redbrick wall is a small plaque commemorating the Victorian circus star Pablo Fanque. Born William Darby in Norwich in 1796, somewhere in the area of Ber Street, and immortalised in the Beatles' *Sgt Pepper's* song 'Being for the Benefit of Mr. Kite!', Pablo Fanque was an equestrian performer who went on to become the first non-white circus proprietor in Britain, owning the most popular circus in the Victorian era. Born of an African father, Fanque's personal history is uncertain but he was either orphaned as a boy or brought up in a workhouse. Whatever the true story, this was a remarkable metamorphosis that challenges the commonly held belief that Norwich's history is almost exclusively Anglo-Saxon. Historically, the city has always been ethnically diverse, albeit predominantly white, with successive immigrations of those who were known as 'Strangers' – Dutch, Walloons from the Low Countries, French Huguenot Protestants and Italians. With the exception of the 12th-century anti-Jewish pogroms, tolerance and acceptance of foreigners have long been key ingredients in the city's reputation.

*

My home was nearby now, close to St Stephen's Gate, the medieval city's southwest entrance just a few minutes' walk away. The street dates from the early Victorian period, constructed at the same time as a railway station, one of three that used to serve the city. The street was bombed during the Baedeker raids of 1942, when the city received rough treatment at the hands of the Luftwaffe, although the castle, cathedral and other key historic buildings were all deliberately spared. The rumour – more probably urban myth – was that Hitler so much admired the clean, art deco lines of Norwich City Hall, its design a tribute to Stockholm's own city hall, that he planned to address the conquered people of Great Britain from its balcony once his victory was complete. I tried to imagine the Führer positioned between the heraldic lions at the city hall steps shouting at the ancient market place below as he stood mad-eyed and aloof, one arm raised in Nazi salute. Given this nightmarish scenario, what would have become of the marketplace? Would the chip stall have added sauerkraut to its inventory of garnishes? Would the leather stall have reluctantly turned its skills to producing *lederhosen*, the shoe-repair bar start taking in jackboots for re-heeling? Would I even be here to churn out such banal clichés?

St Stephen's Gate stands where the main road to London meets the inner ring road. The gate itself is long gone, but a reminder of how it might have looked is represented on the wall of the Coachmakers Arms by the roundabout, an intricate mural based on drawings made by John Ninham just before the gate's demolition in 1793. Two hundred years earlier the Shakespearean clown William Kempe had Morris-danced his way through this gate at the climax of his 'Nine Daies Wonder' from London to Norwich, a nine-day journey spread over several weeks in the late winter of 1599/1600. Kempe at that time was a considerable celebrity, as close to a household name as anyone in the land, and each stage of his journey took place in front of an audience of noisy onlookers lining the road. Always one to play to the crowd, Kempe delayed his final victorious entry into the city for dramatic effect:

> *From Barford Bridge I danced into Norwich; but coming within sight of the citty, perceiving so great a multitude and throng of people still crowding more and more about me... I was advised... to stop my Morrice a little above Saint Giles his gate, where I took my gelding and so rid into the city procrastinating my merry Morrice daunce through the citty till better opportunitie.*

Kempe later recorded:

> *I returned without the citty through Saint Giles his gate, and began my Morrice where I left at that gate, but I entered in at Saint Stephen's gate, where one Thomas Gilbert in name of all the rest of the citizens gave me a friendly and exceedingly kind welcome.*

These days the same entrance to the city is utilised by the street procession of the Lord Mayor's Celebration each July, although now the dancing is mostly performed by battalions of baton-twirling schoolgirls and salsa groups atop slow-moving lorry beds. On special occasions such as this the road is closed to traffic, its pavements crowded with cheering observers. Most weekdays though, the same pavements are host to a constant stream of students heading to and from City College on Newmarket Road; three or four abreast, eyes glued to phones as they head like somnambulists to the St Stephens underpass and the steak bake promise of Greggs that lay beyond.

Almost opposite my own street is the site of the old Norwich and Norfolk Hospital, now repurposed as a top-flight city housing development. The splendid mid-Victorian facade of the original building has been retained, as has the chapel and garden, and the result is undeniably attractive; yet the memory of the site as a working hospital is, for me, still overwhelming. Over the years, I visited the sick here, saw new-born babies emerge from its wards, witnessed the death throes of loved ones. Too real, too visceral, it is hard to forgive the zone's rapid transformation from hospital to cosy domesticity.

The ghost wards of the former hospital, their legacy writ large in my own life story, also feature in those of untold others in the city. The writer W.G. Sebald, whose day job was as German literature academic at the University of East Anglia, opened his much-discussed *The Rings of Saturn* in one of the former hospital's wards. The book begins with Sebald describing how he had been 'taken into hospital in Norwich in a state of almost total immobility'. He speaks of a room on the eighth floor and a window through which all he could see was a 'colourless patch of sky'. Dragging himself to the window, and mindful of Kafka's Gregor Samsa character in *Metamorphosis*, he gazed out to find 'the familiar city, extending from the hospital courtyards to the far horizon, an utterly alien place'. Both Sebald and hospital are now gone from this world, although the alienation provoked by the view he described is still something I can identify with. It is, after all, almost identical to the view of chimney pots, inner city housing and main road that I have from the window of the attic where I work.

Avoiding the temptation to turn left and pop back home, I crossed the road to head down the medieval cobbles of Timber Hill. At the bottom, in the shadow of the Caen-stone cube of the Norman castle on its mound, I followed the pedestrian thoroughfare of Back of the Inns past Castle Mall, before turning left onto Gentleman's Walk in front of the striped canopies of the stalls of Norwich Market.

Almost anyone in the city will tell you with pride that this is the largest and oldest daily market in the country (others might also tell you that Norwich was the first British city to introduce pedestrian precincts, when London Street went controversially car-free back in 1967). Many of the market stalls are certainly long established, like the chips and mushy peas franchise that is well into its third generation of fryers and mushers. Locked in place between the looming splendour of St Peter Mancroft Church and the castellated, flint-faced Guildhall, and flanked by the art deco, Hitler-fancied City Hall at the top, the marketplace has stood here since shortly after the Norman Conquest. The original Saxon marketplace had been further east at Tombland but this was shifted wholesale to make way for the ambitious 11th-century development project that would become the Norman Cathedral. In a city like Norwich, where memories are long, there are probably still some who favour the earlier location.

Of the city's many medieval churches, St Peter Mancroft has always been my favourite. With a glass-door tower entrance that opens onto a wide, paved square favoured by teen Goths and skateboarders, and an elevated position beside the Norman market, it stands as a towering Perpendicular omphalos for the medieval city core. Its interior is a glittering light show of fine stained glass and what seems like an impossibly high hammer-beam roof from which a celestial host of carved wooden angels cling like fruit bats – angels that flew too high for the attention of medieval iconoclasts and Puritan muskets. Like round-tower churches, angel roofs are an East Anglian phenomenon – the very best found in the oversized churches of small villages like Blythburgh on the Suffolk coast. In my more imaginative moments I sometimes fantasise about the wooden angels coming to life after dark – launching into the night air like wakening owls to circuit the parish before returning to their perches in the rafters. Anything crepuscular with silent wings – life-breathed angels, wooden or otherwise, owls of any stripe – is always high in the pecking order of my personal bestiary.

St Peter's best known parishioner was the 17th-century polymath Sir Thomas Browne, author of *Religo Medici* and *Urn Burial*, whom Sebald discusses in detail a few pages into *The Rings of Saturn*. Browne was buried here in 1682, although somehow his skull ended up on display in the hospital museum and remained there until 1922 when it was finally reinterred in the chancel with the rest of his bones. In tribute, a pigeon shit-covered statue of Browne contemplating a broken urn holds pride of place in the Haymarket, the small square squeezed between the church and Gentleman's Walk; a place largely frequented by those factions of the city's youth that favour McDonald's as a backdrop in preference to the more bookish Forum. Although not a native to Norwich, Browne spent the last twenty-five years of his life in a house on Gentleman's Walk. It was at this house – a veritable 'paradise and cabinet of rarities', according to courtier and diarist John Evelyn – that Browne received a visit from King Charles II in 1671. The king, obliged to honour a local of noble standing on his visit, conferred a knighthood on Browne at the recommendation of the Mayor of Norwich.

I headed down Lower Gate Lane to Pottergate. This is the heart of an area that has been successfully rebranded as 'The Lanes' in recent years. The lanes have been here since medieval times but they are now reborn as a quarter of independent shops, galleries and hipster coffee bars. A part of the city that was old-fashioned and overlooked when I first arrived in Norwich is now hip and dynamic. In practice though, not that much is hugely different – the long-established 'head shop' with its dope-smoking paraphernalia and racks of ever-shrinking Indian cheesecloth shirts is still doing brisk business, as is the fish and chip shop on the corner. Fashion is cyclical: while several music shops closed down with the demise of analogue formats at the end of the last millennium, new outlets have mushroomed in recent years in response to the renaissance of vinyl. Retro is the new modern. What is undeniable is that the coffee tastes better these days.

From Pottergate I steered back towards the river, descending steps at Duke Street to the path that ran along its north bank. The Wensum, a serpentine loop of water, divides the city into two. The northern side of the divide, the half of the city that claims the oldest Anglo-Saxon settlement, is known, somewhat mysteriously, as Norwich over the Water, the name gifting a hint of terra incognito to the territory and a vague sense of being on the wrong side of the tracks.

Since its confluence with the Yare near Whitlingham Broad, a meandering mile or two downstream, the river embraces the whole gamut of city history in its loop. It flows past the football ground at Carrow Road; beneath the 21st-century Novi Sad and Dame Julian footbridges; past the grand Victorian railway station; beneath the three-arched, heaven and hell dichotomy of Bishops Bridge, where martyrs were led to the cathedral in one direction and the killing fields of Lollards' Pit in the other; past the Pictish broch impersonation of the 14th-century Cow Tower that overlooks a bend in the river; past the elegantly Virginia creeper-cloaked Jarrold Printing Works; past fragments of city walls and long-redundant churches; past the quay at Fishergate, where goods were once unloaded from ocean-going barges; past where there used to be a ducking stool to punish women for sins as grave as gossiping; past the Victorian brickwork of the Norwich School of Art; and, finally, beneath Blackfriars' Bridge to the point where I stood.

Across the river on the Wensum's south bank is a building that has the entire text of Thomas More's *Utopia* daubed in white capital letters across its walls. Local artist Rory Macbeth undertook the project in 2006 with the expectation that the building, an old warehouse belonging to the Eastern Electricity Board, would be demolished the following year. But a stay of execution occurred and the building remained standing, and the writing – all forty thousand words of the 16th-century fictional work, translated into English from Latin – is still on the wall. Utopia lives on. Further along is the old Bullard & Sons Anchor brewery, a solidly built edifice converted into attractive, des-res riverside units. The brewery's former sky-pricking chimney is long gone, although I remember it and its vertical lettering *B-U-L-L-A-R-D-S* being as much a city landmark as the City Hall clock tower or Cathedral spire.

Further along the riverbank I passed New Mills pumping station, the upper limit of the Wensum's navigation. A few anglers were gathered dangling lines in the foamy water close to the weir – there are nearly always fishermen here although I don't recall ever seeing anyone catch anything. The inner ring road was now in sight, its honking traffic rattling the cast iron bridge that spanned the river ahead. Beside the bridge, a sealed-up concrete urinal bears a sign declaring the curious hexagonal structure to be the oldest of its type in the country. At the height of its public service this Grade II-listed, concrete Tardis provided relief for men from the nearby factories and the former City Station across the road. In later life, before being finally closed for business, it was strongly rumoured that the urinal had been a popular way station on the city's cottaging circuit.

On the other side of the ring road, just beyond the bridge next to a roundabout, there is a modern iron sculpture on an expanse of grass. Welded together from track runners, the work pays homage to the railway line that once terminated here at City Station, the third of Norwich's former stations, which was demolished in the 1960s. The sculpture marks the start of Marriott's Way – a cycle and walking route that extends from Norwich all the way to the market town of Aylsham.

I know the Marriott's Way reasonably well. Its route provides an uncomplicated journey out of the city, an easy contact with the countryside. I have occasionally made use of it for Sunday afternoon cycle excursions to Lenwade and back: twenty-five miles or so, a couple of hours' moderate exercise without the need for a map. Now that I was on foot, here was a chance to take things slower, to see how the countryside squeezed itself into the city along the track-bed of the old Midland and Great Northern Railway line.

A sign announced that Drayton lay five miles distant and Lenwade eleven. The high walls of an industrial estate framed the pathway to the left. To the right, a narrow belt of woodland and then the river. Across the water, where the battered skeletons of scrapped cars had, until fairly recently, once been piled like shipping containers, stood a brand new housing estate – the familiar new-build mix of town houses and maisonettes, pristine brick walls still awaiting their first coating of lichen and moss.

Young oaks and sycamores shaded the pathway; birds flitted between the branches overhead. The track emerged from the dappled light of the wood to continue over a meadow before it passed beneath the outer ring road at Miles Cross, one of Norwich's largest council estates. Daubed on the wall of the underpass, spelled out in bold black and white letters was the simplest of messages: *SHOOK*. A familiar cipher, Shook's handiwork is ubiquitous around the city. An omnipresent dauber in the graffitist roll-call of the Norwich area, there seems to be no part of town untouched by his five-letter tag. He – I can only presume a gender, but there is undoubtedly something male and territorial about the activity – has left his mark on the bridge over the railway track near my home. Like a dog that cannot rest until it has scent-marked every available surface, Shook has also tagged the lampposts in my street. Once, I even noticed his trademark signature on the wall of a tunnel approaching Cambridge station. Far beyond his usual home territory, I had to conclude that this must have been the product of some sort of awayday excursion.

The underpass heralded the western edge of the inner city. Further along, an iron girder bridge spans the River Wensum at Hellesdon, the city's most northwesterly suburb. A kingfisher flashed by close to the water, a cobalt blue bolt of electricity. Beyond the bridge, rough grazing and horse paddocks edged the track on both sides. Woodpigeons flapped away lethargically at my approach, wings clapping clumsily in muffled applause. Then, in the stretch between Costessey and Drayton, at what would once have been a railway cutting, trees enveloped the way completely, wrapping it in a silence that was only broken by the distant roar of a plane taking off from Norwich airport a few miles distant.

At Drayton, effectively a dormitory suburb for the city, I left the Marriott's Way to head into the village and catch the bus back into Norwich.

Chapter 5

Concrete Ghosts, Winding Wensum

River Wensum, Norfolk

Wensum (Old English *waendsum*): *winding*

Back in Drayton the following day, the mechanical drone of the traffic from the A1067 soon dissolved as I followed the old railway track west to skirt Thorpe Marriott, a late 20th-century private estate of lead-windowed, double-garaged town houses at Norwich's north-western fringe. The housing estate and the long-distance footpath are named after William Marriott, the chief engineer of the Midland and Great Northern Railway and a 'concrete pioneer', according to an information board. Concrete is also firmly associated with Lenwade, a village on my itinerary for the day.

The track continued through the deep shade of sweet chestnut trees, the path littered with the spiky green shells of fallen nuts. Autumn was already starting to leave hints of its imminent arrival. Mushrooms littered the ground in earth-fragrant clumps. Apples ripened on bird-sown trees in the hedgerow, their green-red fruit a bonus for an already plentiful harvest that included a rich heft of haws and sloes.

Walking purposefully, I received furtive looks from some of those I met coming the other way. My mumbling into a voice recorder must have appeared strange to some but I was already an oddity as I did not have a dog with me, nor was I dressed in sports gear and jogging, like many of those I encountered. It was hard to know the correct etiquette for greeting fellow path users:

a friendly 'Morning' or just a distracted nod. Once outside an urban area, a mutually exchanged greeting is the usual practice but it depends on which part of the country you are in, the age of those you meet, how rural the territory is. What might appear as a friendly greeting on a footpath in rural East Anglia could be viewed as highly suspicious on a London inner-city towpath. It is a very British problem.

Just before Attlebridge a sign by the wayside pointed out that I had reached the highest point on the old line between Norwich and Whitwell. In Norfolk, where undulations of landscape are subtle, it is necessary to state such things. A bench poem – *Lines ploughed cursive in Black Earth* – neatly summed up the landscape of corduroy-ribbed fields that lay beyond the confines of the track.

At Attlebridge's former station a man, sitting in what was now his living room but which once would have been a signal box before conversion, eyed me as I approached. Completely unfazed when I returned his gaze, and happy in his role as self-appointed overseer of the Marriott's Way, he had the look of someone who would only grudgingly sell you a ticket.

The River Wensum edged closer as I approached Lenwade. Eventually, the path crossed over the river to lead alongside the walls of industrial units. Little seemed to thrive along the clinker-strewn path other than stunted birch trees and ragwort; the whole area felt like a toxic dead zone, a place ghosted by heavy industry, the ground beneath it contaminated. And well it might: it was here, back in the 1960s, that many of the concrete pillars that propped up North Sea oil rigs were constructed. Cast in the yards alongside the track, the pillars were loaded in sections onto Great Yarmouth-bound freight trains at the station that used to stand here. Other concrete precast components manufactured here included panels for East London tower blocks (one of which collapsed after a gas explosion in 1968, which precipitated a dramatic reduction in demand for the Lenwade-made product) and pre-stressed beams for motorway bridges, a growth industry in the 1970s. Although the bare high walls gave a sense of its industrial past, heavy duty manufacturing on such a scale now seemed improbable in a rural setting such as this.

Beyond Lenwade the old railway route curves sharply eastwards at Themelthorpe towards the market town of Aylsham. The route consists of two different railway lines: the line between Norwich and Themelthorpe that was once operated by the Midland & Great Northern Joint Railway, and the route to Aylsham formerly run by the Great Eastern Railway. The two lines – both unprofitable – stood separate until 1960 when they were conjoined by the Themelthorpe Curve section, courtesy of British Rail. The curve, now marked as an improbably sharp kink on the OS map, is believed to have been the sharpest bend in any line in the entire British rail network. The idea behind its creation was to provide a short cut for concrete goods from the Lenwade yards to reach the North Sea coast by the most direct route possible, via Aylsham, Norwich and Great Yarmouth. The last concrete beam travelled by rail from here in 1981 – the line was closed for good in 1983 – so the bizarre sight of huge concrete monsters gliding past the hedgerows of rural Norfolk was a spectacle that lasted for little more than two decades.

*

I took my leave of the Marriott's Way to follow a lane into Lenwade village. From here, I picked up the Wensum Way, a newly devised network of footpaths that rambles westwards. Promoted as the missing link in a Norfolk east–west, cross-county walk, the route links with the Nar Valley Way at the village of Gressenhall, from where it follows the River Nar all the way to King's Lynn.

The route, marked with pristine and expensive-looking wooden signposts, starts not far from the bridge that crosses the

Wensum. A sign pointed me along a shady driveway towards a country hotel before diverting along the perimeter of a chain-link enclosure that held dozens of turkeys. The birds eyed me from behind the fence, some boldly approaching for a better look. They resembled the prisoners they clearly were, although thankfully they lacked the wherewithal to count down the days to Christmas when they would all be leaving this sorry compound.

This part of Norfolk is turkey central: the headquarters of Bernard 'Bootiful' Matthews' turkey empire is down the road at Great Witchingham Hall. While Matthews, who died in 2010, will forever be associated with cheesy 1980s television adverts and the reconstituted, fat-drenched Turkey Twizzlers much derided by TV chef Jamie Oliver, the multi-millionaire poulterer, thanks to a generous endowment, has also been immortalised by an exhibition gallery that bears his name at Norwich Castle Museum. Not for the first time, food production and arts philanthropy are connected – the name Henry Tate is now more associated with refined art galleries than it is with refined sugar.

After the turkeys, a wooden boardwalk led me through poplars and a tangle of Himalayan balsam towards the river. Walking along the raised boards – well constructed from seasoned wood and clearly built to last – felt oddly Zen-like, as if a cotton robe and wooden sandals might be a more appropriate choice of clothing. Beside the boardwalk, a cairn of old tyres long overgrown with moss stood proud of the mud as if marking some long-forgotten sacred spot. A hyperactive party of long-tailed tits whispered in the trees just ahead of me, always a pace or two in front as I approached the open water of the flooded gravel pits at Pockthorpe.

Greening nicely around their edges, the deep pits left behind from gravel extraction had been left to transform into small lakes. Now the preserve of fishing clubs and wildlife charities, the lakes still have a faintly artificial look about them but this is to be expected considering their youth. A natural succession will inevitably follow: the trees will grow larger as reed beds and aquatic plants establish themselves; fish will spawn, birds will breed; perhaps, with luck, otters might visit. JCB diggers, tip-up trucks and pyramids of gravel will have made way for newts and skulking herons. These lakes are similar to the other, longer-established broads just outside Norwich – UEA Broad at the university campus and Whitlingham Broad, which I had passed on my way into the city. All were created by gravel extraction and became convincingly feral, if not actually 'wild'. The Broads proper are different. The well-known network of lakes and connected waterways in northeast Norfolk were formed by the flooding of medieval peat diggings. The Norfolk Broads seemed to be such an integral part of the landscape that their manmade origin was not discovered until the 1960s. The scars of landscape are reassuringly ephemeral; nature often heals more rapidly than might be expected. The idea of wilderness, the truly wild – in England, at least – is pure fantasy. Virtually every inch of the land has been worked, tamed, cultivated, grazed, planted or trodden on at some time in the past – the handiwork of human colonisation is everywhere, even those places that seem on first glance to be natural and untamed.

Another signpost pointed me in the direction of Swanton Morley. It felt good to be walking less familiar territory – free now of the weight of memory in the city and the bicycle-outing familiarity of the Marriott's Way. Here was new ground to cover, although one of the villages along the Wensum Way came with a hint of recollection, albeit little more than a glow in the dark. Lyng, I remembered, had been the location for a summer festival in the early 1980s, a 'faerie fayre' reincarnation of the well-attended Barsham Fayres that had taken place the previous decade in the Waveney Valley along the Norfolk-Suffolk border.

The fayres occurred at the tail-end of the decaying Albion dream – the early Thatcher, post-punk, Miners' Strike years when the building of Jerusalem in England's green and pleasant land no longer looked to be just over the horizon. In a time of collective denial, of clinging to the belief that the broken dream was nothing more than a spiritual hiccup in mankind's destiny, events like the fair at Lyng did their best to keep the vision alive. It was hard to pinpoint precisely when hope for a better, kinder world, along with flared trousers and long hair, was finally abandoned, but the three-chords-and-the-truth, year zero revolution of 1976 was no doubt a bold signpost that pointed to the future.

At all the fayres, electricity was more or less outlawed, camping and bonfires were de rigueur. The ethos was do-it-yourself: attendees in medieval dress were given free entrance, while everyone else paid just a pound or two to get in. Goblins and gentle optimism abounded; the Norfolk soil was danced upon and celebrated, anointed in patchouli, real ale and Afghan resin. As a backdrop to an earlier version of self – bearded, long-haired, flare-flapping limbs – its recollection provoked a faltering, pre-millennial vagueness. My emotional memory of the Lyng event – which I may or may not have confused with a similar fair elsewhere – has been self-obfuscated. Most likely I experienced it as an uneasy blend of pastoral delight and repressed alienation.

I reached Lyng, where there is a bridge over the river and a pond next to a large mill complex. Unabashed, a fisherman was setting up his rods right next to a *NO FISHING* sign. On the opposite bank, a line of anti-tank blocks suggested that the villagers of Lyng had been fully prepared for an invasion during World War II. As well as any inconvenient concrete obstacles, any German Panzer division that made it this far inland would have had to contend with *Dad's Army* conscripts armed with pitchforks and heirloom rifles. The village centre was somnolent – barely a sound other than an unseen barking dog and a waft of guitar jangle from a garage transistor radio. On the green, the village sign depicted sprigs of heather ('ling', hence Lyng) surrounding a representation of the village's four-arched bridge and flint church – a neat pictorial summary of the village's particularities. On the reverse was a roll-call of all St Margaret's past vicars.

From Lyng, the Wensum Way leads through the patchy agricultural land of central Norfolk, a countryside that is a little scrappier than the clichéd picture postcard view of the county. Shallow valleys are interspersed with sloping fields of pig units and marginal land that has been given over for use as motocross circuits – rural economic diversity in action.

At Elsing, the next village, the Mermaid pub stands opposite the church, or rather, immediately below it. An earlier Saxon church had stood on the same spot at the time of the Conquest but St Mary the Virgin's position high atop a grassy mound seems to suggest that a sacred site existed here long before England was Christianised. In Decorated Gothic style, and with an unusually wide nave, the church has attracted visitors as distinguished as T.E. Lawrence, who visited here on a brass-rubbing cycling tour of Norfolk with his father in 1905. The brass that the pair were most probably interested in would have been that of the church's founder, Sir Hugh Hastings, who died in 1347. St Margaret's lay on one of the main pilgrimage routes to the shrine at Little Walsingham in northwest Norfolk and its wide nave provided ample begging space for the mendicants who would have once congregated here. The church's importance has lapsed since those days but there are signs that it still serves as a focus for the village community. The remnants of a recent harvest festival had been left in the porch, and the old village sign, presumably deposited here for want of a better resting place, was propped up in the nave along with collection boxes and leaflets on the West African Ebola crisis. A box of toys and circle of tiny chairs had been put in place for children, and a cardboard box that collected on behalf of the East Dereham food bank held a few tins of sardines and packets of biscuits. Charity, as ever, started at home.

The Mermaid seemed to be almost as ancient as the church, although whether or not an underage Lawrence popped in here for a post-brass-rubbing pint with his father is debatable. I had visited the pub when the Wensum Way first opened a couple of years earlier. It had been quiet and I remembered that the sandwich I ordered was slow in coming – 'the sausage-cooking machine isn't working properly' – but the beer was fine and the landlady welcoming. She seemed to have known my business.

'Are you here doing that new trail then? I read all about it in the paper. That'll bring in trade, hopefully.'

Her interest was well founded – pub business was visibly slack and, apart from me and two locals, the only other customers were some men from the Midlands who had come for the fishing at Sparham Pools. When I attempted to make a phone call and couldn't get a signal, the landlady looked at me knowingly.

'Go up to the church and hold your phone as high as you can in the air – that helps sometimes.'

I tried; it didn't.

From Elsing, I followed a path beside the meandering Wensum to Swanton Morley. Big-horned but docile-looking white cattle half-blocked the way in places; the swallows that memorably skimmed the water in great number here on a previous visit were noticeable by their absence. Swanton Morley's All Saints Church, standing aloof on a bluff ahead, could be seen in the distance, a domineering Perpendicular building that looked far too big for the small village it served. It may be that it was a small village with big ideas. It was, after all, the home village of one of Abraham Lincoln's ancestors: Samuel Lincoln, the great-great-great-great-grandfather of the man who would go on to become the 16th President of the United States.

The final stretch to the village crossed damp meadows enclosed by sagging willows – a mid-Norfolk imitation of Constable Country. I had arranged for Jackie to pick me up at the village's farm shop. The shop's butchery section sold cuts of meat from the same gentle White Park cattle I had tiptoed around at the river. The breed is an ancient one, quite likely the oldest in the UK and a descendant of the wild indigenous cattle imparked by the aristocracy in the medieval period. Here was rare beef in the broadest sense of the word.

*

Travelling back to Swanton Morley the next day, I walked out of the village along a bridleway lined with coppiced lime trees. After passing a junior school that was having morning break, its pupils running around and shouting excitedly in the playground, I started to hear sporadic gunshots in the distance. Then I remembered: it was pheasant open season, the time of year when the Norfolk countryside rings with the crack of shotguns and hedgerows suddenly explode with fleeing, panicking birds.

I passed two Land Rovers parked up by a gate. In the distance, a party of beaters were walking in a broad line across a field. Decked out in waxed cotton jackets and flat caps, brandishing sticks and guns, with dogs in their wake, there was no mistaking the business at hand. A green lane led me to a farm track where another vehicle was parked next to a tarpaulin-covered trailer. Hung from its roof like totemic offerings to an insatiable deity were dozens of barely cold pheasants. These, I assumed, would be counted, taken for plucking and gutting and then sold at a considerable loss to local butchers; some – perhaps many, if the stories of profligacy are true – would end up uneaten and buried as rotting landfill. It is an itemised slaughter that is easier to quantify than qualify. The hunting fraternity that subsidises such practice – and it is mainly a male thing – pays generously for the privilege: the value is in the thrill of the kill.

Heading west towards the hamlet of Hoe, I came to the small flint Church of St Andrew's, set in an overgrown graveyard.

With small windows and a truncated tower it resembled a barn as much as a place of worship. The village's eponymous hall was secreted out of sight behind a tall perimeter wall. Hidden away from the public gaze, it was easy to imagine that the hall might serve as a clandestine location for dark practices – a readymade *Hammer House of Horror* film set. A more likely scenario is that the building is biding its time before being repurposed as a conference centre or wedding venue – the inevitable fate of many unmanageable hereditary piles in East Anglia.

A concrete bridge led me over a disused railway line. On the far side the footpath led across a field that took me a full ten minutes to cross, the way marked by sprayed vegetation. I crossed more fields before joining a farm track that skirted apple and plum orchards on the way into Beetley.

The village sign stood in a small triangle of mown grass. Alongside was a large sandstone boulder: brownish, partly moss-covered and rectangular in shape. In a region where the only naturally occurring rock is the flint that glistens on the fields, the stone was clearly not of local origin. The boulder was a glacial erratic, a remnant of the Pleistocene when rocks that originated in Scotland and Scandinavia were transported great distances on icy moraines. Such strange and mysterious stones, their origins unexplained before the relatively recent development of geological science, usually come with a modicum of folkloric baggage.

Whether or not this stone has rested in exactly the same location since being deposited during the last glacial period is debatable. According to W.A. Dutt, author of *Ancient Markstones of East Anglia* and an authority on such things, it is likely that a local antiquarian placed it here in the 19th century after it had been unearthed somewhere nearby. Local folklore claims that the stone represents the dead centre of the county. While a cursory glance at the map makes this seem a reasonable assertion, it is doubtful that it corresponds precisely. A more recent, and probably more accurate, reckoning has placed Norfolk's geographical centre in a supermarket car park in East Dereham, a few miles to the south. This claim is oddly reassuring: if there is anywhere that might suitably average-out the county as a whole, its glories and ignominies, its glamour and humdrum, then a Tesco car park in Norfolk's most central market town seems wholly appropriate. Besides, in recent years car parks have gained status as focal points for the new archaeology. Who knows what they might reveal?

The Beetley stone is not the only documented erratic in this part of the county. The previous day I had passed close to the 'Great Stone of Lyng', which lies just south of the flooded gravel pits at Sparham Pools on the Wensum Way. The Lyng stone has all manner of romantic legend attached to it – tales of a great battle between St Edmund and the Danes on the site, of buried treasure and supposed Druidic sacrifice. A dozen or so miles further south in the Brecks is the largest of all the glacial erratics in East Anglia. This stone, located in a hedgerow near the village of Merton, comes complete with the legend that if it were ever moved – not an easy task, given its bulk – it would release waters and flood the entire world.

East Dereham, a few miles south of Beetley, is the town where the poet and hymnodist William Cowper lived and died. John Craske, the Sheringham fisherman turned celebrated embroiderer and outsider artist, lived here for a while too, running a wet fish business. But the absence of the sea sickened Craske and it was not until he returned to the coast at Blakeney, at the suggestion of his doctor, that he found relief from the psycho-neurotic state that the inland location had provoked in him.

East Dereham was also the birthplace of the Victorian writer George Henry Borrow, an exceptional linguist who was fluent in languages as diverse as Russian, Hebrew and Welsh. Generally preferring the company of gypsies, whose Romany language he also knew, Borrow was an outspoken figure. He was also a prodigious walker who zealously ate up miles of footpath and roadway on long tours around the country. On one occasion, Borrow walked all the way from Norwich to London for an interview with the Bible Society. Covering 112 miles in twenty-seven hours, the walk was not only testament to the writer's indefatigability but also to the briskness of pace that he was able to maintain. At the interview, he convinced the panel that he was fluent in Mandarin (he was not – not yet, anyway), was given the job, and then walked straight back home. Suffering periodic bouts of depression, Borrow, like many before and after him, had come to realise that walking was an effective means of assuaging what he termed 'the horrors'. Although it was Borrow who coined the phrase 'Norwich – a fine city' in his autobiographical novel *Lavengro* – an epithet that still greets visitors on every entrance to the county capital – the writer's relations with the city fathers were not always so cordial. Writing 'with such ugly figures and flat features that the devil owned he had never seen them equalled, except by the inhabitants of an English town, called Norwich' in his translation of Friedrich Maximillan Klinger's *Faustus: His Life, Death, and Descent into Hell* did little to endear him to the city's great and good. The work was subsequently burnt in outrage by Norwich public conscription library, although the slighted city in the German language original had, in fact, been Nuremberg.

*

On the outskirts of Beetley, over the bridge that crosses the River Whitewater, a tributary of the Wensum, is the Gressenhall Museum of Rural Life. Until 1948 this large Georgian complex served as one of the main workhouses in the county. Originally built as a 'house of industry' for the poor, the 1834 Poor Law

Amendment Act downgraded it further to the status of workhouse, a feared place of degradation for those unfortunate enough to be ensconced within its high brick walls. The ethos was simple: poverty itself was tantamount to being a crime, and descent to the lowly state of becoming dependent on the parish was to be strongly discouraged. A last resort, the workhouse was but a single rung up the ladder of destitution; an institution to be despised and feared; a place without love or much in the way of empathy. The regime was harsh and strictly controlled: men, women and children were separated on arrival; the work was hard, monotonous and unpleasant. These days, the former workhouse and its neighbouring farm make for a pleasant day out – an interesting museum of rural life, a hands-on working farm for children, even a play and picnic area – but it takes little effort to imagine the dread that those who came here in the past must have felt when they arrived by cart, the institution's high walls and stern windows glaring down on them at the gate. While it was true that rudimentary health care and education would have been provided, along with sufficient food to survive, to enter its unforgiving gateway must have engendered an abandonment of hope that is hard to imagine.

A sign on the road outside the museum announced the beginning of the Nar Valley Way, the long-distance footpath that traces the course of the River Nar, a chalk river that flows west to eventually join the Great Ouse close to King's Lynn. Here was the route I would follow to continue across the county on my way to the Fens.

Gressenhall village had the feel of a place occupied mostly by pensioners, a Dunroamin generation. An enclave of bungalows, village green, pub – The Swan – and bowls club; a cardboard sign for *FREE BRAMLEY APPLES* (across the road, with gently competitive altruism, another was offering windfall eaters). A signed footpath out of the village morphed into a densely shaded green lane that led past a fishing pond and a shadowy copse sheltering quacking, half-hidden mallards. The lane would have once been a well-used thoroughfare that connected the village with the market at East Dereham. Now, with the exception of occasional dog-walkers and hikers, it was all but abandoned. Enveloping creepers of ivy engendered a sense of eeriness to the path's deep shade. In the hedge, a single branch of dogwood vibrated furiously in isolation, as if possessed by a spirit – in actuality, a mini vortex created by a quirky flow of air. Strange to behold, it was the sort of thing the Gothic imagination would have seized upon, a living thing possessed by dark magic and in need of propitiation.

I wanted to photograph the lane's slightly sinister womb-like embrace but discovered that the memory card on my camera was full. Stopping to delete a few images, I came across some pictures of a place Jackie and I had visited the previous year – Pendle Hill in Lancashire. Pendle Hill and its luckless witches – the whispered voices of its heathery slopes: there seemed to be a correlation of some sort here, an uncanny happenstance.

I emerged on a minor road at Bittering, where according to the map a medieval village had once stood. Its remnants were now reduced to little more than bumps in a field. What would once have been houses were now just nettle-filled depressions and low grassy hummocks grazed by sheep. Formerly one of the most densely populated parts of the county, the area northwest of East Dereham became seriously depopulated in the medieval period to leave only scattered hints on the OS map: a handful of DMVs (deserted medieval villages), a few gothic-lettered moats and an earthwork named Launditch ('*ditch and bank, Early Saxon, possibly Iron Age*'). Another nearby place name, Hungry Hill, hinted at soil impoverishment, a common problem in the medieval period and as much a reason for the abandonment of land and settlement as plague and the later enclosure clearances.

This still feels like an abandoned countryside in some way – bleak in aspect, a constituency dominated by gravel pits and the ghosts of lost villages.

The sound of earth-moving machinery grumbled softly from a quarry somewhere in the distance. A small herd of roe deer were grazing nervously far away in the fields to the left. Rooks flapped noisily around the tree-tops of a small wood straight ahead. I diverted briefly to follow a mossy driveway to the long dormant Church of St Peter, a small chapel no larger than a cottage. Flint-walled, pan-tiled, tall Early English windows; no tower but a single bell in place at its gable, St Peter's no longer had a congregation to speak of now that its parish has been largely given over to gravel extraction.

I returned to my planned route, heading towards Mileham. The village has its own ruins – the motte and bailey earthworks of a Norman Castle. In paddocks next to the appropriately named Horse Wood, just outside the village, chestnut horses grazed peacefully. The oaks and beeches were just beginning to turn, leaves turning brittle, yellow and gold. A deep, fungal tang was in the air: autumn was imminent.

Chapter 6

God's Holy River

River Nar, Norfolk

Norman saw on English oak.
On English neck a Norman yoke
Sir Walter Scott, *Ivanhoe*

Autumn or not, the weather was unseasonably balmy when I returned to Mileham the following day. It was late October yet dog roses were still in bloom and only the ripening hips and haws in the hedgerows reminded that the season was already well underway. In the fields, sharp blades of winter wheat were starting to emerge, casting a green blush over the bare furrows of newly ploughed land.

I set off along a footpath that climbed gently away from the village, a wide sweep of farmland opening up below. Understatedly bucolic, modestly attractive, I had reached that part of the county that some like to call 'High Norfolk', even though it stands little more than sixty metres above sea-level. A plateau is a relative thing, and viewed from the Fens further west this was comparatively elevated land.

The path looped around a marl pit by a wood, close to where the OS map marked the deserted village of Grenstein. There was nothing to be seen of the medieval village yet it occurred to me that these were the sort of plough-turned fields where something ancient and perhaps even valuable might be found – a Roman coin wedged in a clod of clay, perhaps even a Neolithic hand tool for the taking on the surface. But I possessed neither the expertise nor the patience to search for such things, even if almost every shard of flint looked like it might be an artefact that had been fashioned millennia earlier.

I headed south across the fields, doglegging in the direction of Litcham, gluey clay adhering to my boots to weigh me down like a deep-sea diver. At Litcham I followed the evocatively named Druid's Lane before leaving the village by way of a nature reserve that was being kept in shape by grazing Dartmoor ponies. A buzzard briefly appeared above the trees before vanishing just as quickly. After the briefest of views of Lexham Hall at the end of an avenue of trees, I encountered four young men with large backpacks coming the other way. Duke of Edinburgh Award initiates, they did not speak but just looked miserable, as if the outdoor adventure they were having was someone else's idea of fun.

The next village, East Lexham, was cosily wrapped around a green with a bandstand-like butter market as its centrepiece. The business of trading butter or any other commodity other than occasional jars of WI jam seems improbable in such a place but it is easy to forget that modern-day commuter villages like this were once the centre of the world for the majority of the population.

St Andrew's, the village church, is round-towered and indisputably very old. It is, according to no less an authority than historian Nikolaus Pevsner, of Saxon origin, and the ditched, circular mound on which it stands may have originally been a site of pagan worship. The church is plain – a flint round tower with belfry windows, cement-plastered exterior walls – but there was something of a sense of time standing still here, of ancient tenure, as if it were a glimpse through a wormhole to pre-Conquest Britain. According to some sources, and it is easy to believe, the church is the oldest Saxon church in the county, the second oldest being just down the road at neighbouring West Lexham.

Another accredited Saxon church – this one with a squat, central square tower – stands nearby at Newton. Why such a concentration of ancient churches was clustered here in this quiet corner of west Norfolk is something of a mystery, especially given the proximity of the Norman stronghold of Castle Acre, where I was heading.

As I left East Lexham, the bells of St Andrew's chimed the half-hour behind me. I was just beginning to reflect on the serenity of the place when a brace of jet fighters screamed overhead like vengeful dragons. There had been no warning of their coming: just a momentary clamour, a vapour-trail tearing of sky, and the planes were gone, the stillness of the day shattered in their wake.

At West Lexham no less than four buzzards were circling above the church, their high-pitched mews fluttering down to earth like cast-off feathers. The ancient church, another Saxon jewel tucked-away from the rest of the village in its own undisturbed green acre, seemed to have such a numinous presence that, walking away, I felt the need for an over-the-shoulder glance to check it was still there.

A quiet lane led into Castle Acre. Castle Acre is Norman to its core. How many villages of this size can boast a motte and bailey castle *and* a Cluniac priory? Both castle and monastery were founded by William de Warenne, one of William the Conqueror's main henchmen, shortly after the conquest. There is also a trace of a defensive town wall – a fortified medieval gateway that straddles the top of the high street next to the village green. The high street, which drops sharply downhill towards the river, is hardly standard Norfolk. Its slope too steep, its houses a little too picturesque, it resembles more an idealised Dorset hamlet: Thomas Hardy country, Hovis adverts – cue nostalgic brass bands and cloth-capped boys on trade bikes. But Castle Acre is hardly typical in many ways. Since time immemorial the village has stood at a crossroads of tracks – the Peddars Way runs north–south through the village – and it is easy to see why the newly arrived Normans took such a strategic interest.

The Peddars Way, originating in the Brecks close to Thetford and terminating at Norfolk's coast at Holme-next-the-Sea, is an ancient thoroughfare. Although improved, paved and utilised by Romans as a supply route to its Saxon Shore fort at Brandoninum (latter-day Brancaster), it almost certainly is of even older pedigree. An extension of the Icknield Way, which connected Norfolk with the south coast by way of the chalk escarpments of the Chilterns and the Ridgeway, the same route may have served as a conduit for the flint trade in pre-Roman times. Long-established by the time the Normans arrived in Norfolk, the Peddars Way would have held importance for the regional transport of people and goods akin to that of the modern-day A11. The Nar Valley Way, in contrast, is a recent creation, although the Nar river itself has long served as a channel for traffic, trade and religion between inland Norfolk and The Wash.

I arrived in the village just in time to catch the bus back to Mileham. Waiting for the twice-weekly bus service, its timetable sourced online, I grew anxious about whether the vehicle would actually turn up, the very existence of such a service seeming increasingly improbable with every minute that passed beyond the designated arrival time. The bus eventually showed up, just ten minutes late, a 1960s vintage coach full of pensioners on a weekly trip to market in King's Lynn. The driver, a youth who looked to be about fourteen years old, seemed a little taken aback when I flagged him down, as if no one had ever got on the bus in Castle Acre before. I enquired about the fare to Mileham and the fresh-faced driver, whom every passenger knew as Jack, plucked a figure out of the air – a perfectly reasonable one – suggesting it more as a polite bartering gambit than a demand.

We set off, rattling eastwards along minor roads through burnished countryside that everyone else ignored. In the seat in front of me, an elderly woman showed her neighbour photos of a newly purchased sewing machine on her mobile phone, pleased with her recently acquired mastery of the device. Pulling up in Mileham to let me off, everybody on the bus bade me a cheery farewell. The bus and its microcosm of old-fashioned courtesy then clattered on to its home base somewhere in deepest central Norfolk. Almost immediately, the journey felt as if it had been some sort of apparition – a ghost-bus; my travelling companions, agreeable revenants of a bygone rural England.

*

I returned to Castle Acre on the last day in October, driving there with Jackie and her friend. It was Halloween yet the day was disarmingly mild, warm even, with the temperature broaching twenty degrees Celsius. Before I set off walking the three of us had coffee together at a tearoom by the church. Sitting at an outside table to make the most of the weather, the only visible sign of autumn seemed to be the thin carpet of curling leaves that had fallen from the lime trees outside The Ostrich pub.

I walked out of the village along the edge of Castle Acre Common. Then an oak-lined lane led me into woodland, where I ploughed a furrow through fallen beech leaves. I crossed a footbridge over a stream close to a three-storey mill building tucked away in the deep shade of willows, the tranquillity tarnished slightly by the insistent bleat of a car alarm from an unseen vehicle.

Not to be outdone by its neighbour, the next village, West Acre, also has its own ruined Norman priory. An Augustinian fraternity founded in the 12th century, its buildings were abandoned and left to the elements at the time of the Dissolution during the reign of Henry VIII. Little now remains other than a fractured arch that stands next to the church (in a field full of belligerent-looking bulls). A dark corridor of yews led to the church's main entrance, which has a skull in the keystone of its stone arch, a purposeful reminder of mortality for parishioners. The clock on the tower spells out *PRAY AND WATCH*, each letter marking an hour of the day. In the churchyard, the closest I could get for a view of the ruins, a cherry sapling was bursting into bloom, fooled by the unseasonably warm weather.

With cottages clustered around a small green, West Acre is certainly pretty but, like many rural settlements that have largely been given over to commuters, the village is just a shadow of what it once must have been. The 'Old Post Office' is now a domestic dwelling, as is the 'Old Nurse's House'. I looked for an 'Old Smithy' but failed to find one, although I have seen the equivalent in no end of similarly gentrified villages. Such once-important foci of rural life now exist in name only – nostalgic call-backs to a less complicated past. The tropes are deceptive. There is little work to be had in the modern-day countryside: most rural post offices closed for business years ago, medical practices are now only usually found only in towns, and these days very few require the services of a blacksmith. Contemporary agribusiness employs precious few labourers and any short-term seasonal work is usually carried out by European migrants. Community has dissipated – many village pubs have either closed or been upgraded to gastropubs or 'eateries' with an emphasis on posh nosh. Most villagers drink at home now, supping pinot grigio or cheap foreign lager purchased at an out-of-town supermarket some way from where they live. The romantic notion of unchanging village life is a deceit, albeit a sometimes charming one. In extreme cases, living in a village, rather than being part of a viable community, has become akin to having tenancy of a residential theme park. True, there is still a patrician aristocracy – benign or otherwise – in place at the big house but very few can find employment on the land these days. Country life has increasingly become the preserve of the well-heeled – those with sufficient means and the wherewithal to run a car – whilst the old, the poor, the young and unskilled are inevitably left behind. The pervading rural idyll of a cottage with roses round the door and a Labrador by the Aga has become an *Escape to the Country* fantasy for upwardly mobile suburbanites. Much of what remains is merely an imitation of an idealised past.

*

A farm track that skirted meadows of grazing cattle led the way out of West Acre. One field was set up for a Halloween event taking place that night. There was a large Samhain bonfire – a solid pyramid of logs, tree clippings and broken palettes – and a couple of marquee tents equipped to distribute beer and barbecued meat. With no rain on the horizon to dampen bonfires or spirits, and with enough booze and burgers on hand to satisfy even the most insatiable of ghouls, it looked set to be a fun evening.

The track rose gently through sheep pasture and beneath a string of pylons that crackled with electricity as I passed underneath. Despite the season, the sun was summer-warm on my face. Leaning momentarily on a fencepost, I noticed that it was covered with ladybirds that had been lured from hibernation by the unseasonably warm weather.

I met a middle-aged couple with a dog coming the other way through the woods. Stopping to talk, they told me that they were from Southend and on holiday in the area, staying at a converted priory near Pentney. Our conversation turned to Narford Hall and the estate that we were walking through. The estate is open to walkers but Narford Hall, Grade I listed and built by Sir Andrew Fountaine in the early 18th century, is inaccessible. The hall has long been closed to outsiders; even Nikolaus Pevsner had been unable to gain entry to catalogue its charms. The hall's previous incumbent, also called Andrew Fountaine, had fought on

Franco's side during the Spanish Civil War and was well known for his far-right sympathies. These had supposedly gone as far as allowing estate land to be used for John Tyndall-supervised Aryan boot camps in the 1960s. Disillusioned by the Tories who disowned him for his extremism, Fountaine eventually stood as National Front candidate for a succession of seats. The last of these was at Norwich South in 1979. Falling out with Tyndall in the same year he went on to form his own splinter party, the Nationalist Party, but this met with little success. Fountaine, who was also rumoured to have dabbled with witchcraft, had regularly entertained a local aristocratic witch called Monica English – both were keen on fox hunting and hunts were organised regularly at the hall. He also happened to be uncle by marriage to Tony Martin, the Fenland farmer who shot dead a sixteen-year-old burglar at his home in Emneth in 1999.

The Essex couple told me to look out for the folly on the estate, where they had seen a barn owl, and spoke of their favourite place for a meal in the area, a west Norfolk gastropub that was apparently favoured by the rich and famous.

'Do you know who goes there regular? Sir Alan Sugar! You know – him off *The Apprentice*. He sometimes flies in special in his helicopter. The staff told us that we just missed him last time we were there for a meal.'

They enthused about the area, of which they were clearly very fond.

'We come back here three or four times a year. It's lovely and peaceful – a nice change from all that noise and racket in Southend. It's just like a city there these days. You can't hear yourself think.'

We parted company and I soon arrived at a road where a track led into gloomy coniferous forest full of oddly distorted trees. Reaching a clearing, Narford Hall came into view to the south, resplendent in its setting by a lake. At the edge of the clearing stood the folly the couple had told me about – a viewing pavilion that commanded a favourable view of the hall and estate.

The folly is suitably grand – a neoclassical pavilion with art nouveau tiling and an alcove with a missing statue. In essence, it is little more than a façade constructed specifically to take in the view over the lake and hall, a viewpoint from which to gloat over one's domain. There was no sign of the owl the Essex couple had mentioned, other than splashes of guano on the tiled floor that could have been the work of any bird. Like the gatepost I had seen earlier, ladybirds had come out of hibernation to bask on the tiles of the sun-warmed inner wall. In Celtic mythology there is a threshold to the underworld across which the souls of the dead and supernatural creatures venture forth on Samhain, a 'thin time' when the worlds of spirit and materiality are fleetingly closer than usual. Were the ladybirds a portent of something that might emerge later that night?

At Narborough, the bus I had hoped to catch back to Norwich was late, and it was forty minutes before one finally arrived. As I waited at the stop, I was entertained – perhaps not the right word – by a group of sweary schoolchildren who were hanging round waiting for someone's mother to turn up. The children, maybe eleven or twelve in age, were mostly boys, and in time-honoured tradition they were all doing their best to impress the two girls in their company by behaving in a way that they imagined tougher, older boys might.

I was relieved when an elderly man crossed the road to join me. He asked how long I had been waiting before tutting in response, remarking that bus drivers sometimes did not bother coming off the bypass into the village if they were running a bit late. Standing at the stop together, periodically checking our wristwatches, we soon fell into more general conversation about the sort of things that preoccupied the folk of rural west Norfolk – sugar beet, wind farms and the thorny subject of Eastern European immigration.

The bus finally arrived just as the sun was setting. After such a warm, light-filled afternoon, the sky darkening at such an early hour seemed almost absurd. Then I remembered that the next day would be the first of November.

We headed east along the A47, the last traces of daylight catching the hay bales that were coiled like giant slices of Swiss roll in the fields. This was the same Norfolk as portrayed in *The Goob*, a 2015 film shot in the west of the county that managed to make the flat, open countryside look simultaneously beautiful and just a little menacing. The film deals with coming-of-age and the more general matters that affect the lives of those who inhabit the small towns and villages of the region – immigration, seasonal agricultural work, the inescapable sense of entrapment that rural environments can sometimes provoke. Much of the film's action takes place at a transport café alongside a busy main road. This fictitious setting made use of an abandoned garage complex at the entrance to the village of Necton, a familiar sight to those who regularly travel the A47 between King's Lynn and Norwich. We passed this just after it grew fully dark, the semi-derelict buildings and pot-holed forecourt forlorn in the cold beam of car headlights.

*

It was almost the end of November by the time I managed to return to Narborough. The weather had changed markedly by now and the days had slipped from balmy Indian summer to a fugue of gloomy skies and ever-shortening daylight. A grey eiderdown of cloud lay low over the land as if to mulch it in readiness for the winter to come. It just happened to be 'Black Friday', the super-discount shopping day that had recently been imported from the United States and in the wake of relentless media promotion seemed to be gathering momentum in the British psyche. I felt honour-bound not to waste time or money on what was effectively early Christmas shopping, so I absented myself from Norwich's retail fever and instead took the King's Lynn bus from the bus station.

The westbound X1 had its usual weekday demographic of students, young mums with prams and OAPs. This one, with comfy faux-leather seats, also had the novelty of a recorded voice announcing the stops. The voice brought to mind the cheery male commentator on Cilla Black's erstwhile Saturday-night show *Blind Date*, and pronounced Swaffham as 'Swaff-Ham', much to the amusement of tittering passengers for whom the correct Norfolk pronunciation – 'Swaarf'm' – was more or less genetic.

I got off the bus at the same stop in the village and made my way towards the river. On the edge of the road next to the village hall was something that looked to be a dried-out chamois leather. Then I noticed a pair of horns: a squashed and largely desiccated muntjac deer. At the side of the village hall stood the detached cockpit of a RAF Canberra trainer, a reminder that the airbase at RAF Marham is nearby. Narborough is one of the closest villages to the airbase, although all it could provide in the way of R&R was the Chinese restaurant that had taken over what used to be the village pub. While many rural Norfolk taverns have closed or gone the way of the, now ubiquitous, gastropub, this one has opted for serving up food by numbers.

Down at the water, I took the riverside path upstream. A little way along it, spanning the Nar on both sides, are the brick footings of a onetime bridge, a remnant of the East Dereham to King's Lynn railway line that used to cross the river here. On the opposite bank of the river, on a site now occupied by industrial units, were the maltings that had once been the village's main employer.

Further ahead, looming over the water, is a large cast iron mill wheel detached from any of the grinding equipment it would have once driven. I had come across the wheel a couple of years earlier when, walking the same river path, I met a couple of women who were members of the local Ramblers group. The wheel, they told me, marked the site of the former Narborough Bone Mill where bones were brought from local slaughterhouses for grinding into fertiliser in the early 1800s. What surprised me was to learn that whalebones had also once been transported here upriver from King's Lynn.

It seemed odd to be reminded of giant sea-dwelling creatures here in rural Norfolk but whales had once been part of the county's economy, albeit in a fairly minor way. There is still a Whalebone pub in Norwich, an inn that supposedly took its name from a whalebone arch that once stood nearby. There is also a Yarmouth connection. Prior to the building being bombed and virtually destroyed by a 1942 air raid, Great Yarmouth's Minster Church of St Nicholas had housed a whalebone throne upon which it had been a tradition for newly married couples to sit after their wedding ceremony. The seat had been fashioned from the skull and vertebrae salvaged from a sperm whale carcass found washed up on the beach at Caister-on-Sea in 1592. Originally placed outside the Guildhall that once stood close to the entrance to the minster, in 1606 the seat was painted and dubbed the 'Devil's Seat', together with a concocted backstory that anyone who dared to sit on it would face disaster. It stood there for over two hundred years until the Guildhall's demolition in 1844 when the chair was moved inside the church to a niche by the west door. By this time it had somehow overcome its sinister reputation to become an object of better fortune for those who sat upon it.

Great Yarmouth was never a whaling port but King's Lynn was. Although of lesser importance than other east coast ports like Hull and Grimsby, the west Norfolk town was involved in the whale business in the late 18th and early 19th century and Lynn boats frequently set sail for the Greenland fisheries in search of cetacean bounty (little remains in Lynn today to remind of its whaling days other than the ghost of a name, Blubberhouses Creek, just south of the town). Whaling was a lucrative but a perilous business that dealt fortune and hardship in equal measure. Whales harpooned in the icy waters of the North Atlantic were laboriously cut up in sections for transportation back to port in boats groaning under their weight. King's Lynn was one such centre for onshore processing. Blubber was boiled down for fuel oil – at one time, whale oil illuminated the town's St Margaret's Church – while bones were extracted for use in chair backs, butchers' blocks and ladies' corsetry. The bones that remained were then transported upriver to the mill at Narborough for grinding into agricultural fertiliser. The River Nar was dredged back then, deeper and more navigable than today. The stench involved in the process must have been literally breathtaking and so Narborough's relative isolation may have been to its advantage. It painted a curious picture: the image of barges laden with shattered, stinking whale carcasses moving slowly upstream against an agricultural backdrop. While it would have been a strange sight to behold, its olfactory impact would have been even more extraordinary.

Whales still turn up on Norfolk beaches from time to time – sperm whales, minke whales, fin whales, Sowerby's beaked whales. It has been an increasing trend in recent years, although the reason for their beaching is rarely very clear – perhaps a problem with their navigation system, disorientation, disease or trauma. Solar storms have been blamed, as has military sonar and seismic exploration for oil. A stranded whale is a difficult thing to save, a tricky thing to manoeuvre back into the water. Almost invariably, they die. Considerable effort then has to be invested to remove them from the shoreline before their flesh putrefies and stinks up the beach. What is it that drives them into shallow waters they cannot escape from? It is almost as if it is some sort of ancestral haunting, a response to memories held in the cetacean collective unconscious of their one-time pursuit by whaling ships in Greenland waters; a defiant gesture that says, 'All right, here you are then, here is my flesh, here are my old bones, do what you will with them.'

There had been another source of bone meal that was stranger still – macabre, in fact. The Ramblers women had alluded to it when I spoke with them at the mill wheel; a Google search revealed that what they had heard rumoured was in fact true. When the international whale trade fizzled out in the 1820s, alternative sources of bone were required, and there is strong evidence that human remains exhumed from cemeteries in north Germany were transported here via King's Lynn for grinding in the mill. A popular saying of the time, presumably to mitigate the grisly nature of the enterprise in straight-talking economic terms, had been, 'One ton of German bone-dust saves the importation of ten tons of German corn.' The ghastliest of grist to bring to any mill, the bone dust of dead Hamburgers had once enriched these same Norfolk fields that I now walked through.

The Dereham to King's Lynn railway that opened in 1846 largely superseded the river as the main conduit to supply the mill, and the Nar navigation was abandoned in 1884, although barges probably still plied the route for a few years afterwards. The mill stopped production around the same time although its buildings survived into the 20th century before being demolished, their bricks recycled for local building work or rubble for farm tracks. Wheat and barley still grow well here. Yet so much lies under these fields as historical sediment – the fabric of the works that carried out the milling, the track-bed of the railway that took over from the river trade, the bone-dust of whales and Germans.

*

The path followed the river's edge for the next few miles, a binary landscape of tall poplars alongside water with soggy fen beyond. At the sluice at Marham Fen a family of swans were bobbing contentedly in the bubbling water as if enjoying a Jacuzzi. Complaining squadrons of crows flew up from the fields in every direction: ragged silhouettes against the sky. Every now and again a few of them would take time out to mob a gull, more out of force of habit than a response to existential threat. When the noise of the birds subsided I realised that I could no longer discern the rumble of traffic from the now-distant A47. Such peace was short-lived, shattered in a moment by the banshee shriek of a fighter from RAF Marham screaming overhead and putting all the birds to flight.

At Abbey Priory the riverside path was colonised by docile sheep that eyed me indifferently as I ploughed my way through them, parting only reluctantly at the very last instance. Across the water, the medieval stone façade of the gatehouse was all that remained of the Augustinian priory that once stood here. When I had last been here the building had been covered in scaffolding but now it was fully repaired and re-purposed as a holiday apartment complex, its pale stonework still gleaming from recent sandblasting. Cromwell's army had been responsible for the destruction of several religious institutions in this part of the country, and many pot shots from Roundhead boats were fired at offending establishments such as this one. Somehow, the abbey gatehouse managed to survive intact, either because it had been beyond the reach of artillery or simply as a matter of pure luck.

Just beyond the priory, I crossed a footbridge over to the opposite bank. The path continued past flooded gravel pits that still bore the rough edges of the extraction industry, although a proliferation of *KEEP OUT* and *PRIVATE FISHING* signs suggested they had already been earmarked for fishing. The OS map showed one of the man-made lakes as 'Geneva' (no *jet d'eau* or mountain backdrop here) and another was named Priory Lake. These were names that conferred a romanticism that was largely absent from the view on the ground where pyramids of builder's sand and gravel conferred all the aesthetic appeal of a building site.

Beyond the gravel pits, the soot-black soil of the Fens started to show in the fields. Overhead pylon wires crackled eerily. A cormorant perched in a dead tree positioned itself to dry its wings, its silhouette resembling a miniature pterodactyl that had somehow found its way from the Jurassic.

Finally, I reached Setchey, hard up against the hyperactive A10, the main route between King's Lynn and Cambridge, and representing just as much of a tangible frontier as the River Ouse. This was not yet the Norfolk border, even if in my mind I tend to associate anything west of King's Lynn to be part of a different county, a different country even. Before reaching that other country it was first necessary to cross the wide, low-lying region that sat impassively between East Anglia and the Midlands: the water-drained flatlands known as the Fens.

Chapter 7

Postcode Country

Norfolk Marshland

A frontier region... the resort of brigands and bandits
Sir Clifford Darby, *The Medieval Fenland*

The winter was marred by all-too-familiar arthritic aches and pains but with the steadily increasing ration of daylight that came with the onset of spring I started to think about walking again. On May Day, stepping out like the protagonist of an English folk song, I returned to Setchey, back to the territory that held the uncertain frontier between 'High Norfolk' and the Fens.

Before starting on this journey, I thought I knew most of Norfolk well. The map of Norfolk was the back of my hand: its rivers etched by veins; my knuckles, the Cromer Ridge. But the Fens, a territory that spans the margins of three counties, was another matter. This was a region I knew only fleetingly, mostly from the window of a car or train. Passing swiftly through without apology, unwilling to stop, this vast flat expanse of open fields did not seem a territory ideally suited to exploration on foot. And why should it? As I understood it, the Fens region was little more than dried-out wetlands given over to intensive farming; a place of no-frills functionality, of borrowed land and borrowed time. Before Dutch engineers were recruited to drain the land in the 17th century, the indigenous population was largely made up of eel catchers and wildfowlers who lived pretty much outside the law. Some might say that this aspect of the Fens has still not vanished entirely – the whole region is at the edge of polite society, the sort of place looked down upon even by west Norfolk farmers with attitude (and also a little altitude, to accentuate their perceived superiority), a region where taciturnity might be worn like a badge of honour.

Before draining and transformation to a region of intensive arable farming, the Fens was a swampy hinterland of marshes, rivers and low-slung islands. The northern reaches bordering The Wash – an area usually referred to as the Marshlands but sometimes called Silt Fen because of its silt-rich loam soils – were laid down under salt water but now stand slightly above mean sea level. It is a region where, as late as the 16th century, the shore of The Wash extended as far as Wisbech and Spalding; a region where the Situationist slogan '*Sous les pavés, la plage*' might be modified to read '*Sous les pavés, la mer*'. South of here were the true Fens – the Black Fen – that lay just below sea level, a vast growbag of fertile black peat punctuated with scattered centres of population like Ely, Thorney and Crowland on 'islands' that were slightly higher in elevation.

Contrary to popular belief, the Fens had not been largely unpopulated in the much-misunderstood 'Dark Age' period between the end of Roman colonisation and Norman rule. In the Anglo-Saxon period, the Fens was a managed landscape, with island-living inhabitants engaged cooperatively in *gamaene worc* – 'mean or common work' – to maintain seasonal meadows and manage the water with controlled inundation. The main land use during this period was cattle rearing, and the seasonally flooded land, enriched annually with fresh silt deposits, made for excellent grazing. It was not until the late 11th century that the economy and land tenure of the region changed dramatically, a consequence of the widespread gifting of land to the Norman aristocracy and the Church.

The whole region, Fen and Marshland, has long been considered bandit country (a prejudice confirmed by pioneering historical geographer Sir Clifford Darby, the first to gain a PhD in geography from Cambridge University). Impenetrable, unknowable to outsiders, this was the region where the semi-mythical nobleman Hereward the Wake organised his raids on the hated Norman invaders and where, six centuries later, embittered eel-wranglers lurked in wait to attack the Dutch engineers that had been employed to drain the land.

Even today the region's public image is little better. To some, this low-lying frontier zone remains a territory where outsiders are both unwelcome and ill equipped to survive; a modern day realm of Little Englanders, Eastern European farm workers and marginalised Romany travellers. True, the well-educated affluence of Cambridge is just down the road, but no boater-hatted punter ever ventures further north than Ely unless absolutely necessary.

All this is, of course, conjecture: the image that some Fenlanders like to project to the outside world – a misunderstood region with the collective persona of Millwall FC ('No one likes us, we don't care'). But the same accusations of insularity and belligerent xenophobia can be attributed to many other parts of the country, almost anywhere, in fact – so what of the reality? I really could not say as I had never spent much time in the region other than passing through it on journeys between Norfolk and the Midlands or the North. All I knew was that, travelling in either direction, the Fen landscape engendered a vague sense of unease in me and it always felt a relief to start to notice even the most modest of slopes once more after having travelled for miles under an enormous sky through often dreary flatlands. It was always a relief to be free of the tyranny of the horizon, a relief to see *relief*, either the modest swell of High Norfolk or the undulating countryside that signified arrival in the East Midlands.

*

Setchey was unchanged from how I remembered it: a bridge over the river, a linear sprawl of houses and bungalows on either side of the lorry-rattled A10 that shot through the village like a sciatic jolt of pain.

I waited for a break in the traffic and crossed the road to make my way down to the riverside path on the western side of the bridge. The path traced the River Nar for a mile or so before following a farm track that led away from the river, past drainage channels and through vast yellow fields pungent with flowering oilseed rape. Electricity pylons ran along a distant field edge like a perimeter fence. It was difficult to say how far-off they were as it was almost impossible to scale distance in this two-dimensional landscape. Seen across the vast prairie-like fields, the pylons might well have delineated the very edge of the world or, at the very least, the beginning of a 'Here be Dragons' territory of the imagination.

I crossed the Cambridge to King's Lynn railway line and, just before arriving at the Great Ouse, passed a lay-by where several plastic bags of crockery had been discarded among the ragwort and flattened Coke cans. Curious as to what sort of tableware local folk considered disposable, I took a look. Many of the pieces appeared to be the sort of promotional merchandise you might have found gracing a 1970s pub lounge: ashtrays with the name of a whisky manufacturer clumsily applied by transfer, a candle-holder that bore images of Nelson and an advert for 'British Navy' Pusser's Rum – the sort of thing that generally finds its way into the bargain box at car boot sales. I picked up the candle-holder and put it in my rucksack, a souvenir for Jackie, who after years of marriage has grown accustomed to my instinct for collecting worthless found objects such as this.

At the wide channel of the River Ouse a group of newly arrived swallows glided and cavorted high above as they effortlessly scooped flies from the air. Before crossing the river, I diverted a little way south to investigate the ruin of Wiggenhall St Peter's, one of three churches that stand in godly collusion within a mile of each other along the river here. St Peter's abuts the raised riverbank half a mile south of the bridge at Wiggenhall St Germans. Slowly, firm but resolute, feral nature was taking over, and elder bushes had sprung up in the stony niches of the graveyard, levering gravestones out of kilter as their branches arched skywards. Skeletal stone arches give way to a roofless nave that is open to the sky. Small carved-stone heads bookend the arches, each bearing the gloomy medieval face of those doomed to a pious yet disagreeable life. Here, set in weathered limestone, their solemn likenesses are already half a millennium old and destined to outlast the building whose portal they guarded.

I headed north along the riverbank to Wiggenhall St Germans where, clustered next to the church, is a pub with a beer garden, a shop and a repairs garage. I crossed the bridge and, walking out of the village, skirted the edge of an enormous field that took me a full half-hour to cross: a prairie of oilseed rape that had just a couple of stunted trees to break the monotony. A distant line of pylons stitched the yellow monoculture to the blue-grey sky. The effect was a binary illusion, a landscape draped with a faded Ukrainian flag.

I came to Islington, which too small to describe as a hamlet let alone a village, is little more than a parish with a signpost. The village sign depicted a woman in country dress sat on a bank with herons flying about her. Next to this stood a dog waste bin, an expensive-looking concrete bench that had been neatly inscribed *DR PUNSFER GIFT*, and a notice board that had parliamentary election notices securely locked behind glass. A three-way signpost indicated the direction of the two Tilneys – All Saints and St James – the three Wiggenhalls – St Mary's, St Mary Magdalene,

St Germans – and Marshland St James. A focal point in a huge land-sea of yellow and green, it felt as if this tiny island of information and signage marked the earthly coordinates of some sort of uncharted East Anglian pole of inaccessibility. It also made me wonder how many resting backsides would ever polish Dr Punsfer's civic-minded bench.

This same Islington, I later found out, was a late Anglo-Saxon settlement that had once been sufficiently populous to have its own church and warrant inclusion in the Domesday Book. St Mary's, a 14th-century replacement of the original church, still stands within the parish, although it is now redundant and partly ruined. Islington itself has been reduced to just a few cottages and isolated farmsteads, a long way from its namesake in the capital; although that urban borough (originally *Giseldone* – 'Gisla's Hill') was also an Anglo-Saxon village, hence the shared name.

Approaching Terrington St John along a footpath, a hand-painted notice screamed out *THIS IS NOT A PUBLIC FOOTPATH* with Magritte-style, '*Ceci n'est pas une pipe*' logic. The work of a local Dadaist or – more likely – a curmudgeonly farmer, the forbidding message contradicted the two Norfolk County Council public footpath arrows that adorned the broken post to which it was fixed. I followed it anyway.

It was starting to look as if the Marshlands did not necessarily 'welcome walkers' as places in more traditional hiking country, like the Peak District or Yorkshire Dales, were wont to declare on their village signs. Certainly, this was not natural territory for pedestrianism of any kind: footpaths were scarce and few lanes or byways criss-crossed this drained and repurposed marsh country, which not so very long ago had been an unpopulated watery realm of eels and waterfowl.

*

I took the bus to King's Lynn with Jackie a few days later. We spent a couple of hours together wandering around South Quay admiring the Hanseatic buildings of the old port then, after lunch together on the quay, I caught another bus to Terrington St John to pick up from where I had left off.

The stretch between Terrington St John and Wisbech had troubled me as there was no obvious route to follow. While there were country roads and farm tracks that seemed to head in vaguely the right direction, the OS map showed no clear footpaths or the like. In the end I resorted to Google Earth and traced what looked like the most direct route between the two settlements, zooming in like a spy satellite to see if any of the field boundaries marked on the OS map looked feasible to walk along in lieu of a properly defined way. They did, but it was all a little uncertain.

I left Terrington St John in light drizzle and, after following a dual-carriageway for a short way out of the village, turned south along a zigzagging concrete farm track. The air was sweet and musky with May blossom, the frothy heads of verge-side cow parsley brightening up the gloom of an otherwise dreary day. In the distance, beyond a wide, whiskery expanse of barley, stood lines of pole-straight poplars; beyond these, breaking the horizon, were half-dead willows with shattered trunks and twisted boughs. As a bank of foreboding dark clouds gathered in the east, a low shaft of sunlight broke through momentarily to illuminate a distant white cottage, making it glow preternaturally as if it were the end of the rainbow or the location of buried treasure. Even here, in the monocultural world of agribusiness, nature asserted itself. A yellow wagtail perched atop the haulms of a broad bean field; a skylark clattered noisily overhead while a kestrel broke cover to fly up from the poplars. As I watched the kestrel hover above some unseen prey, a roe deer appeared as if out of nowhere, dancing in swift leaps and bounds through the barley as if it were jumping over waves of water. Delicate in its movement, and as nervous as a kitten, the animal rapidly skirted the dyke I was following before vanishing from view when it became engulfed by the barley once more.

The OS map showed a minor track that led up to a farm. This, I had ascertained from Google Earth, was the only possible route I could take to reconnect with the road, so I climbed over a gate and followed the concrete track towards the farm buildings I could see in the distance ahead. A short way along the track I found something quite disturbing, something that had a touch of folk horror menace about it: a solitary crow entrapped in a small wire cage, the bird kept alive with a grain feeder and water dish like an awkward over-sized budgerigar. The crow was an unwilling decoy, a hostage intended to lure its companions into the cage that served as its gaol. I was aware that many farmers considered crows to be vermin, but this was the first trapping device of its kind I had ever seen. The fact that the bird was still alive did not make it any less awful.

The trap was emblematic of other gamekeeper's ploys I have witnessed over the years: birds with broken necks hanging from posts, velvety lines of dead moles suspended from a fence – disquieting totems to repel unwanted fauna. An Internet search later revealed this portable Guantánamo to be a Multi Catch Larsen Trap (about £100 on Amazon, which stocked a good range of magpie traps, too, and plastic decoy birds for those who did not want to take the trouble of baiting their trap with a live one). Despite my repugnance, the trap was legal. I was tempted to try and free the bird although, realistically, this could not have been achieved without a serious pair of wire cutters. Crows are notoriously intelligent; I wondered: did this hostage have the wherewithal to signal to its fellow birds to keep well away? At least it seemed to have managed this so far as the bird remained alone, miserable in its caged isolation.

Arriving at the farmyard, I came across a worker climbing down from a tractor. He seemed affable enough, albeit a tad curious as to what I was doing there.

'Are you having a bit of a walk round the area, then?'

I affirmed and asked the way to the road ahead, although I could see it plain enough. The two elephants in the farmyard-room – my trespassing, the farm's antipathy to crows – went unmentioned.

I followed a narrow, grass-centred lane where half a dozen chickens wandered distractedly, unafraid of traffic. This took me past Ten Trees Pig Farm, a name that struck me as over-specific although detail is everything in this minimalist landscape. A fine drizzle started to fall again as I skirted an enormous field that had been marked with a mysterious square of fence posts – a building plot? Then, at West Drive Farm (another beige descriptor), I took a track through wheat and mustard fields beneath a line of pylons that marched Godzilla-like towards the horizon.

Another minor road led me past a traveller caravan site. There was no one about, just a few loose-tethered horses and dishevelled Shetland ponies. A signpost pointed to Emneth, a couple of miles distant. Emneth is a name that comes with a reputation: the wrong sort of notoriety. Although the Reverend Wilbert Awdry, creator of *Thomas the Tank Engine*, had once been vicar of the village's St Edmunds Church, Emneth was better known these days as the home village of Norfolk farmer turned intruder-shooter Tony Martin. It was a place where, simmering with rage after several attempted burglaries on his property, Martin had lived as an isolated bachelor in a rundown farmhouse (presciently named Bleak House). Newspaper reports in the more sensationalist press at the time of the 1999 trial had gone to town on Martin's background, relishing the freedom to play fast and loose with the hackneyed Norfolk tropes of inbreeding, straw-chewing stupidity and rampant xenophobia. Martin's murder case had introduced new material with which to embellish the stereotype – far right politics, the wilful insularity of Fen folk and, perhaps most fancifully, the apparent lawlessness of a frontier region where Norfolk met Cambridgeshire and where the respective constabularies of either county were not very much interested in policing. More disturbing though, was the view in some quarters that Martin was a modern-day folk hero, and that the sixteen-year-old traveller boy shot running away from the crime scene had got all he deserved. An unlikely, and unlikeable, celebrity, Martin's subsequent infamy drew many would-be reactionaries out of the woodwork. A have-a-go hero poster boy for the likes of demented xenophobes like Britain First, it seemed only a matter of time before some aspiring Andrew Lloyd Webber acolyte scored *Tony Martin: the Musical.*

The track past the caravan site led to a junction of paths from where I could hear the faint rumble of traffic on the A47 in the distance. It was becoming clear that road traffic in the Fens, however far-off it might be, could always be just about discerned if you listened hard enough. Perhaps it was this vague, almost sub-audible thrum – the constant taunt of an ever-present escape route – that contributed to the region's contrarian outlook?

I headed down what looked to be a private road, past industrial-scale farm buildings and a solitary bungalow. I half expected to be challenged but there was no one about. The road terminated at a metal gate, and then continued as a heavily overgrown farm track, which took me to the raised bank of the A47, where trucks and white vans rattled by at sixty miles-per-hour in both directions. Darting across the road, eyed up by passing drivers, I felt like a fugitive, an outlaw traversing forbidden territory. Even to me, this seemed to be a strange place to be walking.

Across the road, a narrow path brought me to a large expanse of orchards. A tractor was towing a trailer between the trees, spraying something that was swirling up in the wind. Seeing me approach, the driver stopped to let me walk by before recommencing. The orchard ended abruptly at the edge of a new estate of pristine detached houses that looked so freshly occupied that it seemed unlikely the cellophane was off the three-piece suites yet. This sparkling new development marked the edge of Walsoken, Norfolk's most westernmost outpost and a village that is effectively a suburb of the Cambridgeshire town of Wisbech.

Clouds were starting to gather threateningly and it seemed a good idea to go into the centre of Wisbech as quickly as possible to get the bus home. I managed to navigate my way to the Lynn Road but after diverting down a cycle path – a shortcut that turned out to be anything but – I found that I was lost. It was about this time that the rain started to fall in earnest. Disoriented and uncertain which way to go, I followed a long, curving road through suburban housing estates but it seemed to lead nowhere in particular, certainly not the centre of town. Coming across two men sheltering in the porch of a house, I asked for directions. Was the town centre far? Was this the right direction? By now I was rain-bedraggled and this did not go unnoticed. The men just smirked at each other and told me that the town centre was miles away, back in the direction that I had just come.

Tired, wet and not a little aggrieved by such thinly disguised Schadenfreude, I sloped off in search of the mythical town centre. Perhaps I was doomed to perpetual circumambulation – a human satellite locked in unbroken orbit? More petulant rain-walking ensued. Finally, I arrived at a main road where a *WALSOKEN* road sign marked what must have been the town's northern boundary. There was a bus stop, too, which I managed to reach just in time to flag down an eastbound X1 for the long, damp journey back to Norwich.

Chapter 8

Islands in the Fens

North Cambridgeshire/South Lincolnshire

We passed the Fenn country to Wisbich, but saw nothing that way to tempt our curiosity but deep roads, innumerable dreyns and dykes of water, all navigable, and a rich soil, the land bearing a vast quantity of good hemp.

Daniel Defoe, *Tour through the Eastern Counties of England*, 1722

Another X1 bus wheeled me back to Wisbech a few days later. Not wishing to take any chances on getting lost in the town's outer reaches this time, I stayed onboard until it reached the bus station.

The historic town centre, which clusters around the River Nene riverbank, is solid Georgian and early Victorian brick. Pevsner had lauded the town as possessing 'one of the most perfect Georgian streets of England', and the assemblage of fine buildings that flanks the river close to the bridge is certainly impressive, if just a little down at heel. In particular, the Phoenix Hotel, across the river on North Brink, with a couple of letters missing from its sign to diminish itself to 'Oenix', looked to be an institution unlikely to be rising from the ashes anytime soon. The hotel, which had become home to a highly rated Chinese restaurant, is now little more than a façade having been reduced to its ruinous state by the work of an arsonist in 2010, one of several, possibly linked, fire attacks in the town in that same year. Following the fire, the remaining walls were supported by steel girders to make the building safe but by the time the work was completed by Fenland Council its owner had left the country and could not be traced to foot the £100,000 bill. The cruel irony of the former restaurant's name was lost on no one.

With a high proportion of young Eastern European agricultural and food processing workers in Wisbech's ethnic mix – Lithuanians and Poles mostly, but also Czechs, Slovaks, Portuguese, Bulgarians and Romanians – the town and hinterland was prime pro-Leave territory during the 2016 EU referendum. But it is not as if everyone else in Wisbech are tenth-generation descendants of the Fen Tigers, the fenland inhabitants who fought against the 17th-century drainage schemes that brought prosperity to the town. Many of the 'indigenous' population are recent arrivals, too. A small but steady flow of migrants from Essex moved into the area around Wisbech in the late 1990s. The East Europeans started to arrive shortly afterwards, in the first decade of the current century, following the accession of their countries into the EU. It did not take long for resentment to build, nor for sensationalist stories to surface in the media. In 2008, the *Daily Express* printed an article that claimed that the influx of immigrants had brought increased crime and illegal activities to Wisbech. Not to be sidelined by its rival, the *Daily Mail* ran a story in 2012 about 'the Baltic mafia... terrorising local residents and ensnaring teenagers' in the town. Whatever the truth of this, the frenzied media attention was sufficient for the idea of an 'immigrant problem' to be firmly lodged in the collective psyche of many of the economically disadvantaged natives of the region. Guilty or not, the hard-working and better-educated incomers, with their incomprehensible speech and willingness to toil at monotonous and poorly paid agricultural work, were tailor-made to be scapegoats. Perhaps as a measure to counter the town's dubious reputation, the *Guardian* featured Wisbech in its 'Let's Move To...' column in 2011, but the town did not fare too well in terms of schools, connectivity or culture, although property was gleefully described as very cheap by metropolitan standards.

However, it was important to check my own prejudices. Both town and region are all too easy to dismiss with an inflexible mindset. The environmentalist Barry Lopez has written that what one thinks about a region comes down to 'what one knows, what one imagines, and how one is disposed' towards it. My own disposition towards the region was already unwholesomely negative. But what did I know? What did I imagine?

*

Heading northwest out of the town, I was soon plunged back into an agricultural hinterland of isolated farms, tall stands of poplar and vast fields of sugar beet. Hand-painted roadside signs advertised potatoes and straw bales for sale. With the exception of a couple of small garden centres and used car dealers, farming was everything.

I passed a battered old car with Bulgarian licence plates parked in a lay-by. In the distance, a gang of workers were industriously picking roses in a field. It may be that Bulgarians have the monopoly on rose-picking in the Fens – niche work in this land of sugar beet and corn. Bulgaria is, after all, the world's premier rose oil producer so it makes sense to employ native expertise.

While orchards characterised Wisbech's eastern hinterland, its fruit trees thriving thanks to accumulated silt rather than the peat found elsewhere, the landscape west of the town soon gave way to the peat-rich soil of the Black Fen. This is a landscape of plain functionality: a giant outdoor grow bag with no concessions to beauty, no rural quaintness; just modest houses, nothing older than Victorian, tucked behind tall windbreaks of rampant leylandii. In the fields, huge prefabricated hangars slumped over the land like forsaken crime-scene tents and the sun-bleached plastic of abandoned polytunnels flapped raggedly in the breeze. *NO ENTRY* signs started to become more numerous, as did warnings that proclaimed *FARM ALARMED* and *DOGS RUN LOOSE.*

There were, at least, birds to remind that agribusiness did not have a complete throttle-hold on the land: high swooping swifts and yellowhammers that perched atop bushes chirruping their dairy-free refrain ('a little bit of bread and no chee—ese'). Swallows skimmed low over the wheat fields picking off insects, although Bird's Drove, a shady lane hemmed in by rampant, eight-foot tall hemlock, was more given to butterflies than its name suggested.

The landscape opened up a little; larger fields, still table-flat but gradually rising. Walking along a bridleway, I startled a skulking heron that rose just a few feet in front of me, close enough to look into its fierce orange eye before it flapped away in irritation. Nature, tamed but not defeated in this conquered realm of straight lines, presented itself in bite-size chunks: the heron, the swallows, the eye-gladdening sight of purple loosestrife in the ditches, the mustard-yellow chain of ragwort along the field edge. Above, in a faraway cerulean sky, a kestrel hovered like an aerial signpost.

Back at a minor road, I walked past paddocks and more new housing. One of the new-builds had been designed to resemble a barn conversion, although it was unlikely that any farm building had ever stood on the same spot before. A new house constructed as a simulacrum of an old farm building, this was faux history, not so much reinventing the past as making it up: the desire for heritage in virgin territory, a fresh take on the mock Tudor leaded lozenge windows favoured by suburbanites. The paddocks came with signs that, rather than names, simply bore the postcode: PE (Peterborough). No village, no hamlet, no proper address, this was almost nowhere... although it did possess a postcode.

I reached the North Level Main Drain, an unwaveringly straight water channel that marks the border with Lincolnshire. On the roadside, the black letters of a sign marked 'Harold's Bank' had been redacted by mustard-yellow lichen to render it almost illegible. At the bank itself, the *FISHING IS PRIVATE* notices came with a very detailed Polish and Lithuanian translation, and in case things were not clear enough there was also a crossed-through cartoon that showed a fish on a cooking griddle along with a crossed-through depiction of a man running with a large fish tucked under his arm – graphic signifiers of native Fenlander versus Eastern European cultural differences. As I was examining these, a couple of red-headed teenage boys passed by on bicycles; both were carrying fishing rods, clearly with intent. One of them greeted me cheerily but the other looked wary, as if I might be some sort of informer. The pair stopped a little further along the bank to peruse the water for its fishing potential but thought better of it when they saw me coming their way and remounted their bikes in search of a more secluded spot.

At the twin-arched bridge at Clough's Cross I crossed into Lincolnshire and walked a mile or so along the road to Throckenholt. The village, a scattering of houses with no obvious centre, had a hand-painted board at the roadside advertising *RASPBERRIES, NEW POTATOES,* and *HOME GROAN POTATOES!* Home groan! Was this a Freudian slip, an unconscious allusion to the enervating tedium of domestic life, the unchanging and perhaps dispiriting view of the horizon out the window? The Fens, though, do have a thing about potatoes – they are, after all, a sizeable part of the region's bounty as the tubers grow well in the fertile black soils. I remembered an occasion driving through the Lincolnshire Fens when I tuned into a local Spalding radio station and heard the retail price of spuds being discussed earnestly for the best part of half an hour.

Another time, close to Ely cathedral, I had seen a sign planted in a meadow that forbade their cultivation: *DO NOT PLANT POTATOES HERE.* It seemed an unnecessary prohibition unless there was something in the blood that provoked Fenland folk to propagate tubers wherever the opportunity presented itself – guerrilla gardeners, perhaps? Sir Walter Raleigh, the man responsible for introducing Britain to its favourite carbohydrate, has much to answer for.

Throckenholt was my finishing point for the day, as I had planned my walk to coincide with the infrequent bus service that connected the village with Spalding. As ever with bus stops on irregular routes, I was troubled with uncertainty as to whether the service really existed. While I waited, I perused the OS map of the area. I was aware that the point where I stood was more or less at a county boundary but closer inspection revealed that it was pretty much astride the Prime Meridian, too. A figure in the top margin of the map simply read '0°'. From a longitudinal point of view, this was where east became west, a coordinate on the arbitrary and imaginary line of zero longitude that ringed the globe; a point where time – or at least GMT – was fixed by the time lords at the Royal Observatory at Greenwich. (It might, of course, have been the more westerly Paris meridian instead had history been just a little different). A veritable no man's land of a county boundary at 0° longitude, a place where I stood at approximately zero metres above sea level, did the Throckenholt bus stop qualify as some sort of geographical threshold, a turning point? Certainly, it seemed an unlikely place for a bus to pick up passengers.

Mercifully, the bus arrived on cue – an empty double-decker with me the only passenger on board until we picked up a young mother and baby at another village on our way into Spalding.

*

It was cloudy and drizzly on the day I returned to Throckenholt. It also happened to be July 15th, St Swithin's Day, which did not bode well for the weather to come. The view from the train window as it passed through the Brecks west of Thetford was foggy and dispiriting. In the fields, pigs were huddled in the mud in front of their units, hardly able to see each other through the murk. One of the pigs, I noticed, had a magpie perched on its back like a weather vane, although the animal really did not seem that concerned about it.

On Spalding's main shopping street small groups of Eastern European men were huddled together in conversation. A busker was singing a Richard Thompson song outside a bank, although no one seemed to be paying attention. Other than Polish and Lithuanian, the voice on the street was the vaguely northern flat vowels of the East Midlands rather than anything that sounded remotely East Anglian – the local dialect already noticeably different having stepped just a short way beyond the Norfolk frontier.

There was time for a coffee and a snack before my bus left. In what seemed to be an earnest attempt at British-Mediterranean fusion, the panini I ordered came with a portion of garlic chips on the side. It was too much to cope with this early in the day so the friendly woman behind the counter offered to wrap half of it up in foil for me so that I could eat it later.

The bus dropped me off by the 'Home Groan' sign in Throckenholt. I took the road west out of the village, which led past scattered homesteads and paddocks of contented chestnut horses, before I continued along a lane that followed the track-bed of a long-redundant railway line tracing the Lincolnshire-Cambridgeshire border. At a house called Crossing Keeper's Cottage, the old railway line ghosted into the fields, its former track-bed reduced to little more than a crop mark. From here, I followed the northern bank of the winding Old South

Eau, a channel that traced the county boundary west beside an enormous expanse of grassland. Summer heat had cracked patches of bare soil into a rough matrix of dun polygons. Tiny brown butterflies clustered around the blooming ragwort, clinging on with hair-breadth legs in the strengthening breeze. The repetitive jangle of a skylark filtered down from above, the bird so high to be almost invisible to the eye. Across the fields, a troop of woodpigeons clapped their wings in lazy stalling flight. Unseen beside the path, a pair of kestrels rose up suddenly from cover to swoop to a solitary tree before taking flight again, one to rise ever higher on a thermal, the other opting to hover determinedly above the wheat. Above them, a buzzard circled slowly, keeping an eye on both.

After a while, the tower of Crowland Abbey started to show itself in the distance. I followed a lane that zigzagged in its direction to arrive at the A16 that skirted the town. My OS map indicated a footpath that led from here directly into the centre but this proved to be elusive, perhaps even non-existent. In my futile search for the path I clambered through overgrown vegetation to end up surrounded by six-foot-high thistles. Pursuing a little further, I found myself knee-deep in the stagnant water of a hidden ditch. Abandoning my search as hopeless, I retraced my steps back to the main road, where I hoped no one would notice my ignominious re-emergence from the bog I had haplessly stumbled into.

With wet feet, and still brushing storm flies and thistledown from my hair, it occurred to me that my involuntary plunge into the ditch was a timely reminder that, in the past, all routes to Crowland were of a watery nature. Crowland, like nearby Thorney, and Ramsey and Ely to the south, was formerly just one of several 'islands' in the Fens – insular pockets of land that, protected by the region's awkward topography, were of value as safe bases for religious communities. For early Christians facing the constant threat of attack and premature death at the hands of Viking raiders, water was their friend, even if the isolation and hardship concomitant with life in the mosquito-plagued marshes must have made everyday existence in such places far from comfortable.

Although Crowland, hard against the Cambridgeshire border, lies just a few miles north of Peterborough, its ecclesiastical allegiance is to the diocese of Lincoln. The once powerful Crowland Abbey, whose surviving tower I had seen from afar on my approach to the village, has long lain in ruin although most of its surviving stonework has since been absorbed into the parish church.

Founded by St Guthlac in the early 8th century, the abbey's early communities suffered frequent Viking raids in the centuries leading up to the Norman invasion. Little by little, land was drained and reclaimed around the abbey for agricultural use during this period and none other than the anti-Norman guerrilla leader Hereward the Wake is reputed to have held land here as a tenant during the early years of the occupation. As elsewhere, the abbey was dissolved and partially demolished in the mid-16th century, leaving just the nave and aisles for use as part of the village's parish church.

Hereward, a semi-mythical figure, eventually became fictionalised as a *Boy's Own Paper*-style hero in Charles Kingsley's eponymous novel of 1865. In Kingsley's tale, Hereward, along with his newly acquired 'the Wake' epithet, is presented as 'the Last of the English': a swashbuckling hero fighting the repressive Norman yoke, a patriotic force to be reckoned with. Hereward's rebellion against the occupation, both actual and fictionalised, centred on the once water-surrounded Isle of Ely in Cambridgeshire. The son of Anglo-Saxon nobles, Leofric, Earl of Mercia, and Lady Godiva of Coventry – she of naked equestrianism fame – Hereward was probably better known as

Hereward the Outlaw in his own lifetime. But the veracity of any stories that involve Hereward is contentious as they rely heavily on 12th-century Latin sources that purport to be a translation of earlier lost Old English texts, which, in turn, are based on oral accounts of his supposed Norman-bashing activities.

Whatever the true facts of Hereward's life, his name has been wreathed in legend since Kingsley's fictional reinvention. In an episode of the 1950s television series *Hancock's Half Hour*, Hancock's sidekick, Sid James, in a ploy to get the house renovated by the National Trust, makes the claim that Hereward once stayed at the Hancock residence in East Cheam. Another fanciful version of the man is portrayed by human foghorn Brian Blessed in the 1990 TV movie *Blood Royal: William the Conqueror*. Hereward has also resurfaced in recent years as an off-stage presence in Paul Kingsnorth's 'shadow language' historical novel *The Wake*, in which the protagonist anti-hero Buccmaster, 'socman of holland', is sceptical of the abilities of any other potential leader in the struggle against the Normans.

Given such a patriotic pedigree, whether factually correct or not, it seems only a matter of time before Hereward's legacy is claimed by the same far-right nationalist groups that fancy themselves as latter-day Knights Templar. A timeless English hero, a warrior archetype, a reincarnated Harold Godwinson, resurrected and reassembled from the Hastings battlefield to continue the fight against the invader, one of Hereward's major legendary feats, later fictionalised by Kingsley, was to slay a caged polar bear in the north of England. The legendary white bear of the Hereward story, sometimes referred to as the 'Fairy Bear', is just possibly a forbearer of the Whittlesey Straw Bear that is still put to the fire annually each second Sunday in January in the eponymous Cambridgeshire town.

*

A sizable gathering of crows had assembled on the power lines that flanked the road into town. Perched like musical notation on a stave, it felt as if the birds were some sort of a welcoming committee and this was their fanfare. Crowland: the name was wholly appropriate as, like the Yare Valley back in Norfolk, this too was crow country par excellence.

The town, small enough to be a village, is a cosy oasis of honey-coloured, Barnack stone houses and pub clustered around Crowland's most notable feature, the ruined arches and stumpy spire of its church and former abbey. The poet John Clare, who lived not far away in Helpston, wrote a sonnet that celebrated the 'awful and sublime' atmosphere of the abbey and its 'tottering stones':

Of this old Abbey, struggling still with Time,
The grey owl hooting from its rents the while

Today, though, the church tower on which the spire's base sits was clad in scaffolding, which diminished its grandeur, but the town's other main historic site, Trinity Bridge, stood unadorned and proudly eccentric in the town centre. The bridge, an odd triangular structure now shipwrecked on dry land, once ferried pedestrians over the confluence of the River Welland and its tributary, the River Witham. Both rivers have since been diverted away from the town to leave the bridge high and dry, a white elephant of civil engineering.

Although no longer an island adrift in a sea of impenetrable bogs and marshes, Crowland still possesses a sense of insularity, despite its proximity to Peterborough just eight miles to the south. Built of the same warm-toned limestone, the town brought to mind a smaller version of Whittlesey, the town of Straw Bear fame. Whittlesey, at festival time at least, is all about pubs, Molly dancing and tipsy crowds on the streets. A winter spectacle of Englishness at its most wilfully eccentric and contrary, the festival is, despite a hint of self-consciousness, a fully licensed *Wicker Man* with dancing straw bears substituting for sacrificial virgins (at Whittlesey, the bear dancer at least gets to vacate the straw suit before it was incinerated). Crowland, in contrast, was anything but lively. In fact, the town seemed deserted. I could only imagine that everyone was out visiting retail outlets in Peterborough's sprawling hinterland.

Planning my route across the Fens I had been at pains to avoid being sucked into orbit by Peterborough's gravity, choosing to skirt the conurbation to the north. But Peterborough was to become a necessary hub for the next couple of days' walking as I needed to change buses there on my way back to Norwich from Crowland. I was also obliged to return to the city before I could continue my way west from Crowland on foot. Oddly, for a city less than two hours' drive from where I live, it was somewhere I knew almost nothing about.

Travelling into the city by bus from Crowland was disorienting and I seemed to lose any natural sense of direction as soon as we entered its suburbs, although I knew that all city-bound buses would eventually end up at Queensway next to the railway station. On our way in from the north, we passed through a neighbourhood called New England, which brought to mind the Billy Bragg song. Had this modest suburb been built as some sort of vision of the future, a paradise found?

Closer to the centre, the bus passed through Millfield, a multicultural city ward that still bears a stain on its name because of the killing of a seventeen-year-old white boy by British Pakistani youths back in 2001, just ten days after the 9/11 attacks in the US. Such blemishes are hard to remove and the crime still stands as hard evidence of the failure of multiculturalism for those determined to discredit it.

Peterborough has grown rapidly over the past three decades

as a result of immigration. First, it was Italians, who came to work in the city's brick works, then Commonwealth Asians. These were followed by Iraqi and Afghan refugees and latterly Eastern Europeans, and for a while all the classic symptoms of racial ill-ease seemed to rise to the surface in the poorer sections of the city. Racial tensions had already been a serious issue before the Millfield killing, and these worsened for some time afterwards with sporadic street riots and ethnic in-fighting between youths of Pakistani, Afghan and Iraqi origin. For all I know, the problems are still there, but driving past a group of teenage girls in bright *salwar kameez*, heads tossed back in laughter as they played on the swings in a children's playground, the area looked peaceable enough, harmonious even.

At the bus station itself, there was a number of Polish speakers milling around, which came as no surprise as many Eastern Europeans arrive in Peterborough before spilling out to the fields, farms and food processing factories in places like Spalding, Boston, King's Lynn, March and Chatteris.

It turned out that Peterborough – 'The Gateway to the Fens' – was even better connected than I thought. As I waited for my bus home to Norwich, a Polish coach pulled in ready to take on passengers for a direct trip to Warsaw.

Part Two

East Midlands

Chapter 9

Crowland to Clare Country

South Lincolnshire/North Cambridgeshire

But it is a 'far cry' from Lynn to Crowland, and by the time I reached the end of my journey I should probably have had more than enough of the fat, flat fens.
William A. Dutt, *Highways and Byways in East Anglia*

From Crowland, I was walking west into Clare Country. The name was official, not just poetic fancy on my part, as even the map on the Peterborough tourist information website referred to it as such. John Clare, the inaccurately branded 'Northamptonshire peasant poet', spent all of his early life in the village of Helpston, a little way northwest of Peterborough, and had written with great passion and tenderness about the modest countryside that surrounded his home territory in what is now part of north Cambridgeshire. A man who in early life rarely travelled far from his village, Clare would end his days ensconced in a Northampton asylum. Before this he had been incarcerated for several years in High Beech asylum in Essex on the edge of Epping Forest, an institution from which he would eventually escape to make his way back to Helpston by means of a desperately tough, eighty-mile, three-day journey on foot.

Clare's fateful journey is well documented but questions remain about the character of the poet's so-called madness. Was it the result of heartbreak due to the unrequited love for his childhood sweetheart (who died while he was interned in the Essex asylum)? Was it purely a hereditary condition, or was it what would now be called bipolar disorder? Or could it be put down to the fury and sense of loss that Clare felt as extensive farming enclosures took hold of the countryside he loved so deeply? The answer is probably a combination of all of these. During his lifetime, Clare had seen the enclosure movement transform the territory he called home. With vast tracts of common land taken into private ownership and fenced off by landlords, the enclosures of the early 19th century traumatised the English countryside and disenfranchised a workforce for whom life was always an uncertain struggle in the first place. Within just a few years the already restricted world of agricultural labourers and the non-landowning rural class shrank dramatically. Geography shifted, borders were drawn, fences erected; a peasant's sense of place and belonging bludgeoned into allegiance with a brutally imposed new world order. As a one-time labouring man, Clare was both bereft and angry by the changes foisted upon his class in the name of progress. His raw indignation at the dramatic social and environmental change he witnessed was baldly expressed in his poem *The Mores*:

Inclosure came and trampled on the grave
Of labour's rights and left the poor a slave

Even now, more than a century and a half after his death, Clare's ability as a poet is still open to debate. There are those who find no charm in his rusticity and use of the vernacular, and who baulk at his sometimes clumsy rhyme and approximate spelling. What seems to be beyond question though was his estimable skill as a nature writer. Clare's powers of observation were immense and many of his poems celebrated the natural world with charmingly lapidarian detail. Writing about a nightingale's nest, Clare notes:

... so famed a bird
Should have no better dress than russet brown
Her wings would tremble in her ecstasy,
And feathers stand on end, as 'twere with joy
And mouth wide open to release her heart
Of its out-sobbing songs.

And what a world it was that Clare had to write about. His home territory in those days would have been alive with wildlife that most modern-day naturalists could only dream about: corncrakes skulking and breeding in the hand-scythed wheat fields; nightjars and wrynecks a common sight, along with glow worms in the fen. The natural world, free of chemicals and mechanised farming practices, was writ large, unfettered by modern technology and petrochemical 'progress'. Lest we get too dewy-eyed about what might seem to have been some sort of Eden before the Fall, it should be remembered that life for the average early 19th-century farm labourer was relentlessly tough and comparatively short compared to today: harvesting crops by hand was back-breaking work, and diseases like malaria were still rife in the wet, swampy Fens.

*

Leaving Crowland, I followed the raised bank along the New River Channel south of Crowland High Wash, a large area of marginal grazing land that has served as emergency drainage for the area since the reign of George III. The River Welland, now diverted to flow a little way north of the town, lay just out of sight at the northern edge of the High Wash. With the exception of the abbey, whose spire slowly diminished behind me, and a white water tower that rose in the distance, the bank, standing a few metres above the surrounding land, was the most elevated thing around for miles. A glance at the OS map confirmed that

I was traversing a landscape almost entirely devoid of contours, the only exception being a few isolines that circled a '0' to show where the land dipped even lower. Then I realised that, not just here in the Fens but ever since Narborough in west Norfolk, I had been walking at more or less sea level.

A strong, warm westerly confronted me head-on as I walked along the bank. The track formed part of the Green Wheel Cycle Route that circled Peterborough but there were no cyclists to be seen today though, or fellow walkers apart from a solitary jogger and a woman struggling to control four lively dogs on leads. The track also served as a local heritage trail, and spaced at regular intervals along it were carved wooden posts with Perspex panels that depicted local wildlife – flora, owls and, of course, crows. Wildlife was certainly abundant. A little way ahead of me, a pair of kestrels methodically worked the edge of a plantation, hovering flawlessly despite the strength of the wind, tail feathers fanned to anchor the birds motionless as they froze time in the air. A dozen goldfinches flashed past before alighting on a bed of thistles, their collective voice an almost imperceptible chiming of tiny bells.

Further along was an isolated piece of sculpture, an iron 'Charm Tree' whose branches bore dangling metal charms that clanged gently in the wind. A sign explained that the charms had been designed by local schoolchildren who had been given the brief that they should show what they thought made Crowland special. The charms depicted the various things they associated with life in their home village: musical instruments, fish, a hand and what I first thought was a pair of Y-fronts until it dawned on me that it was a representation of Crowland's Trinity Bridge. Hanging lower than the other charms was a black metal crow. On the bank ahead, a dozen or more real crows were pecking at something on the path. They rose as a mass as I approached and were immediately joined by scores of others from the fields below to make a wheeling protestation of harsh-voices above my head. Was this some sort of corvid farewell to the parish, a valediction to signal my departure from Crow Country? The wind, which was noticeably stronger on top of the bank than just a few metres lower at field level, made it difficult for the birds to fly and it was not long before individuals peeled off untidily from the throng to return to the land's natural windbreak. In contrast to the crows, the equally numerous swallows seemed to savour the turbulent conditions, taking advantage of the wind's lift to swoop high before accelerating down on unsuspecting flies at astonishing speed. The same blustering wind played havoc with my voice recorder: listening to the barely intelligible playback later, I sounded like an Arctic explorer struggling across tundra in a blizzard.

I walked on beneath a sky that Clare might have described as 'vaulted'; a sky hung with stratocumulus that sported grey tracksuit bottoms and fluffy white tops. What I found baffling was the way that the clouds did not seem to move despite the strong wind that sheered beneath them.

To the north, I could make out skeins of greylag geese flying along the course of the unseen River Nene. Like fish and eels, wildfowl has always been part of the Fens' rich harvest. A little way south of the bank, my map showed a pentagonal plantation surrounding an eight-pointed star of water – a former decoy for wildfowl in which each point of the star would have been a net-covered ditch into which ducks were enticed from the central pond. Borough Fen Duck Decoy is one of the oldest of its kind in England and lured wildfowl to aristocratic dinner plates from the late 17th century until as recently as 1951. Now, somewhat ironically, it is a bird reserve. All that I could make out of it from my viewpoint on the bank was an isolated group of trees among the fields.

I came across a sign for Borough Fen earthworks: *One of the most impressive ancient sites in the region*. According to Historic

England, this is a plough-damaged Iron Age lowland fort which, *despite damage to the interior, protected by later alluvium, preserves a nationally important Iron Age occupation with waterlogged features.* It is the sort of feature that archaeologists sometimes describe as a 'hill fort', although there was nothing that remotely resembled a hill in this dead-flat terrain. It was not necessarily a fort either. It may not have had a defensive function at all but, rather, have been a centre for tribal gatherings or for the performance of ritual – a complete horse's head excavated from the outer enclosure ditch certainly suggested the latter. Either way, here was another case that proved the value of being able to see the world more flatly, as from my low viewpoint I was only able to discern the vague outline of a raised bank. While I was pondering how the site might have looked more than two millennia ago, a man coming the other way noticed me and put his Alsatian on a short leash. I must have appeared worried, but his owner just said, 'It's all right, mate. He just gets a bit excited when he sees someone.'

A farm track beside a large pond led away towards a distant farmstead. Unheralded, I had crossed the county boundary and walked back into Cambridgeshire. This was the part of the county that had once been part of Northamptonshire; that far-flung northeast corner of the old county where John Clare had lived and poetised.

The bank veered south, edging ever closer to the course of the River Welland. At Sissons Farm, just outside Peakirk, an information board described the extensive drainage work carried out in the 17th century by the Dutch engineer Cornelius Vermuyden. Fearing an end to their traditional way of life, many of Vermuyden's men had been murdered by antagonistic marshmen – an echo of the violent resistance that had taken place centuries before in the time of Hereward the Wake, and a precursor of the later enclosure protests witnessed by John Clare in which, once again, the rural poor feared for their liberty and livelihood.

Just beyond the farm, where a sign bore the cheery valediction *SEE YOU AGAIN SOON*, I crossed a bridge and level crossing into Peakirk. The direct route to Glinton was cross-country from here. I followed a footpath out of the village, past well-attended allotments and then alongside wheat and sugar beet fields before I found myself confronted by something I had not encountered for quite some time – a gentle slope.

I stopped for a break and sat down on the grass at a field edge to have something to eat. The smell of my sandwich was enough to instantly draw the attention of two sniffling, friendly but hungry dogs. 'You don't want to let them near your food,' said their owner cheerfully, although that had hardly been my intention. I was doing nothing untoward but I felt a vague sense of embarrassment, as if I had been caught trespassing in some way. It seemed that, somewhere deep within, I harboured an atavistic urge to tug my forelock in the same way that John Clare might have involuntarily found himself doing had he been caught poeticising in the fields. It may be that it takes centuries and numerous generations to unlearn the deeply entrenched habit of knowing one's place.

I now had the sense of approaching the edge of something – the intimation of a change of air and landscape in the offing. The contours proved it. At Glinton, I was finally leaving the Fens behind and heading into the chalklands. But the chalklands of where, exactly? The East Midlands? No, not quite yet. This was still East Anglia – just about – yet it was somewhere around here that the transition started, where the landscape eased from low fen to chalk valleys and modest slopes – a brief geographical hiatus before arriving in territory that could be more easily labelled. At Glinton and the villages that followed I would be walking into a Cotswolded world of cosy brownstone, a shift that seemed dramatic after so much brick and flint.

Cresting a low rise, the towering spire of Glinton's St Benedict's Church showed itself between the clustered cottages of the village below. It was a sight that must have been very familiar to John Clare, who, not surprisingly, had a sonnet for it:

Glinton, thy taper spire predominates
Over the level landscape – and the mind,
Musing – the pleasing picture, contemplates
Like elegance of beauty, much refined

Everybody in Glinton seemed to have at least one dog. Walking through the village, I was painstakingly overtaken by a man riding a bicycle as he walked his terrier on a lead, an impressive feat of balance considering that he moved so slowly that stepping up my own pace just a notch would have been sufficient to keep up with him.

A footbridge at the end of the village took me over the A15, the trunk road that connected Peterborough with Lincoln and Hull. Only the heavy traffic on the road beneath the bridge gave a clue to the proximity of a city of nearly 200,000 – that and the surprisingly busy railway line that I had to cross just before Helpston. I watched four trains pass as I approached the level crossing, and then another three as I waited for the barrier to lift.

John Clare was already ensconced in Northampton Lunatic Asylum when the railway arrived in his home village in 1846. This was probably for the best, as not long before his incarceration he had been horrified to witness men laying out the plan for an 'iron railway' between London and Manchester, a route that would have passed close to his beloved Royce Wood. For Clare, the coming of the railways, like land enclosure, spelled out irremediable change to the gentle countryside he had grown up with. It seemed a terrible irony then that, after his death in Northampton in 1861, the last journey that his body would ever take was to be returned to the village of his birth by railway carriage.

The outlying part of Helpston was unremarkable: bungalows mostly, and small businesses – a florist's, a sign promising *GENTLE DENTISTRY* and another, *WASP PROBLEMS DEALT WITH.* Eventually, I reached a crossroads where a monument to Helpston's most famous son stands next to St Botolph's, the parish church. The road to the left led to the village pub, The Bluebell, and, almost next door to this, the poet's cottage museum.

The museum was still open, so there was time to look around before catching my bus back to Peterborough. The rooms were presented as they might have looked in Clare's time, filled with his personal possessions, like books and writing equipment. An audio guide related snippets about his early life here with his mother. Standing in the courtyard is a life-sized statue of Clare, a diminutive man swaddled in a large coat and carrying a satchel, his hand resting on a *KEEP OUT* sign, the bane of the free-ranging country poet. The courtyard led onto a well-tended garden filled with hollyhocks, and a smaller yard that held a wooden bench inscribed with the poet's words in lower case: *fields were the essence of song.*

On my way up to the bus stop, I called in at the church to see Clare's grave. In a graveyard redolent with lavender and filled with the hum with bees, Clare's gravestone is a modest affair: a mossy, roof-shaped stone carved with the simple axiom, *A POET IS BORN NOT MADE.* Around the stone were withering posies of flowers, tenderly placed there to commemorate the poet's birthday the week before.

The Peterborough bus arrived on time, its driver never seeming to draw breath in the interminable conversation he was having with the young woman who sat up front with him. Rattling at speed through the northern suburbs into the city, the rapid shift from rural peace to urban clamour came as a jolt to the senses, a disorienting transition between two disparate worlds that would have troubled Clare deeply.

*

A few days later, I caught a train back to Peterborough. Thanks to a lengthy period of dry, sunny weather, most of the wheat had been harvested and the countryside was already starting to develop a weary, burned-out appearance even though it was still only July. As if in sympathy with the landscape that lay beyond the window glass, everyone on the train seemed to be exhausted too – fatigued and despondent, as if every one of us were on their way to the dentist.

In his book *The Moth Snowstorm*, Michael McCarthy writes about his feeling that summer really ends around August 15th, and of the period that follows being like a 'post-coital depression in the natural world'. I tend to feel much the same, especially after the wide-scale harvesting that takes place around the time of my birthday in late July. Coincidentally, this is also the time of year when swifts, the most transitory of migrants, leave Britain for their African wintering grounds. Modern science has turbo-charged the maturation of crops to the extent that the harvest period has been brought forward considerably – a triumph of the late 20th-century's Green Revolution. The trouble is, following such an early harvest, it sometimes feels as if the natural world is biding its time until autumn comes. The end of summer marking the time of harvest is something that has been lodged in mankind's consciousness since the birth of agriculture back in the Neolithic. A vague sense that things are out of place is perhaps a natural response to a change in what is a deeply entrenched seasonal rhythm. After all, harvest festivals, adhering to tradition, still take place in September just before the autumn equinox, not at the start of school holidays in late July.

From Peterborough, I caught a bus back to Helpston, where I arrived to find two middle-aged women seated in camp chairs sketching the spire of St Botolph's Church at the crossroads. The high street led me west out of the village, past almshouses and honey-toned cottages that had hollyhocks swooning over the pavement. As if to remind passers-by of the village's genius loci, one property had carefully positioned a Clare poem in its street-facing window. Such reminders were unnecessary though, as everything in the village – the cottage museum, the church, even the pub – seemed to have some sort of intimate connection with the poet. Even the village school, John Clare Primary, bore a cameo image of the poet's head on the banners advertising its 50th anniversary. But the Clare connection was but only one aspect of the village's tangible self-esteem. Displayed on the wall beside the entrance to the village hall was a gallery of plaques that boasted of the accolades Helpston had collected in recent years: *Best Kept Village 1986, Peterborough Village of the Year 1997, 1998, 1999, 2000, 2001* – the turning of the millennium, a purple patch in terms of local civic pride. The plaudits seemed reasonable enough; the village – neat stone cottages, thatched roofs, Barnack limestone – is fine-looking in a Cotswolds sort of way, even without its poetic heritage.

Long, dry-stone walls at the edge of the village enhanced the Cotswolds image. Across the fields on the skyline, a caravan of railway freight wagons was wheeling slowly west. I left the road to follow a footpath through fields along a route called the *Torpel Way*. In one of the fields, a group of people were haymaking, shifting pitchforks of dry grass into loose heaps. It was a sight Clare would have been familiar with but the people involved, in smart casual clothes and expensive wellingtons, looked more like middle-class country folk than farm labourers. The haymaking, a glimpse of bygone days, was plainly some sort of well-intended revivalism that offered a hands-on taster of the past.

I had wondered about the name and my question was answered when I passed Torpel Manor. A signboard indicated that here was the site of a fortified Norman manor house and deer park that once belonged to Roger de Torpel. Deer parks and hunting forests were, of course, the original enclosures – Norman land snatches that, gifted as favours to loyal henchmen, created an aristocratic class that still has hold today.

I followed the way through meadows and harvested wheat fields. Chalk country now, with a different variety of flowers – burdock, knapweed, field scabious – this was already a markedly different landscape to the Fens. In Ashton, a man on a bicycle overtook me, announcing, 'Coming through,' to no one in particular. I continued through more fields, where a man waved at me from a tractor as a buzzard glided overhead. Across the fields to the south, the church at Ufford stood out clear on the far side of the valley.

I left the Torpel Way to walk into Barnack. For medieval stonemasons, the village had been a lithic Mecca, its pale limestone much sought after as high-quality building material. The Romans were the first to mine here and, later, in the medieval period, industrial scale extraction of 'Barnack rag' provided stone for the cathedrals at Ely and Peterborough, the monasteries at Crowland, Ramsey, Sawtry and Bury St Edmunds, as well as for domestic dwellings in many nearby villages and for most of the town of Stamford, where I was heading. Such was the demand that the best of the stone was all used up by the mid-15th century, although the dissolution of the monasteries in the following century meant that much of the Barnack stone used to construct Fenland religious institutions ended up being recycled for use in the new college buildings of Cambridge. Later excavation of lower-quality stone was used to build the Great North Road between London and Edinburgh, a route that partly traced the course of Ermine Street and paralleled much of the modern A1.

Barnack is as handsome as you might expect of a settlement that has limestone at its heart. On my way into the village I passed a fetching stone dovecot, a Wesleyan church that had found new life as a community centre, and a wedding dress shop called Bridal Dreams – a niche market in a small village if ever there was one.

Just outside the village, Hills and Holes, the former quarry area that had been so busy with mining activity in the early medieval period, is now a nature reserve. The name is fitting: the old mine pits had created numerous small bumps and depressions in the land that made it appear like one of those fruit box inlays found at supermarkets. The limestone just beneath the surface had rendered the soil alkaline and consequentially the site was resplendent with bright clumps of chalk-loving flowers like agrimony and dog rose. A brochure I had picked up proudly boasted that the site is also home to no less than eight species of orchids. Most of these had long finished flowering but I managed to find several clusters of pyramidal orchids lurking in the grass, their pink tapering flower spikes resembling a group of jelly babies attempting a Catalan human tower.

In my attempt to leave the site, I became temporarily lost and ended up on the wrong side of the large stone wall that separated the reserve from the woodland of the Walcot Hall estate. Eventually, after several *PRIVATE LAND* signs, I came to a gateway that led onto a footpath and a route called the Hereward Way. Like the Boudica Way in Norfolk, the Hereward Way is an appealing fiction: a concocted juxtaposition of place and local history designed to attract walkers. I was almost surprised that John Clare had not yet given his name to a route in the vicinity but perhaps that is just a matter of time, a project in waiting for an underemployed rural planner.

The footpath led to a road with a protected verge – more pyramidal orchids – and I followed this awhile before heading off across fields blackened with the stubble of the oil seed rape harvest. This led to a gently climbing path that followed the perimeter of Burghley Park. I noticed a red kite circling overhead. Then I made out three more arcing even higher above, unmistakeable even in silhouette with their crooked wings and sharply forked tails. These were the first kites I had seen since setting out from Yarmouth. As with buzzards, their range has expanded markedly, from an upland stronghold in central Wales a few decades ago, to southern England, especially the Chilterns, and beyond in more recent years. Once, of course, red kites had been widespread, common even – perhaps especially – in cities. The birds had been commonplace scavengers in the filthy, offal-rich streets of Victorian London. But, scavengers or not, they are extraordinarily beautiful birds, especially seen close up.

Burghley Park was somewhere John Clare had occasionally come to labour as a youth. More significantly, it was also where he had once jumped over a wall to find a secluded spot to secretly read the book he had walked all the way to Stamford to buy. This was an act that spoke of the embarrassment of a humble man compelled to rise 'above his station', as if the idea of a labourer reading of a book of poetry was somehow shameful, or worse, pretentious. Such class-ridden bias and fear of affectation still persists. As an occasional labourer in younger life I had sometimes found myself in work environments where to read a book or broadsheet newspaper during breaks was considered to be a bit 'up yourself', although tabloids or soft pornography were just fine. A phenomenon of class, to some extent, my own father, a bright but sparingly educated, self-made man, who rose from apprentice to middle management when it was still possible to do such things, claimed, not particularly proudly, to have never read a book in his life. For his generation and class, education was passive, something that was done to you when you were young; in my dad's case, up to the age of fourteen. Beyond that you were expected to go out and earn a living. His was a generation that had to learn to grow up quickly – hard times, a long economic depression and then a world war saw to that – but when the more meritocratic 1960s came along, social boundaries became more blurred. Grammar school children like me went on to become first-generation middle class almost by default, which gave licence to embrace some of those things that had been denied to those like me a generation earlier: books, foreign travel, art – lofty aspirations that lay beyond concerns for possessions, a decent pension and suburban stability.

A track led me along the edge of Burghley Park, past a meadow with horse-jumping fences and then through a golf course where smartly uniformed public school teenagers were teeing up on the green. The A1 was audibly close now – a faint, yet persistent murmur beyond the trees. Just beyond the golf clubhouse I reached the Old North Road, the precursor of the A1, where a mysterious sign announced *ST MARTIN'S WITHOUT*, 'without' in this case meaning outside the parish of Stamford.

On the Old North Road was a sign for *LINCOLNSHIRE WOODCRAFT SUPPLIES*, although by my reckoning we were still within the bounds of Cambridgeshire. Stamford's multiple spires had come into view by now and it all seemed a little incongruous: a mini Oxford, a town on the edge of the Fens that looked as if it had been uplifted and deposited here from a valley in the Cotswolds.

The final approach to town through fields of sheep pasture helped consolidate the Cotswolds association. I came to a road in front of the town's football club (*Stamford AFC Welcomes You to Wothorpe Road. Home Of 'The Daniels' Est. 1896*), which, with weeds scrambling up its corrugated iron fence and a boarded-up window on the ticket wicket, had the look of a club still waiting for some *Roy of the Rovers* inspiration to help it climb up the divisions. What I did not know but found out later was that the club had moved to a new ground in late 2014. I would also learn later that the team's nickname did not derive from biblical references to martyrs and lion's cages but came instead from a local man called Daniel Lambert, the fattest man in English history, who lived and died in Stamford. It seemed an odd choice of image for a sporting club.

Chapter 10

Lost from the Map

Stamford, Lincolnshire to Rutland Water

The absent has a geography too
Ken Worpole, *The New English Landscape*

Stamford took me by surprise. Part of it was down to my own amazement that I had never actually visited the town before, although I had occasionally caught a speed-blurred glimpse of its honeyed stone buildings from a car window on the A1.

Stamford is, according to Sir John Betjeman, 'the most attractive (town) in England', and similarly, was described by Sir Walter Scott as 'the finest stone town in England' and by Nikolaus Pevsner as 'the climax of Lincolnshire in terms of historical as well as architectural significance'. Pevsner might better have said 'very edge' rather than 'climax', as the town, while belonging to Lincolnshire, sits close to the meeting point of four counties. Certainly, the town is picture-perfect English pastoral, a toothsome selection box of biscuit-coloured stone; the sort of wholesome market town favoured by building society advertising and colour supplement property porn (Stamford was voted 'best place to live' by *The Sunday Times* in 2013).

Barnack stone, tidy streets, a medieval core that sports an elegant juxtaposition of towers and spires, the town's architectural appeal is tangible. If Stamford resembles a pint-sized exclave of Cambridge or Oxford then there is good reason. A group of disgruntled Oxford academics tried to establish a rival college here in the 14th century but were thwarted in their ambition when Edward III ordered its closure. The site of the short-lived Brazenose College is now incorporated into Stamford College, the town's public school, some of whose students I saw practising their golf swing on my approach to the town.

Standing proud of the paved area next to Sheep Market is Queen Eleanor's Cross, a tall, tapering stone monument that resembles one of those cruel spikes employed for human impalement by Vlad Dracul. Sprawled on stone benches around the memorial was a group of Spanish teenage students, who appeared nonplussed to have so much history and architectural elegance distracting them from important business on their phones. Happier-looking were the tourists and pensioners enjoying pub grub and pints of lager at the tables outside The Golden Fleece opposite.

There was just enough time to visit one of the tearooms before it closed for the day. I also ordered a scone with jam, although, thirsty from the day's walk, what I really wanted was a larger pot of tea: a pot of tea for two... for one. But it was obvious that the proprietors were eager to shut up shop so, feeling a little pressured, I drank and ate as quickly as I could. The two elderly women at the next table seemed less troubled by the hovering waitresses and sipped their tea unhurriedly as they discussed post-war rationing as if it had only just ended that year. It reminded me of the sort of conversations I used to be party to as a bored child, who even then rather wished that adults would not bang on about the war quite so incessantly. It was a cue to go, so, jam-full, I took my leave of the 1950s to make my way across the river to Stamford's railway station and wait for the train home.

*

On the night before my return to Stamford I dreamed of a little owl and awoke with the vague recollection that in my dream I had remarked that this was the first I had seen for decades. This was true – it had been years since I had seen one and I had been hoping that I might encounter the bird somewhere on my walk through the Fens. I checked a dedicated website that monitors sightings of little owls in England and it seemed that the area I had just passed through was one of the most likely areas in the country to see one. Alas, such a sighting was not to be.

In Greek mythology the little owl (*Athena noctua*) represents Athena, the goddess of wisdom. The same species also accompanies Minerva, Athena's Roman counterpart. Athena, who is sometimes portrayed with a little owl on her arm, was originally a goddess of night and her association with the bird was probably down to the relationship with dusk and the passage from day to night that many owl species have. It is a bird of thresholds, of brinks of time and space, and I can recall an occasion decades ago when, travelling overland to India, I had crossed a footbridge in the no man's land between the Greek and Turkish borders. Halfway across, perched unblinking in a bush just a few feet away, was a little owl observing me. It felt like an omen, a good one. I was crossing the threshold between West and East for the first time in my life, so the sighting seemed noteworthy, as if the bird were some sort of familiar guarding my passage. To have glimpsed a little owl somewhere in the border territory that separates East Anglia from the East Midlands might have had similar significance but instead I had to be content with a cameo appearance in a dream.

*

I took the train back to Stamford via Ely. It was a dreary, grey day with a dimpled canopy of cloud weighing heavy over the Fens, a match for the gloomy frame of mind I seemed to have woken up with. It was a mood I was more accustomed to experiencing in winter but there was never any way of knowing when the black dog might pay a visit. This was no Shuck, the legendary fire-eyed hound of terror that is said to prowl lonely footpaths along the East Anglia coast. This dog was an altogether meeker beast, a timorous mutt that was frightened by harsh words and alarmed by sudden noises; a yapping lapdog with attitude. Sometimes it helped to take the black dog for walk.

In Stamford, before setting out walking, I had breakfast outdoors at a café by the river. A young family were seated silently at the neighbouring trestle table, the dad and son both sporting replica MUFC shirts – a badge of loyalty to signify tribal membership. Despite fanciful notions of individuality, I was not so different myself. My tribe were those in fleece and walking boots who went out into the world carrying rucksacks: usually lone males in later life who idled their time pouring over maps. Far more animated than me or the Man United family were the group of chipper pensioners who were busily discussing how they would spend the day that lay ahead. I found myself envying their cheerfulness of outlook and the easy conviviality they seemed to share.

Heading out of town, I crossed back over the bridge to follow a footpath that led west alongside the River Welland. The path, which threw up the cloying scent of mayweed, was part of the Jurassic Way, a route that extends all the way to Banbury in Oxfordshire. Its name was a confirmation of the chalk geology beneath my feet. The riverbank was thick with burdock and Himalayan balsam but many of the other wayside flowers had already finished blooming for the year and gone to seed. The gentlest hint of autumn was already in the air, and the downy heads of spent thistles were attracting the attention of small flocks of goldfinches that fluttered across the path in front of me in painterly flashes of yellow, red and black.

A little way along the path, a plaque set in a brick plinth marked the original location of what was known as The Roman Ford, the place where the Roman road between Lincoln and

London had once crossed the River Welland. In 61AD, Roman soldiers fled across the river at this same spot pursued by a blood-crazed Boudica thirsty for retribution. Once a place of fear and panic, any lingering ghosts seemed to have long been exorcised and the only traffic on the river was a family party of mute swans gliding silently downstream.

Another significant crossing loomed ahead: the A1, a contemporary version of Ermine Street, the once-important Roman road that plied north–south close to the town. As I drew closer, the sight and sound of commercial traffic thundering in both directions became more pronounced with each step. In the distance across the meadow I could make out what looked like a tunnel. Half overgrown with vegetation, it appeared to offer a safe route across – or rather, beneath – the dual carriageway. I could also discern a figure with a large rucksack walking in my direction. As our trajectories met we stopped to have a word.

Dave was a middle-aged Suffolk man from near Bury St Edmunds. Dave did a lot of walking, especially long-distance routes: 'About nine hundred miles a year on average,' he told me. His wife always stayed at home but was sympathetic to his needs as long as he spent enough time with her, too. His manner was a little downbeat, shy even, and he seemed to be weighed down by baggage other than the seventy-litre rucksack on his back, but his eyes lit up when he talked about some of the walks he had done and the sort of terrain he favoured. The greatest walking of all, he confided, was the Lincolnshire coast between tides: 'Hard sand, the best of all.' I admired his tenacity, his willingness to carry a heavy pack day-in, day-out along long-distance trails that did not necessarily lead anywhere; like the route that he was currently following, the Macmillan Way, which just seems to meander fairly aimlessly around the East Midlands. One of my own tribe, albeit far more hardcore. Was Dave a typical long-distance walker? Probably not, although I had met very few others as I flitted from trail to trail on my own haphazard westering route. But there was something about Dave that made me feel as if I had just met another version of myself coming the other way – a man more single-minded than I was, someone less easily distracted by zeitgeist and the whims of catholic interests; a striding doppelganger for whom the walking itself, the intimate contact with the ground, the immersion in a map, meant more than the destination. I suspected that we both walked the same dog sometimes.

Walking, as we both knew, is a therapy of sorts. This is nothing new. In the aftermath of the Great War many young men whose youth had been devastated by the savagery of conflict turned to walking as a means of coming to terms with the damage inflicted on them – injuries that were both physical and psychological. Walking was a way of making some sort of sense of their young, yet already troubled, lives, a dependable means of coping with trauma.

There is something to the speed and rhythm of walking that encourages reflection and clarity of thought. Not for nothing has the notion of *solvitur ambulando* ('it is solved by walking') been in the mind of thinkers since time immemorial. The philosopher Jean-Jacques Rousseau is credited as saying, 'My mind only works with my legs,' and similarly, Charles Dickens, Henry David Thoreau, Bruce Chatwin, Patrick Leigh Fermor and several of the Lake Poets – all indefatigable foot travellers – have embraced the value of walking as a practice that facilitated creativity and inspiration.

The poet Edward Thomas, whose life ended abruptly at the Battle of Arras in 1917, was another great walker. A man haunted by severe bouts of depression and feelings of existential isolation, Thomas would regularly go off on day-long walks, often without maps, in an attempt to ameliorate the 'melancholy' that he carried within him. Thomas did his walking in the years that led up to the Great War that would tragically end his and millions of other young men's lives. A close friend in those pre-war years was the Welsh poet and 'super-tramp' W.H. Davies, whose own work ('*What is this life, if full of care...*') reflected the joys of a rambling life. Thomas became a kind of protective guardian for the older man, paying the rent for a cottage close to his own home in Kent and even arranging for a replacement wooden leg to be made for the poet. Another friend and walking companion was the American poet Robert Frost, whose most famous poem *The Road Not Taken*, intended by Frost as a playful swipe at indecision, would influence Thomas sufficiently to encourage him to sign up for military service in 1915. This was a fatal decision; in this case he had chosen the wrong road, one that led to his death. For Thomas, it was a matter of honour rather than obligation: as a mature married man there was no compulsory requirement for Thomas to enlist.

Thomas's pre-war rural *dérives* were carried out decades before Guy Debord and the Situationists put their stamp on the urban equivalent in their attempt to subvert the geography of the city – in this case, Paris. Later, Richard Long's *A Line Made by Walking* made disciplined walking an art form and helped confirm what we already knew of the human urge to make pilgrimage even when there was no religious goal at the end of it. As Sinclair McKay remarks in *Ramble On*, 'Walking is sometimes a form of religious practice in itself; a meditation or even prayer, but at a steady pace.'

We each walk alone and carry losses and absences along with us. But walking works as a healer, too: a mender of wounds, physical and emotional; a tonic for body, heart and mind. If pilgrimage is an arduous and often dangerous journey undertaken to awaken hidden spiritual depths then the walking of it is, as much as the final goal of the destination, an important factor in its efficacy. Walking, the heart gets in step with the rhythm of the stride; the mind paces itself accordingly. The world looks different at a steady three miles an hour.

*

I took the foot tunnel beneath the A1, traffic grumbling noisily overhead, to reach a railway line where I had to wait for a freight train to pass before I could continue. Across the track, a tractor was working a field of oil seed rape stubble, chipping it into fragments that mulched the soil like wood bark and rendering the air pungent with the stale-fart reek of cabbages. I followed the footpath uphill towards a patch of woodland. Remarkably, this was probably the first real incline of my entire walk so far – the most modest of slopes yet sufficient to momentarily shorten the breath.

I walked south for a while, climbing gently uphill into Easton-on-the-Hill, a comely dormitory village of well-scrubbed limestone that had a pub (another Bluebell) and cottages with neatly clipped bay trees in tubs beneath shuttered windows. Sitting in the garden of one of the village's houses, enjoying the sunshine and eating lunch from a plate, was a middle-aged Black woman dressed in a turban and bright robes, suggesting she was of West African origin. Perhaps realising our mutual incongruity in a village that resembled an exclave of the stockbroker belt, we briefly exchanged greetings as I walked past, neither of us any the wiser about the other. It was not really my business to ask but I wondered how long she had lived in the village. Did she live here alone? Where had she come from? Where would she end up? Her presence brought to mind the Somali refugees I had seen in isolated villages in Arctic Norway. Small groups of displaced men with nothing to do, they had stood out in every way imaginable: separate from the other villagers, separated from their womenfolk; listless, un-rooted, painfully far from any semblance of home in those remote northern communities. Every one of them was waiting for something to happen, for something to change, but time weighed as heavy as stone in such comprehensive exile. Would these men eventually become Norwegians? Would they ever come to love pickled herring, saunas, birches and the savage beauty of the Nordic tundra? What situation was worse: refugees housed in an incongruous rural environment like the Norwegian Somalis, or those who were transplanted without ceremony to a hard-to-let council flat in a run-down neighbourhood of a post-industrial city? It was an honest question – where would they settle best? Where would they have the better opportunity to integrate, to find work, to successfully educate their children, to avoid the bitter resentment of an already disenfranchised community?

For the next couple of miles I walked through arable land across the northeastern extremity of Northamptonshire, the western border marked by the River Welland. In the village of Ketton, an overambitious three-arch bridge spanned the modest trickle of the River Chatter, a tributary of the Welland that, truth be told, whispered more than chattered. This was Rutland, and the new county was quick to assert itself: a window poster in a limestone cottage advertised Rutland Morris Dancers, and beneath the shadow of the spire of St Mary the Virgin Church, a flyer on a notice board urged me to *Walk Rutland for Jesus.*

Heading uphill from the village I followed a bridleway through Ketton Quarry, a dusty expanse of pits and diggings that flanked both sides of the track. The site was busy with JCBs and lumbering, heavily-laden lorries but it was plain to see that some areas of the quarry were already exhausted and starting to turn feral, reverting slowly to unsanctioned havens for wildlife.

From the quarry I dropped down to a minor road that led into Empingham, close to Rutland Water, although there was as yet no sight of the water itself. Empingham, a well-heeled settlement of thatch and limestone, seemed staid and conservative, a place of twitching curtains and 4x4 envy – a village not quite pretty enough to be a tourist draw but too much of a commuter settlement to have much in the way of a community feel.

I caught a bus back to Stamford and walked to the railway station to wait for a train heading back east. As my train drew into the station I spotted a familiar face in a window: the former Archbishop of Canterbury and sometimes poet, Rowan Williams, who was gazing out wistfully from the crowded carriage. Instantly recognisable from television appearances – dog collar, kindly face, horned eyebrows and flyaway hair – he sat with someone I assumed to be his wife at a table seat. I boarded the same carriage to head across the Fens, to Ely (for me) and Cambridge (for him, I presume). The carriage was almost full but I seemed to be the only passenger who recognised the celebrity cleric in our midst, much to the relief, no doubt, of the former archbishop.

*

A few days later I came back to Empingham to walk along the north shore of Rutland Water. Previously I had not so much as caught a glimpse of the horseshoe-shaped body of water that took up a sizeable share of this diminutive county. A short walk out of the village soon put that right.

The reservoir, which was originally named after this same village at its eastern end, was opened in 1976 to provide drinking water for the East Anglia region. To create the 11km^2 of open water that constituted the reservoir, the Gwash Valley west of Empingham was dammed using clay from the area of the valley that would subsequently be flooded. Two valley villages were expunged in its creation. The largest reservoir in England in area (although Kielder Water in Northumberland holds a greater volume of water) and one of the largest artificial lakes in Europe, Anglia Water has long promoted Rutland Water's virtues as a place of recreation. Now there are boating marinas, bathing beaches, car parks and carefully maintained perimeter walking and cycling tracks galore. There is even a pleasure cruiser, *Rutland Belle*, and wildlife too, some of which was invited or – or rather, reintroduced – and the crowning glory is a nature reserve with its very own breeding ospreys. But, like almost any reservoir, it is hard to lose sight of the fact that it is a manmade entity superimposed on the landscape. It may be that it just needs more time to bed into Rutland's gently rolling scenery. After all, nature needs time to heal and the reservoir is barely forty years old – my *Bartholomew World Atlas* is older than that and still boldly shows Rutland as an entirely dry county, a contemporary of now extinct political territories like Yugoslavia, USSR and Czechoslovakia.

The footpath out of Empingham dropped down through fields of ragwort and thistles towards a long raised bank, the reservoir's eastern dam wall where I could see cyclists and people walking dogs silhouetted against the skyline ahead. Reaching the bank, the breadth of Rutland Water opened up in front of me. It was a sunny day, and groups of people were clustered together at a beach whose bathing area was neatly demarcated by a string of bright yellow floats. Beyond the bathers and canoeists, the water was busy with sailing boats, some of which were tacking around the water quality-monitoring limnological tower that stood proud of the water some distance offshore.

I followed the northern perimeter track past crowded car parks where families were carrying picnics from their car to the beach. The beach was clearly the thing; the sun and water, the objects of worship. I must have stood out as one of the few men over a certain age that deigned to keep their shirt on, although I noticed that some visitors chose not to visit the beach at all but instead sit in deckchairs next to their car in the shade of trees.

The further west along the shore I went, the quieter it became. At Barnsdale, I climbed up through woodland to a memorial bench that was inscribed *In memory of happy days with Jim*. Alongside the inscription was a photo that showed a middle-aged man looking blissfully content as he paddled a canoe. I sat down on Jim's bench to eat a sandwich and admire the view across to the Hambleton Peninsula. The flooding for the reservoir had reshaped the local topography and what was now a peninsula had once been a ridge above a valley. The village of Upper Hambleton is still there but its less elevated neighbours, Nether and Middle Hambleton, now languish beneath the water. Nether Hambleton, sometimes known as Lower Hambleton, had only been a small hamlet yet it was the location of what was thought to be Rutland's oldest home, a tiny thatched building called Beehive Cottage. This, along with other historic and picturesque dwellings dating from the 18th century or earlier, had been demolished in 1975 in advance of the flooding. While Upper Hambleton survived and Nether Hambleton drowned, the halfway village of Middle Hambleton suffered mixed fortunes. Two of its farms were lost to the reservoir scheme, as were several of its cottages, although the 17th-century mansion, Lyndon Hall, managed to survive as it was just above the high water mark. The hall's owner, Sir John Conant, who lost farm buildings, workers' cottages and 217 acres of farmland in the scheme, had been one of leaders of the 'Don't Dam Rutland' campaign that followed the 1970 parliamentary act to approve the reservoir's construction.

Back at the water's edge, I walked to Eglington and then on to Rutland's only urban centre, Oakham. It is easy to joke about Rutland: the county's diminutive size ('*Multum in Parvo*' is the council's motto) and slightly odd name gifted it an unfair start in terms of ridicule. Back in the 1970s the county had been considered sufficiently comical to have inspired the creation of *Rutland Weekend Television*, a short-lived television sketch show that starred ex-Python Eric Idle and launched The Rutles, a Beatles parody rock group (*Can't Buy Me Lunch*).

While Iain Sinclair dismissed Rutland – 'a Monty Python joke location. It doesn't officially exist except in the memory segment of Deepest England' – Arthur Mee, writing in *The King's England: Leicestershire and Rutland* in the 1930s, was kinder about the county, describing its pint-sized capital, Oakham, as possessing 'a peacefulness unruffled by the 20th century'. An updated edition might observe that this same tranquillity has persisted into the 21st, although my own appreciation of the town's serenity was short-lived as I arrived just in time to catch the bus back to Stamford.

Chapter 11

The Unhorsing of Kings

Leicestershire

I swooped through leicestershires of swift green light
J.A. Baker, *The Peregrine*

It was raining when the train pulled into Leicester station but the sight of a group of jolly girls running a charity cup cake stall in the arrivals hall warmed me to the place immediately.

The city had barely been on my radar. Apart from passing through it by train a few times, I could only recall two previous occasions when I had ever visited Leicester. Both were decades earlier. The first was when I had hitchhiked from Norfolk to visit a former girlfriend who was at university there. All I remembered of this encounter was a vague sense of disappointment, although I hardly think I had travelled there with any great optimism in the first place. The second occasion was travelling there by car with my father to buy a second-hand camera lens. This was on the day before I flew to Sudan to teach English for a year, and Dad had driven me to Leicester in pursuit of a telephoto lens. He may have seen it as an opportunity for a bit of father-son bonding before I went off into the great unknown. I was on the brink of something; I would be away for a year and it was an obvious source of worry for my mother. We were both a little wary of each other, not wishing to cause any upset: the years of father-teenage son friction were still a fairly fresh memory and we had not yet really found a way of talking to each other openly and without judgement.

In Leicester, a suitable lens was found but neither of us had enough cash and so we went to a high street bank where my father, without any proof of an account, tried to convince the staff that this was the same bank with which he always did business. The staff, unimpressed, demanded some form of documentation and this annoyed my father to the extent that he very nearly flounced out of the door declaring words to the effect of: 'Do you know who I am? I'll take my business elsewhere in the future.' I do not recall what happened next but somehow the money, a relatively modest sum, was arranged and the lens was purchased. I remember feeling quite shaken by the experience. This was a side of my father I had never witnessed before. It seemed almost a revelation that a mild-mannered family man with a dry sense of humour had another face that he sometimes showed to the world. For all I knew, as soon as he left home for the office each morning, he morphed Janus-like into some sort of anti-hero: Middle-Manager-Man, an impatient boss who expected results. At home he was always just Dad, an easy-going, albeit perennially worried man who, like his son, usually did his utmost to avoid conflict. Middle-aged, (lower) middle-class, middle manager from the Midlands – the societal centre ground was the territory I had grown up in and knew best. My own part in this unstinting middle ground tradition was reflected by a school career of almost textbook mediocrity, such was its utter lack of distinction. Middling, mediocre, moderate: it was world that I had thought I was comfortable with.

*

I ventured out of the station into the drizzle, and a brief glance at the rain-stained buildings made it clear that Leicester was no Samarkand or Rome, or even Oxford. But it was certainly no blighted urban jungle either.

Close to the station entrance stands a statue of Thomas Cook, the Baptist preacher turned travel agent whose first booking in

1842 was to organise a rail trip from Leicester to Loughborough for fellow supporters of the temperance movement. The line still exists, unlike the travel company that went into administration in 2019. Cook's first endeavour using the service of the Midland Railway Company was so successful that he went on to arrange further alcohol-free trips to Derby and Birmingham, and in 1845, an excursion to Liverpool that came complete with its own handbook, a sort of proto-travel guidebook. Cook, of course, went on to much greater things but what this devoted teetotaller would have made of the conspicuously non-abstemious Club 18-30 holidays that his company provided in the latter part of the 20th century is anybody's guess.

I made my way through rain-splattered streets to the city tourist office where I was given a map, then, following this, made my way to the newly built Dynasty, Death and Discovery museum dedicated to Richard III, whose connection to the city has come sharply into focus over the last few years. On the way, I walked past the market place where *Match of the Day* presenter Gary Lineker once bagged up spuds on the family fruit and veg stall.

Until recently, a mention of Leicester might invoke a handful of well-known names from the man in the street – footballers Lineker (goal hanger) and Shilton (goal keeper), the Attenborough brothers (Richard, the film-maker; David, zoologist and world-saver), crooner Engelbert Humperdinck, fashionista Gok Wan and playwright Joe Orton. Perhaps also Simon de Monfort, the father of parliamentary democracy; maybe even John Merrick (the 'Elephant Man') or the Teddy Boy rock 'n' rollers Showaddywaddy (a name that would always be remembered as pronounced in the staccato Leeds accent of an unmentionable, creepily eccentric DJ on *Top of the Pops* – 'Shooh-wadd'eh-wadd'eh'). But such connections are relatively inconsequential compared to a chance discovery in 2012 that made the city newsworthy for weeks on end.

King Richard III, the last Plantagenet monarch, died close to the city at Bosworth Field, defeated in the last decisive battle of the War of the Roses in 1485. His body was buried without ceremony after the battle, but the precise location of his Leicester tomb was lost by the time the Reformation had run its course. More than half a millennium later, the grave was finally discovered by accident beneath a city centre council car park on a site that was once a priory church of the Franciscan order. The skeleton was without feet, as these had been inadvertently removed during the upheaval of earlier building work. An archaeological dig exhumed the skeleton, and in early 2013 the University of Leicester announced that, beyond reasonable doubt, these were indeed the bones of the king. After some debate as to where his royal, if footless, remains should finally be laid to rest – Richard III was the son of Richard of York, after all, and York Minster had a stake, as did Westminster Abbey – a grand televised re-interment took place at Leicester Cathedral in March 2015.

Outside the entrance to the museum someone had gone to the trouble of creating a large equestrian sand sculpture of the king. This was a bittersweet tribute considering that Richard's undoing came about by being unhorsed in the field of battle, an event that would never be far from the lips of those fond of quoting Shakespeare. Richard III is not the first Plantagenet to be remembered by a sound bite. Richard's father lent his name to a mnemonic that helps recall the colours of the rainbow – 'Richard of York gave battle in vain' – which is apt as Richard Plantagenet, the Duke of York, had, like his son, also died on the battlefield.

The museum was filled with screens that showed actors in medieval dress telling the story of Richard III. Several of the talking heads made an effort to counter the commonly accepted Shakespearean depiction of the last Plantagenet as a crippled and bitter tyrant – the 'poisonous hunch-back'd toad' pantomime villain of the serious actor's repertoire.

It seemed only proper to visit Richard's tomb now that I was here, so I ventured back out into the rain to make my way to the cathedral. I had been abroad when his bones were moved here and had missed seeing the televised pomp and circumstance of the internment ceremony. At the cathedral a greeter welcomed me in hushed tones and pointed out the tomb. I took my place in the queue. As I waited, the ever-worsening rain fell loudly on the pitched roof high above – a rhythmic thrum that in different circumstances might be taken for distant cavalry crossing hard ground. The tomb is suitably austere: modern marble with a French motif, Richard's coat of arms and, fittingly, the white rose of Yorkshire. With light streaming in through the stained glass windows, and freshly painted golden angels supporting the ceiling beams above, the setting was a marked improvement on an unmarked grave beneath an unloved car park.

Leicester was to serve as the base from which I would cross the county east to west. To continue where I had left off, I had first to return to Oakham in neighbouring Rutland. There was no obvious route to follow, although the OS map revealed an ample scatter of footpaths. I decided that from Oakham I would first head west to Knossington before striking southwest to the villages of Tilton-on-the Hill and Billesdon, from where I could catch a bus back to the city. The next day, I would continue southwest to reach the old Roman road at Little Stretton, which would take me past the airport into the city's eastern suburbs. Having passed through so much low-lying country beforehand in the Fens, the promise of walking to somewhere that was '-on-the-Hill' engendered a gentle thrill in my being.

My base in Leicester was a guesthouse just off Narborough Road in the west of the city. A fairly basic sort of lodging, the window of my small single room looked out onto the pantiles of the roofs of neighbouring buildings – the same humdrum outlook that might be seen in a residential area of any city. Although it was geared up for trade with itinerant overnighters, the guest-house felt like a student bedsit property, with plenty of muffled comings and goings of other lodgers that I heard but never saw. Lying in bed on my first night, I found myself feeling inexplicably anxious when I heard unseen guests come up the stairs to use the shared bathroom. Barely audible voices, the unsettling hiss of running water, taps running, a toilet chain being pulled – strangers just a few feet away on the other side of the thin wall. I do not know what initiated my anxiety but it felt as if I were in hiding from the world, as if it were somehow crucial that I kept my presence secret. Such feelings are uncommon but, like the black dog that casts a gloomy shadow occasionally, anxiety is an unwelcome visitor that sometimes comes to call. I can hide from it as much as I like but it will always manage to find me.

*

I woke to bright sunshine on my first morning in the city, although the radio weather forecaster suggested it probably would not last. When I went to the station to buy my ticket, the man at the counter responded, 'Oakham, really? Are you sure? It's a terrible place.'

I felt that some sort of rejoinder was necessary. 'Oh, I'm not going to stay there. I only want a one-way ticket, thanks.'

He smiled and countered, 'Oh, it's all right. I'm only joking. I actually live there.'

The train went via Melton Mowbray – *Rural Capital of Food*, according to the station sign – and passed through a rolling countryside of corduroy-ribbed fields. By the time we reached Oakham the sky had clouded over and rain seemed imminent, although as things turned out I encountered nothing worse than light drizzle on the twelve-mile walk to Billesdon.

I did not linger in Oakham (*Twinned with Dodgeville, USA; winner of Britain in Bloom*) but walked straight out of the town along a narrow lane that led to a hilltop radio mast. From here, I followed a footpath through fields of placid Friesian cows and fly-swooping swallows. The gleaming mass of Rutland Water soon came into sight as the green valleys of Leicestershire's cattle country opened up to the south. At a fenced-in wood, a *Hunt Staff Only* sign served to remind that, however cosily pastoral it appeared, this was prime John Bull territory – a countryside where, to paraphrase Wilde, the unspeakable and uneatable coexisted uneasily in some sort of dynamic equilibrium.

From Owston, a neat sandstone village surrounded by fields of sheep and corn, I climbed uphill to another radio mast from where I could make out the church spire of Tilton-on-the-Hill straight across the valley ahead. To reach it, I had to descend steeply before climbing again, the steep fold of the valley forming a natural ha-ha that hid the trackbed of a disused railway line long overgrown with hogweed.

My plan had been to stop for lunch in the village pub at Tipton-on-the-Hill, but storm clouds were gathering threateningly by now and it seemed better to carry on to Billesdon, where I knew there would be a bus back to Leicester. Just beyond the village was a footpath that led me through a large field bisected with electricity pylons. The map showed a diagonal route across the field but I was a little concerned when I saw that it also contained a herd of cattle. I was about a quarter of the way across when the animals, which had hitherto been following at a distance en masse, started closing in on me in what felt like a menacing manner. It was important to remain calm, so I walked on slowly, turning around frequently to wave my arms in an attempt to get the animals to back off a little. This is a technique that has usually worked in the past but these animals seemed more hostile than most – it was also quite possible that my arm-waving was precisely the wrong sort of body language to employ. The cattle approached closer, almost to the point of nudging me, and then I noticed one individual, stamping a hoof on the ground, that looked as if he was about to take a run up like a *toro* in a Spanish *corrida*. Seriously outnumbered and with no desire to play the toreador, I edged towards one of the pylons, hoping that its metal base might serve as some sort of protective cage. This worked to some extent but the increasingly curious animals moved right up to the base to surround me, looking as if they had no intention of withdrawing. Seeing no alternative, I edged my way out again and, walking backwards whilst shouting at the seemingly unperturbed cattle, made my way to the corner of the field. Eventually, with great relief, I reached the edge, where I threw my bag ahead of me over the electric fence before shimmying beneath it. Forcing my way through an overgrown bank of thistles, I finally reached the safety of a farm track. By this stage I had stopped worrying about rain. Dazed by the encounter, I walked the rest of the way to Billesdon in a state of bewilderment that lay somewhere between trauma and euphoria.

Although Belgrave Road in the north of the city is home to Leicester's 'Golden Mile' of Indian restaurants, it is fair to say that Narborough Road, which runs southwest from the centre, is probably the most ethnically diverse area in what is already Britain's most multicultural city. The neighbourhood is as much Turkish in character as it is Indian, as much Bangladeshi as it is Pakistani. It is Kurdish, Somali and Arabic too, but a cursory impression suggested that everybody seemed to rub along well enough together, whatever their origin.

When television news teams were lured to the city in 2016 by dint of the meteoric climb and surprise win of Leicester City FC in the Premier League, Narborough Road was the place where the media would invariably gravitate to record vox pop interviews and examine the multicultural element of Leicester's success story. More often than not, the television interviews seemed to be conducted at one of the tables of the cavernous Istanbul restaurant, where I chose to go to eat on my first night in the city. The place was surprisingly busy for a weekday. Unsurprisingly, given Narborough Road's ethnic mix, most of the other customers appeared to be of Turkish heritage. Most were in family groups – mums and dads, aunts and uncles exchanging noisy banter, their kids wandering away from the tables to chase each other around the restaurant. I, as ever on this journey, sat and ate alone. For most of the time on my walk I was untroubled by loneliness and content enough in my own company. Evenings though, meal times especially, were different. I felt conspicuously solitary, vulnerable even, an involuntary loner adrift in a sea of warm conviviality. The good-natured bustle of the Istanbul was something that was not mine, nor could I be party to it. Thankfully, my *köfte* arrived quickly, so there was no need to linger.

*

Before setting out next morning I treated myself to a breakfast at the Cafe Two Ten by the railway bridge, a 'greasy spoon' that defied the Trades Descriptions Act in being pleasant and not in the least bit greasy. Suitably fuelled with tea, eggs and toast, I made my way to the bus station to catch the bus to Billesdon, from where I started walking back in the direction of Leicester.

Harvest time was approaching and swallows were gorging on flies, swooping and dipping above the ripening wheat. On some of the hillsides the contoured outline of medieval fields could still be discerned as long narrow strips. Such evidence of one-time intensive farming suggested a settlement that had long been abandoned, its population probably moved out because of new tenure of the surrounding land. The OS map confirmed this, bold Gothic lettering indicating that a medieval village had once stood in the vicinity. Like some parts of Norfolk, this region, once far more densely populated than it is today, is a ghosted landscape.

The tower of Gaulby's St Peter's Church peaked over the hedgerows ahead, a weathervane on each one of its stone finials. With a grand manor house at its core – long gravel drive, *Keep Out* signs, stone walls and fenced tennis court – Gaulby had the us-and-them air of an estate village where the 'big house' still meant something. At King's Norton, the next village, I had intended to follow a footpath through a farmyard but an electrified wire across the path and the intimidating barking of dogs persuaded me to stick to the road, which I followed alongside tall hedgerows weighted with ripening sloes. It was along here that a voice called out to me unexpectedly from a parked car. The voice belonged to a young Asian man – smartly dressed, polite, mild Leicester accent – the vehicle's sole occupant.

'Hey there! Hello, sir. How far have you been walking?'

I told him that I had set out from Billesdon.

'Where are you heading, then?'

'As far as Leicester, if I can. I hope so, anyhow.'

We exchanged a few more pleasantries and as I walked off, he shouted after me, 'Good luck with your walk, sir.' I was a little curious about what he was doing parked up in an isolated spot like this but did not like to ask. All the same, I was touched by his courtesy to a passing stranger.

Little Stretton, just before the main road that led into Leicester, is another well-to-do enclave of stone houses with neat flower borders and a squat church that looks as if it might have been fashioned out of slabs of chocolate cake. The village telephone box was, as its sign proclaimed, ***no longer a working telephone box but a preserved museum piece for the villagers of Little Stretton***. Helpfully, another sign said: *LOST? VILLAGE MAP IN PHONEBOX*. I was not lost, but I peered inside anyway to find a stack of business cards that read, ***Implement a custodial tariff for paedophiles***, along with the Twitter handle and website details of someone called Phil, who clearly had strong feelings on this matter. The cards summoned up an image of a genteel lynch mob – village vigilantes in Barbour jackets armed with pruning shears, rolled up copies of the *Daily Telegraph* and sufficiently good broadband to be able to WhatsApp for backup if necessary. As a reminder of the box's original use, a panel with dialling instructions and international telephone codes had been left in situ as a memento, along with the Samaritans' number and the instruction that the phone box was situated 'adjacent Blacksmiths Shop', although it had been a long time since the cottage next door had witnessed hot metal hissing in a pail. The map, painstakingly hand-drawn, detailed every building in the village. I sensed that nothing went unnoticed in Little Stretton and that any newcomer would have to undergo rigorous DBS checks before they would be permitted to purchase a property.

The main road, of arrow-straight Roman pedigree, took me on past Great Stretton, where traces of another deserted village lay as indistinct mounds under the coarse grass of a meadow. Although built for marching legionnaires, the road was no longer ideally suited for transit on foot. With no footpath to cling to, latter-day walkers were an unwelcome anomaly in this pedestrian-free zone.

At the brow of a hill, just after I passed the entrance gate to the city's airfield, a modest rectangle of concrete and grass that seemed to be mostly devoted to the training of helicopter pilots, a funeral cortege of shiny black limousines drove past. I was in no need of a sign to remind me of my inherent mortality – the speed-crazed traffic and absence of a footpath were already enough for that. Nature did its best to comfort as lapwings flapped up in flashes of chiaroscuro in the stubble fields beside the road, the birds pee-witting mournfully above the din of the traffic. Overhead, I heard a high nasal mewing: a buzzard, which circled down to lurk in the crown of a tree.

Finally, a bridleway led me away from the highway across a field painted blue with borage. Ahead, on the skyline, was the spire of Stoughton church. More wheat fields, more fields of sky-blue borage – the pale green scent of cucumbers... more buzzards.

Stoughton, a dormitory village that seemed to happily exist in denial of its proximity to a major city, had a Silver Jubilee bench on its green and a sign that pointed out a cycle route into Leicester. Better, I thought, to dodge pedal-powered two-wheelers than container lorries with a grudge against pedestrians. So I followed the cycle track uphill and down to Evington, then alongside a golf course into Leicester's eastern suburbs.

Cresting a hill, Leicester lay sprawled in the wide hollow below: semi-detached suburbia beneath a tight scatter of high-rises; no obvious identifying features, just a few redundant chimney stacks punctuating the huddle of concrete and glass that marked the city centre.

A large mosque dominated the crossroads at the bottom of the hill. Opposite the mosque was a smart detached house with stained glass panels that spelled 'Allah' in Arabic script; next door, a doctor's surgery that advertised travel vaccinations and a circumcision service. This was the east end of town, yet it seemed to buck accepted urban geography stereotypes in being both noticeably prosperous *and* predominantly Asian. A topsy-turvy cityscape that defies typecasting, this is no Bolton or Bradford blighted by urban poverty, this is Leicester – a success story. If well-assimilated multiculturalism ever needed a poster girl (modestly attired, of course) then the city was a prime contender.

I headed on through Stoneygate, a more modest area of terraced housing, and then onto Main Road and alongside Victoria Park on to New Walk for the final leg into the centre. New Walk is an eye-catching green thoroughfare lined with fancy wrought-iron lampposts and handsome Georgian properties. Built as a pedestrian promenade in the late 18th century, it traces the route of the Via Devana, the same Roman route linking Colchester and Chester that I had dodged traffic along earlier near the city's aerodrome. Reaching De Montfort Square, a leafy rectangle of property of the sort that only lawyers and solicitors can afford, I went into the neoclassical New Walks Gallery for a drink in its tea-room before summoning up the energy to continue into the city.

At Haymarket, close to the crossroads of pedestrian thoroughfares in the centre, an ex-soldier was doing his best to sell wristbands to passers-by.

'They're to support our boys in the forces fighting for our safety abroad.'

Lurching, foot-shifting towards the constant flow of humanity that streamed by, his determination was apparent, although few seemed to take up his offer.

I made my way back to my room in the west of the city and after a rest and a shower went out for something to eat. I ended up at an Indian restaurant at the city end of Narborough Road.

The Jamal Tandoori was a small, family operation fronted by the eponymous Jamal, a friendly Leicester native who welcomed each guest individually and gave a little talk on how the menu was flexible and could be adapted to personal tastes. Chicken or meat, he assured, could be 'tikka'd' for no additional charge; chillies could be added or subtracted without fuss or judgement, spices moderated. The place was unlicensed, so after the (correct) assumption being made that I would require a beer with my meal, I was dispatched to a nearby takeaway to purchase the BYO of my choice. That night, drinking Russian beer from a Polish supermarket, eating north Indian food cooked by Anglo-Pakistanis, followed by a pint of English real ale in a nearby pub, I enjoyed what was probably the definitive multicultural Leicester experience.

*

Next morning, I took my leave of Leicester. After a farewell breakfast fry-up at the Two Ten, I walked west out of the city towards the M1. Once beyond the railway bridge on Narborough Road, where *WEST END* had been neatly painted across the width of the bridge to signify some sense of community, the neighbourhood morphed from vibrant multiculturalism – Afro Supermarket, Lucky Dragon Chinese Takeaway, Lynn's Cafe – to something that looked a little rougher around the edges. This was a neighbourhood of that would have been at home in the poorer end of any British city – an area of solid semis and decent-sized gardens, some neglected and cushioned with discarded mattresses, others lovingly tended with symmetrical borders of begonia and lobelia.

I made my way across Braunstone Park, an expansive realm of football pitches that slopes up towards a large brick building. The park was deserted apart from a solitary hooded youth on a bicycle, who overtook me so slowly on the path that it made me feel a little uneasy. Braunstone Hall, which stands at the top of the park, was closed to the public. With its classical pillar-framed entrance boarded up, and fronds of buddleia dangling from its pediment, the building has seen better days although it still commands an imperious view.

Leaving the park, I made my way through more suburban streets before walking through a wooded area where tough-looking men were exercising tough-looking dogs. Approaching the edge of the city, I crossed the A47 and followed a public footpath along the edge of an industrial estate. The M1 was close now, audible yet hidden from view behind an embankment. Despite the whine of traffic, the tall hedgerows that bordered the path created an impression of rural calm. Dense thickets of blackberry at the wayside gleamed with clusters of plump, inviting fruit. I tried one, wondering what its petrochemical content might be. It tasted fine – sweet and juicy, and not a hint of diesel.

Finally, I came to an underpass beneath the motorway. Like a doorway between worlds, it led directly into open fields, and for a moment it seemed as if the whole city of Leicester had suddenly vanished behind the curtain blur of racing traffic. The path continued across a buttercup meadow and a signpost topped with an abandoned cloth cap pointed out the route into Kirby Muxloe. The village is now effectively a far-flung outlier of Leicester but it had once it been sufficiently independent of the city to have its own castle during the War of the Roses. A fragment of this still remains and I caught a glimpse of its decayed stonework through the trees as I walked into the village.

From Kirby Muxloe, I followed a footpath that led through an expanse of wheat-stubble fields bisected by humming power lines. A scatter of wind turbines, close enough to hear the low metallic moan of their rotors, completed the impression of a landscape that literally buzzed with energy.

I lost the footpath at a farm complex, so I headed across fields towards the nearest road, jumping a ditch to reach it. I walked the grass verge into Desford, passing Bosworth Academy (*To Learn and To Achieve*) at the bottom of the hill, and the Blue Bell pub and Vicki's Barbers (*Hair Cut, Sir?*) further along the high street. At the end of the village I left the road to cross more fields of stubble into Newbold Verdon, where I found the stop for the bus back to Leicester.

Boarding the bus, the driver, seeing that I had been walking, asked where I was from.

'Norfolk? My daughter lives that way... in Cromer. It's lovely there, isn't it? We visit her whenever we get the chance.'

Back in Leicester, waiting for a bus to take me to the railway station, a young man who must have spotted my rucksack approached to ask if I had been camping.

'No, I'm just doing a bit of walking in the area.'

Not for the first time, I found it hard to explain what it was that I was doing. Leicestershire was not renowned for its hiking opportunities, and someone my age tramping the city with a rucksack on my back probably gave the impression of a footloose itinerant rather than a hiker. There again, Birmingham, where I was heading next, was not exactly well known as a prime walking destination either.

Chapter 12

Ghosts and Stone Memory

Leicestershire/Warwickshire

I have set my life upon a cast,
And I will stand the hazard of the die
William Shakespeare, *Richard III*

It took four hours of combined train and bus travel to reach Newbold Verdon on the day I returned to Leicestershire. By the time I finally arrived in the village I was stiff-limbed and raring to go.

My route out of the village took me through fields of placid white cattle, where swallows were swooping for flies in readiness for their imminent migration south. All of the fields had been harvested by now, leaving wide sweeps of golden stubble in every direction. I followed footpaths and a minor road to reach the outskirts of Sutton Cheney, from where a broad grass track led down to the Bosworth Field battlefield site.

Scattered around the site, wind-up information posts with disembodied voices told the history of how the battle unfolded. One had the story of a Norfolk archer (complete with unconvincing Mummerset accent) who told of his recruitment and journey out west to Bosworth. Another gave a potted history of Richard III and the reasons why the battle took place. Elsewhere, a large sundial set amidst rose beds (an appropriate planting of red and white to represent the opposing factions) commemorated the thousand or so men lost in the battle and the many more thousands who were killed during the thirty-year span of the Wars of the Roses.

Despite the ready association of Bosworth with the critical 1485 encounter, it now looks unlikely that this was the actual battlefield site and there is plenty of evidence to suggest that the actual carnage took place at a site two miles to the south at Ambion Hill. Whatever the location of the true site, the fluttering flags on the hilltop – the war banners of Richard III's and Henry Tudor's respective armies – seemed to reinforce some sort of metaphysical truth, the inference being that the battle had been a wholly noble enterprise, a necessary skirmish to determine the lineage of a future monarchy.

The coordinates for the exact location of the battlefield may not have been correct but, according to Danny Dorling, Professor of Geography at the University of Oxford, Bosworth stands exactly on what he defined as the North/South divide, an imaginary line that separates the poorer north of England from the more prosperous south. In Professor Dorling's reckoning, the line runs more or less diagonally across England between the Bristol Channel and the Humber estuary. Dorling's theoretical division is not without controversy: the author and columnist Simon Jenkins has dismissed the academic as 'Geographer royal by appointment to the left', and no doubt there are Lancastrians and Yorkshire folk who resent parts of the Midlands being described as 'northern'. In the *real* north, the soft south is anywhere south of where you happen to live; for a Geordie or Mackem, Darlington is 'down south' and 'la-di-da'. But in this notional world of North/South cultural and socio-economic variation, physical geography is skewed: Norwich and Leicester are both located south of the line, while Birmingham, Coventry and all of Wales lie to the north. According to Dorling, the transition from north to south is not gradual, as one might expect. The imagined line of partition is, in fact, a fractal division sharply defined by all manner of factors – voting patterns, house prices, wealth, health (average life expectancy is markedly lower north of the line), life chances, Oxbridge university access, language and dialect – particularly vowel sounds – and even preferences for flat or bubbly beer. The theoretical line follows distinct features of physical geography, too – the division between upland and lowland Britain, and pastoral and arable farming – features that have strongly influenced British history and culture. The divide also roughly delineates the southern territory colonised by Saxon invaders and follows uncannily close to the route traced by the Roman Fosse Way. As the angle of the hypothetical divide is sharply tilted and runs roughly southwest to northeast, I was aware that from now on, while I would be continuing westwards at more or less the same latitude, I would be walking 'north' of this invisible yet tangible divide for the rest of the way to the coast.

Diametrically opposed to this imaginary North/South division is another historic line that could be superimposed on the map: the ragged border that once separated Wessex and Mercia from the territory of the Danelaw. A 9th-century treaty between Alfred the Great and the Danish warlord Guthrum established a frontier that more or less delineated the current county boundary between Leicestershire and Warwickshire. So here, close to Bosworth Field and Watling Street, was an intersection of two frontiers that separated contrasting cultural and political worlds. An unsteady, and partly theoretical, 'X' marked the spot on the map: it was a fitting place to host a battle.

Battle sites come with their own attendant ghosts; the more bloody and violent the clash, the more plentiful and visible the ghost presence – or so it is said. At the time of the Civil War, apparitions of spectral battle scenes were claimed to have been widely witnessed at sites where skirmishes took place. Such apparitions have been interpreted as not so much supernatural phenomena – dead souls returning to life – but as traumatic events mysteriously and inexplicably recorded by the landscape itself. The belief is that such events have somehow etched themselves into the fabric of the landscape: a stone memory of place – a battlefield, a (haunted) mansion, a site of execution – generated by human distress and the emotions of fear.

Victorians were especially attuned to this way of thinking and ever-enthusiastic in exploring new ways of opening our eyes and ears to them. Guglielemo Marconi, the Italian physicist and inventor of radio, working in the late 19th and early 20th century, conceived of wireless telegraphy not simply as a useful means of communications but as a spectral science. Marconi was convinced that any sound generated never died but merely became fainter with time, such that our limited perceptions were no longer able to detect it. Thus, even the much-cited hypothetical tree falling in the forest would be detected by the rest of the forest as a fragment of wood memory, albeit one that even the most sensitive of aural devices could neither record nor reproduce. Marconi was particularly fascinated with the music played aboard the SS *Titanic* as it went down (he would have been aboard the doomed ocean liner himself had his circumstances been only slightly different), and at the end of his life still dreamed of one day hearing Jesus' original Sermon on the Mount, reproduced by means of ultra sophisticated listening technology. Marconi was wrong, of course. Sound does die – it does not adhere to place indefinitely like the magnetic memory of a cassette tape or the grooves of a vinyl disc recording. Some humans though, their sensibilities attuned to such phenomena, might be capable of sensing 'an atmosphere' at a particular locality.

Perhaps it was because this was not the precise location, or possibly it was down to my own brutish insensitivity to such things, but there was no perceptible stone memory of the conflict at Bosworth, as far as I could tell.

*

From Bosworth Field I walked downhill to Shenton station. In a single geo-historical instant I stepped over an invisible frontier marking a transition that was socioeconomic (South to North), monarchic (Plantagenet to Tudor), and historic (Medieval to Enlightenment). I crossed the railway line and Ashby-de-la-Zouch canal before following a footpath across oak-planted parkland to reach Shenton, the next village. Here, on the other side of Professor Dorling's North/South divide, things did not look so very different.

Walking west from Shenton, I reached the A444, a remnant of the Roman military highway that once connected Ratae (modern-day Leicester) with the fort at Manduessedum (now the village of Mancetter) just outside Atherstone, where it met with Watling Street.

It remains uncertain but it is likely that Boudica's final action against the Romans, the so-called Battle of Watling Street, took place close to Manduessedum where the two ancient roads intersected. What became of Boudica after this final battle is open to debate. The Roman historian Tacitus writes that the Iceni leader escaped with her daughters to another part of Britain, where they took their own lives by drinking poison. In sharp contradiction to this, Cassius Dio, a Greek source, suggests that, rather than suicide, Boudica died naturally of illness and was given a lavish funeral by her people. Either way, it is unlikely that Boudica's body was ever returned to her native Norfolk and probable that it remained wherever she died, far from home. The warrior queen's grave has never been found but there are some – admittedly only a few – who cling to the belief that her body lies somewhere beneath a branch of McDonald's in Birmingham. A feature in the *Birmingham Mail* in 2013, headlined *Boudica, the burger queen of Brum*, has claimed somewhat tenuously that 'if archaeologists are in the right spot' her remains might be discovered beneath a fast food outlet in Kings Norton. The claim is largely based on the assertion that Parsons Hill, in the Kings Norton district of central Birmingham, is another possible contender for the site of the final Roman-Iceni encounter. Now that Leicester has Richard III as a sort of legendary royal mascot, it seems only fair that Birmingham can claim an iconic monarch for its own. The trouble is, this is not the only place to claim the warrior queen: Birdlip in Gloucestershire has long been mooted as another possible burial site, as a Celtic hoard dating from approximately the same period as her death in 60AD was discovered close to the village in 1879. Yet another speculation, perhaps no less credible than the Birmingham McDonald's claim, is that Boudica's remains lie somewhere beneath London's King's Cross station – beneath platform 8, 9 or 10, to be precise – although other cases have been made for Hampstead Heath and even Peckham Rye. But London has enough dead monarchs already; surely it is not too much to ask that there be just one in England's second city?

*

Despite the road's impressive lineage, walking the unnervingly busy A444 was less than ideal for contemplating Roman occupation and the fate of Iceni queens. I hugged the curb – there was no grass verge – and followed it south as far as Fenny Drayton, where a footpath took me to the A5 – Watling Street, as was.

Although Meriden, not so very far away from here, has both a name and a plaque to prove it, Fenny Drayton's claim on the title of England's most central settlement is probably more legitimate as, in 2002, the Ordnance Survey declared that the geographical centre of England lay on the southeast outskirts of the village at Lindley Hall Farm. The same body erected a plaque to denote this in 2013, much to the annoyance of Meriden folk who had been basking in the glory of their own geo-centricity for centuries. Someone would now have to go and brave the collective wrath of Meriden to chisel 'Almost' into the plaque that stands at the foot of the ancient cross commemorating this in the Warwickshire village.

Having visited the site of one of England's most epoch-changing battles, crossed a hypothetical North/South divide, and passed close to the meeting point of two Roman roads, all in a single day, it felt as if my walk had finally reached some sort of tipping point. There was another transition, too: as I crossed the A5, I entered the county of Warwickshire and the territory of the West Midlands.

If East Anglia – Norfolk, in particular – represents the present and the future, the place where I have lived out most of my days, then the West Midlands is the past... *my* past. It is the place of my childhood, my parents, grandparents and generations before them; my schooldays, teenage years and coming of age. The Birmingham hinterland where I was heading is deeply seamed with family connections, formative experiences... epiphanies. Now I was walking into it, back into the past.

Warwickshire greeted me with a sight of Mount Judd, a Fuji-shaped slagheap, which, long grassed over and now sprouting trees on its slopes, has merged into the surrounding post-industrial landscape to almost give the impression that it has always been there. Known to some in these parts as the 'Nuneaton Nipple', it was voted 'Britain's Best Landmark' in a 2018 *Daily Mirror* poll, beating both Stonehenge and the Angel of the North. A manmade realignment of landscape, nearly 160 metres high, half as high again as Neolithic Silbury Hill, I wondered: did ley lines pass through it or mysteriously swerve around it; did migrating birds use it as a navigational aid, a distance-marking mound beside the Coventry Canal?

Heading south from the A5 along a minor road, I crossed the River Anker and the Coventry Canal to the reach a steep wooded slope below the village of Hartshill. I made my way uphill to find the bus stop. From there, a bus took me all the way to Coventry, where I picked up the Birmingham to London rail service to take me to Northampton.

Northampton was way off-track and might not seem the most obvious choice of a stopover but I had arranged to stay there with my friend Haydn. Given the town's regular rail connections with Birmingham and the rest of the Midlands it seemed as good a place as any to serve as a base for the next stretch of my walk.

*

I barely knew Northampton. My knowledge extended to its ring road, its bus station, and a playing fields toilet block where I used to stop to pee on cross-country drives. As things transpired, I failed to get to know the town any better even after staying there, as Haydn dutifully ferried me by car between station and home on both of the nights that I spent at his house.

There is a Gothic aura to Northampton's reputation, superimposed on the place by its most famous literary son and resident shaman, Alan Moore, who champions the town and still lives there. What I did know is that the town is a world away from the genteel limestone villages of the county that took its name. I knew of its Carlsberg brewery (*Probably the best lager in the world*, brewed *The Danish Way...* in Northampton). I was aware of the town's shoemaking industry, too – its football team's nickname, 'The Cobblers' – and its short-lived revival producing fetishist footwear (there was even a film and musical inspired by this episode, saucily titled *Kinky Boots*). In Victorian times, shoe-making was a cottage industry in the town and many Northampton homes had tiny cobbling sheds in their backyards – Haydn's mid-terrace was no exception. Alan Moore claims that the town was obliged to provide footwear for Cromwell's New Model Army during the English Civil War, although by the time the Restoration came they had still not got around to settling the bill. Whether this is apocryphal or not I have no idea, or even the inclination to investigate further, although it does somehow ring true.

Then there is the town's former lunatic asylum. John Clare, the aforementioned 'Northamptonshire peasant poet', spent the last two decades of his life in the Northampton General Lunatic Asylum, an altogether kinder and more nurturing institution than its name might suggest. Later renamed as St Andrew's Hospital for Mental Diseases (the same saintly dedication as the erstwhile Norwich mental institution where I once scrubbed floors and served up powdered egg to the chemically coshed), inmates included James Joyce's daughter, Lucia, who had been treated by Carl Jung before diagnosis as a schizophrenic, the composer Malcolm Armstrong (who won an Oscar for his *Bridge on the River Kwai* score), the boxer Frank Bruno and Violet Gibson, a woman who shot and wounded Mussolini in 1926. According to the gospel of Alan Moore, Dusty Springfield and actor Patrick McGoohan – the soulful voice and 'the Prisoner' – were also temporary incumbents, although this is most probably mere literary invention on his part.

What I knew of Northampton personally was out of date and came mostly from brief visits in the late 1970s when I used to regularly pass through the town, long before Alan Moore came to prominence as local sage. It was also around this time that the Northampton Development Corporation backed a song competition in a bid to promote the town, which did not have the best of reputations. The winning entry was something called *Energy in Northampton*, a big production pop ditty by Linda Jardim that told, somewhat improbably, of 'aliens from outer space, needing help from the human race' choosing the town for a base on Earth because 'they knew there was energy in Northampton'. The B-side of the single, *(60 Miles by Road or Rail) Northampton*, made use of the same tune and arrangement but had a different, more romantic lyric in which the singer, keen to visit her 'Northampton guy', extolled the town's convenient transport links. It remains unclear whether any aliens ever got the message but there was undoubtedly energy of some sort at work in the town.

Alan Moore has described the town as a sort of 'vision sump', a place that has a tendency for clawing in interesting minds. Northampton, re-imagined in multitudinous dimensions, serves as the centrepiece for Moore's 1,200-page magnum opus *Jerusalem* – clearly, nowhere else would suffice. Watching Moore talk on YouTube clips brings to mind a composite of some of the dopehead philosophers I had known in Redditch in my late teens – not just the hairiness and dolorous expression but the aura of standing outside and looking in. With his chuckling gravity and mage-like baritone delivery of understated wisdom and acerbic wit, along with an unselfconscious pride in possessing an accent that is not BBC-approved RP, what I hear and see is a quality of fearlessness, of valour in the face of the *wyrd*. To Moore, Northampton is *unheimlich* to its leather-working core, but it is likely that he would have said the same of almost anywhere else had he been born and raised there and given the chance to incorporate its place-specific psychic fabric into his grimoire.

*

If Northampton was an enigma then I could not say the same for Coventry (Cofa's Tree, the name's precise derivation long lost but something to do with marking a boundary). I lived in the city for about eighteen months in my youth, but my recollection of the place had been relegated to some sort of black hole of memory, its time-frozen super gravity created by a cocktail of personal circumstances that combined a crisis of confidence, the end-fizzle of a relationship and the post-teen angst of an oversensitive young man. Over time, the very name of the place had turned into some sort of personal synecdoche for unhappiness and uncertainty: Coventry – the lost year(s). The tropes – equestrian nudists, Peeping Toms, enforced silences, phoenix-like resurrection from the ashes of war (collateral damage begun by Luftwaffe bombers in the 1940s, the job completed by cack-handed city planners in the 1960s) – were there for the asking, but these I overlooked. Living in Coventry back then I had barely looked up from my navel long enough to contemplate the looming industrial decline. The Thatcher-era collapse as documented by The Specials' *Ghost Town* was yet to take place, but all the warning signs were there. In many ways the Two-Tone movement initiated by The Specials and other Midlands bands was the cultural antidote the city needed to stymie its slide into post-industrial malaise. Even so, I never returned.

The Specials captured the city's essence and committed it to song; the terrace chants of noisy ghosts caught on tape and scratched on vinyl. Other artists have adopted different means of expressing Coventry's post-industrial poetic. For the Tile Hill painter George Shaw, the medium is paint on wood: Humbrol gloss as used by schoolboys and hobbyists on Airfix plastic models. Shaw's subject matter is invariably the west Coventry estate where he grew up, and he has documented the humdrum and nondescript of that modest borough, although it might be argued that there is little to be done to elevate a suburban West Midland housing estate above the quotidian.

Tile Hill is no inner city landscape of urban squalor but rather a place on the edge, the fringe of the city: textbook edgeland, its periphery bordered by fields and woodland, oak-wood murmurs of the elusive Forest of Arden, marginalised greenwood. The titles of some of the paintings are a giveaway as to what is being celebrated. *Landscape with Dog Shit Bin* tells it as it is, as does *Peephole*, a poked-out knothole in a creosoted garden fence.

Other works veer towards the religious: *The Washing of Hands* entitles a portrait of a council house; *Jesus Falls for The Third Time*, an estate pub. Deserted of human beings, and luminous with a gloss that gives these landscapes a vaguely disturbing, unearthly sheen, the very place-specific scenes they portray might be almost anywhere. The emotional effect is of seeing somewhere that is simultaneously cosily familiar and unnervingly alien. Shaw, who moved from the city many years before he started painting, found he could not leave the haunts of his Coventry youth behind and so periodically returned to paint them. The paintings *are* his youth, a place frozen in a specific time, distilled through memory and reproduced in paint normally reserved for model airplanes. Part of the explanation for the resonance I feel for Shaw's work may go beyond the familiarity of subject matter. Humbrol was the only paint I had ever encountered in a creative context too, albeit used for painting the wing camouflage of 1:72 scale Spitfires and Hurricanes during an early-teen obsession with the machinery of World War II aerial combat.

A chance meeting connected me to a friend of a friend who had also once lived in the city. We discovered that we both had lived in exactly the same student house in the north of the city, his tenancy immediately following mine. Whether we had both occupied the same damp upstairs room I never found out. The house, a rundown Victorian terrace with peeling wallpaper, sagging mattresses and charity shop furniture was owned by an affable, albeit unashamedly mercenary landlord called Mr Askari. The house was in Foleshill, north of the centre, which, even then, was a predominantly South Asian area, with grocer shops selling herbs and unfamiliar vegetables, and window signs in Urdu. Grey-bearded men with turbans stood at street corners, young mothers in buttoned-up Burton's overcoats over glitzy *salwar kameez* waited at bus stops; no one looked very happy. The house was a bus-ride away from the city centre. Foleshill was upwind of the then hyperactive Courtaulds textile works, a dark satanic mill devoted to producing man-made fibres (it was the home of 'Courtelle' fabric, very fashionable in its day), whose enormous chimney belched out the brown and chrome yellow smoke that tainted the air we breathed.

I was a student at what was then known as Lanchester Polytechnic (latterly upgraded in status to Coventry University), in the heart of the city next door to the Cathedral. The layout of the city centre is lost geography to me now but it was Basil Spence's beautiful new Cathedral that made the greatest impact back then, its entrance almost across the road from the polytechnic's student union building. Suspended from the wall above the Cathedral steps is Jacob Epstein's *St Michael's Victory over the Devil* bronze sculpture – St Michael triumphantly on top with wings and arms spread, a spear in his right hand, the defeated Devil cowering beneath, bollock-naked with hands and feet bound, Michael's left foot resting firmly on his satanic brow. The church interior elicits an equally powerful reaction, perhaps as much to do with its almost shocking modernity as anything else. That, and Graham Sutherland's thrilling *Christ in Glory* tapestry, the glorious distillation of a decade's activity. When Edward Thomas wrote of cathedrals, stating that 'when I am within them I know why a dog bays at the moon', he was referring to their ancient counterparts like Canterbury and Salisbury. For me, Coventry Cathedral, resurrected phoenix-like from the carbonised wasteland left by saturation bombing, engenders much the same sort of visceral response.

My clearest recollections come from the leafy environs of the polytechnic and Cathedral, an oasis of sorts tucked away from the concrete brutality of the city centre. I recall concerts at the student's union building: 1970s prog-rock (Van de Graaf Generator), flower-haired singer-songwriters (Bridget St John), the crème de la crème of British jazz artists – once Lol Coxhill and the Brotherhood of Breath on the same bill, a beautiful cacophony of free honking brass sufficient to revive the Devil just up the road. On another evening there was a sort of free musical happening, with percussion instruments and old piano frames scattered around the polytechnic grounds for do-it-yourself improvisation. These memories have stayed with me, persisting beyond the malaise I felt from being trapped in what felt like the wrong place at the wrong time.

I remember too, a tragedy: a student who, for reasons unknown, took his own life by hanging himself from the railings of the concrete bridge that led across to the polytechnic common room. I did not know him but I was on nodding terms with his girlfriend – a beautiful young Black woman with a cut-glass public school accent. Discovered by cleaners in the early morning, dangling within sight of St Michael and the Devil just across the way, it was evident that this ill-fated young man had lost the battle with his own demons.

In contrast to what might happen today, the event was hardly spoken about, barely mentioned in conversation in the common room. But afterwards I felt an even stronger sense that the immediate environs of where I was studying were somehow charged – a conjoining of malign forces that worked through education and religion. Perhaps it is this that explains my site-specific amnesia? Thought and experience accrete into layers like geological strata. Some memories end up like nodules of flint buried in chalk – tough and hard, but separate from one another, not a continuum. For me, Coventry had become a flint lost in the stratum, a scattering of nodules in the stone memory.

Part Three

West Midlands

Chapter 13

Pulped Fiction/ The Ghosts of a Forest

North Warwickshire/Birmingham

Ay, now am I in Arden; the more fool I; when I was at home, I was in a better place: but travellers must be content
William Shakespeare, *As You Like It*

Haydn drove me to the station in Northampton the next day and I took the train back to Coventry. Passing through Foleshill, I noticed that it was now a largely Sikh area, with street market stalls, moustachioed men in turbans and women in glittery saris. It seemed a happier place than the one I remembered. Skinheads were nowhere to be seen, and the tall Courtaulds chimney was long gone too, the noxious smoke that used to billow from it reduced to just a lung-memory. Crossing the motorway heading north we passed close to the Ricoh Arena, home of Coventry City FC, on the northern fringe of the city in an area that had still been green fields when I lived there.

At Coventry, I caught a bus back to Hartshill, passing through Bedworth and Nuneaton en route. Nuneaton's ordinariness seemed to belie the fact that the town has produced notable individuals as diverse as Ken Loach, Mary Ann Evans (aka George Eliot), and TV filth-fighting evangelist Mary Whitehouse. Nuneaton clearly held considerable appeal for some: 1970s TV variety darling Larry 'Shut that door' Grayson had liked the place sufficiently to retire to a bungalow in the town.

Arriving in Hartshill, I followed stone steps down from the ridge and made my way up the other side of the valley through a stand of oaks. The trees seemed too close and uniformly spaced for this to be natural woodland and I wondered whether this was reclaimed land – a former industrial site planted with trees in the hope that its blemish would gradually melt back into the landscape. And it had, more or less: a landscaped landscape, only the woodland's straight-line regularity betrayed the lie of human interference.

I emerged from the trees into the light at Hartshill Hayes Country Park. Colour-coded walking trails led off in various directions. A bunch of cellophane-wrapped lilies had been Sellotaped to one of the benches that looked over the valley – a tribute to someone recently deceased who had admired this view, a vista that had once been shared with a loved one. The view was certainly impressive, albeit murky beneath the morning's overcast sky, and through the haze I could make out the twisting course of the River Anker, the less wavering Coventry Canal and the faux volcanic cone of Mount Judd that stuck out as proud as a pimple to the southeast.

Arriving at a road next to a nursing home, another footpath led me along the bank of an old railway line and into another wooded area. This time there was no doubt about the woodland's pedigree. This was a remnant of the once vast Forest of Arden – a bosky tract that once covered much of Warwickshire and across which it was said that squirrels (red, naturally) could traverse the entire county without the inconvenience of ever having to make contact with the ground. These days the squirrels are grey American imports, and while they are less loveable than the natives they ousted, they are undoubtedly more streetwise, better equipped to contend with the motorways, housing estates and out-of-town shopping centres that have been imposed as barriers to free roaming.

The Forest of Arden had been the real thing, a true forest. Unlike many other wooded expanses of post-Norman Britain, it was never a designated 'royal forest', a usurped territory with hunting rights reserved exclusively for the king and, by invitation only, the aristocracy. More than a third of southern England had been allocated as royal forest by the early 13th century but the Forest of Arden was never requisitioned – its ownership remaining with the descendants of Mercian kings, the Arden family, a rare example of Anglo-Saxon land tenure that survived the conquest.

This same ancient woodland had also been virtually untouched by Britain's previous invaders, the Romans, whose spear-straight military highways – Icknield Street, Watling Street and Fosse Way – uncharacteristically went around the forest rather than through it. Although never quite the magical realm fictionalised by Shakespeare, this 'uncouth forest' was always a place of secrecy and a suitable abode for outlaws. The Knights Templar once owned a lodge in the middle of the Forest of Arden at Temple Balsall, where some of Shakespeare's ancestors originated (his mother's maiden name was Arden). Some villages, relatively safe in isolation, maintained Catholic beliefs well into the Reformation period and none less than Robert Catesby, the recusant leader of the 1605 Gunpowder Plot, hailed from Lapworth, a village that in the early 17th century was still tucked away deep in the heart of the forest.

Emerging from the wood, I came across a woman walking two Alsatians. Both dogs sported spotted neckerchiefs, presumably to codify that they were of a gentle persuasion and guaranteed not to bite. She greeted me cheerily in broad Brummie: 'Lovely walking round here, innit?' I knew then that I was drawing closer to my goal for the day.

I followed a stretch of long-distance footpath called the Centenary Way through more fragments of woodland to reach Birchley Heath, where a mud-caked path continued alongside a stream for a couple of miles. Much of the land was given over to pheasant shooting and areas had been fenced off to enclose breeding birds. At one point I passed a feeding station and a shooting platform within clucking distance of each other – the apparatus of both life and death in the same field, a coexistence that struck me as macabre. Eventually, I reached the B4116, shiny gobbets of clay still adhering to my boots.

After the bucolic tangibility of much of Leicestershire, the shadows of cities loom large over north Warwickshire: Birmingham to the west, Coventry to the east. While unquestionably rural – pastoral, even – with meadows, streams and dung-heaped farmyards, it has the feel of an unlikely countryside, squeezed like toothpaste between two sprawling conurbations.

I turned south to follow the road through Furnace End, then over a river and railway bridge into Church End, where the spire of Coleshill's St Peter and St Paul church started to rise into view ahead. A road lined with smart detached houses led me uphill into Coleshill's centre, where I found the town sign draped with flowery hanging baskets, a dependable indicator of civic pride.

Close to the dotted line on the map that demarks the frontier of the West Midlands, Coleshill lies near the top of the inverted apostrophe that delineates Warwickshire as it curves around Birmingham's eastern limits. The town, which dates back to the Iron Age, was once an important Romano-British settlement. Arthur Mee, in the Warwickshire volume of his *The King's England* county series, describes the town as a 'matchless bit of Warwickshire; we may come to it a hundred times and find something new'. This was my first visit but the description struck me as fair-minded enough. Certainly, its high street looked impressive, with Georgian brownstone buildings, a solid handsome church and a couple of grand old pubs that must have once served as coaching inns. Good-looking and thoroughly provincial in character, it gives little clue to the metropolis nearby.

*

Some cities draw you in by dint of gravity or beckoning pathways – officially designated walking routes or those shaped by regular footfall. Not so Birmingham: here the momentum at the city's outer limits is largely centrifugal – a manic rotation of vehicles around the city rim, a spinning Catherine wheel of inertia that is hard to break through. Much of the infrastructure of England's second city is, as many commentators have observed, purpose-built for motor transport, and unrepentant walkers struggle for footing away from its pedestrian-friendly core around Centenary Square and the newly marketed Jewellery Quarter. Cars have long been a key component of the city's industrial success. Once Birmingham and the West Midlands had been Britain's largest car manufacturer, with popular makes like Minis, MG Rovers, Aston Martins, Jaguars and Land Rovers all produced in factories in the region. Such manufacturing had followed on from the production of rolling stock for railways around the world. The West Midlands had long provided the means for the world to keep moving – and 'world' is no exaggeration: Birmingham-made Victorian rolling stock can still be found in service in some of the quieter corners of what was once the British Empire.

Birmingham's unyielding obeisance to the internal combustion engine has long had comedic value: the Gravelly Hill Interchange, aka 'Spaghetti Junction', is infamous for its pot noodle confusion of tangled asphalt, and some reaches of the outer city give the appearance of a dystopian Ballardian landscape in which the motor car has unfettered dominion. It is the sort of petrol-head utopia that you might imagine would make a *Top Gear* presenter's eyes moisten with emotion. Even so, one of that television programme's erstwhile presenters, Jeremy Clarkson, was unmoved by the city's car-friendly credentials and, never one to knowingly miss an opportunity to cause offence, once described Birmingham as 'like a rugby player's bath after all the water has drained out: empty in the middle, with a ring of scum around the outside'. Offensive certainly, and grossly unfair; but yes, the 'ring' – the multiple lanes of speeding traffic that orbit the city – is problematic for anyone unfashionable enough to chose to approach the centre as a pedestrian.

There are chinks in the armour here and there though – safe passages on foot that reveal themselves through scrutiny of the upper right-hand side of the Birmingham 1:25,000 OS Explorer map. One such pedestrian wormhole appeared to occur beneath the M6 at Chelmsley Wood at the far eastern edge of the city close to Birmingham Airport. A close study of the map showed a footpath heading west from Coleshill towards Chelmsley Wood but the barriers were considerable: no less than three motorways and a major trunk road separated this county outpost from the city that lay beyond.

I left Coleshill high street to weave my way down through a new housing estate towards the din of traffic that emanated from beyond a protective belt of woodland. A muddy footpath led through the trees to the A446, the Stonebridge Road, which I had to cross in stages, resting like a human bollard in the central reservation before dashing across to the other side where the path continued.

The footpath merged with a farm track that led to a bridge spanning two motorways – the M42 and the M6 Toll. Traffic roared by beneath as I walked across – a dozen lanes of cars and lorries speeding north and south, their preoccupied, road-dazed occupants oblivious to the world beyond their windscreens. On the other side of the bridge were a few arable fields that had been orphaned from their farm by the building of the motorway – the bridge and farm track that connected them were merely a concession, a dispensation for bisecting the farm's original acreage.

This motorway island, like Chelmsley Wood, my destination ahead, its high-rise blocks now in sight beyond the pylon wires that framed them, was once another tract of the vast Forest of Arden before it vanished beneath farmland and real estate. Any starry-eyed notion of this transformed landscape ever being the fantastical forest setting for Shakespeare's *As You Like It* now seems risible. This vehicle-shaken, tree-ghosted territory is no place for romance, even given the subterranean presence of 2½ million remaindered Mills & Boon novels that were supposedly pulped to provide bulk for the underlay of the M6 Toll road I had just crossed – bodice-rippers recycled in such a way that their fictitious female protagonists would now genuinely be able to feel the earth move beneath them as the traffic roared by on the tarmac above.

Literary ghosts are just part of the fabric of this liminal zone. The Roman road that once led through here has, according to local legend, its own phantom presence. There have been reports of sightings of wraith-like Roman soldiers, time-slipped and separated from their legion by almost two millennia. Not long after the M6 Toll was completed, one Coleshill resident reported seeing twenty legionaries walking waist-deep through the tarmac as if it were water – military ghosts wading through the pulped fictional lives of pulp fiction heroines.

A reminder of the proximity of Birmingham Airport came when a jetliner swooped in to land ahead, the plane hugging the horizon to create a trick of perspective that gave the momentary illusion of it perching on the roof of one of the high-rise blocks that lay beyond the M6 ahead. But even here, in sight of the airport and in plain earshot of the thunder of three motorways, the land use was defiantly rural: wheat fields stretched productively all the way to the motorway barrier, the hedgerows chirruped with birds, flowers decked the drainage ditches. A few venerable oaks, remnants of the ancient forest and centuries-old witnesses to the concrete and tarmac development that unfolded around them, stood defiant as they soaked up the hydrocarbon-sullied air.

But even that which remains of this uncanny rural islet is under threat. Walking the farm track to a soundtrack of birdsong underpinned by motorway grumble, I came upon a planning notice attached to a tree. This informed me that the land had been earmarked as part of the planned HS2 rail link to connect London with Birmingham and Manchester with a super-fast train service. So, in addition to the numerous lanes of traffic on the ground, and airport flight paths above, there will also be a high-speed railway. It seems unlikely that any other place in the country could possess quite so much raging kinetic energy – enough centrifugal force to send the metropolis of Birmingham reeling off its fulcrum.

I followed the track until a pedestrian underpass came into view ahead, a passageway that led beneath the last of this triptych of motorways, the M6. Graffiti spattered the walls of the underpass – it would have felt somehow wrong if it hadn't – and at the other side an anti-motorbike gate funnelled me direct into the Chelmsley Wood estate.

The underpass served as a psycho-geographical cat flap allowing entrance to Birmingham. Except this was not yet Birmingham proper, as Chelmsley Wood, while effectively Birmingham city overspill, technically belongs to the Metropolitan Borough of Solihull. Such geographical tenure must have sat a little uneasily with the city fathers of Solihull, as the borough considers itself a bit posh and a cut above the rest of the conurbation.

The writer Lynsey Hanley, who was raised on the estate, describes Chelmsley Wood – 'The Wood', as she calls it – a 'proletarian hell' in her book *Estates: An Intimate History*. The estate certainly does not have the best of reputations – a clergyman had been car-jacked in broad daylight outside a church here just a few weeks before my arrival – but on first glance it did not appear threatening in any tangible sort of way. As Hanley notes in her book, council estates are 'nothing to be afraid of, unless you are frightened by inequality'. The high-rises – thirty-nine in total, one of the biggest development schemes in Europe when they were first erected in the late 1960s – looked to be well maintained and sympathetically planned, with grassy landscaping softening the territory between the blocks and cycle-ways tracing curved routes towards the meandering River Cole, which delimits the estate's northern boundary.

Kingshurst Brook, effectively a damp ditch enlivened by blousy pink stands of naturalised Himalayan balsam, leads away from the river to skirt the estate's perimeter. I followed it past Alcott Wood, another remnant of the ancient Forest of Arden that serves as a local nature reserve and gives the Solihull motto *Urbes in Rure* ('Town in Country') a little credence. Before the new estate was built city dwellers used to come here to picnic and pick bluebells on spring weekends, arriving by train at Marston Green station and walking across what was then still open countryside to reach the wood. All this has changed, and despite the best efforts to promote the wood as a place of leisure it was unlikely that many from Birmingham's inner city would bother making the journey out here today.

A road led me out of Chelmsley Wood and into Marston Green, where I made my way to the railway station. The train arrived and I became another anonymous occupant of a fast-moving bubble of humanity that sped southeast away from the city. Past the airport and the National Exhibition Centre, past the cow-grazed fields of Warwickshire, through the ghost territory of the ancient Forest of Arden; back to Coventry, back to Northampton.

Chapter 14

Slouching Towards Birmingham (Another Venice)

Birmingham Grand Union Canal

In Birmingham alone 500 varieties of hammer are produced.
Karl Marx, *Capital*

Brummagem screwdriver *n.* a hammer.
[origin: the supposed oafishness of the Birmingham worker who would rather hammer in a screw than use the correct tool]
Green's Dictionary of Slang

I took the train back to Birmingham next day, walking out from Marston Green station with an A–Z map of the city to help me navigate my way to the Grand Union Canal. In an industrial city like Birmingham, which, as the rest of the world is repeatedly informed, has more canals than Venice, the city's extensive canal system seemed the obvious choice for an off-road route across the conurbation.

I planned to join the canal at Olton but first I had to navigate around the boundary of Birmingham Airport before I could strike out across the city's eastern suburbs. Abutting the airport to the north was Sheldon Country Park and I followed tracks through this to make my way around the airport's perimeter fence through scrubby heath and patches of birch woodland occasioned by dog walkers.

Once I had circumnavigated the airport I found myself in a residential area. This, now, was Birmingham proper. For me, it is a city that, as well as memories, provokes imaginings, fantasies and sometimes unease – a trepidation that was perhaps valid for the canal path where I was heading.

I walked into the suburb of Sheldon, where the street names conjured a ruralism that had long since vanished from the area – Furrowers Road, Barn Lane, Sheaf Lane, Greats Oaks (now a treeless cul-de-sac). On Horseshoes Lane I came upon a modernist church: a reinforced concrete edifice built in a style that could only be Roman Catholic and late 1960s. Stylistically, the Church of St Thomas More was a scaled-down amalgam of Yugoslav brutalism and Liverpool Cathedral-style modernism. Thomas More was, of course, the same sainted statesman and one-time advisor to Henry VIII whose word-coining bestseller *Utopia* has been daubed in its entirety on a wall I had passed back in Norwich. There was also another Norfolk connection, as early in his career, before his hair shirt days as a Catholic zealot, More had represented Great Yarmouth in parliament. On the 'at risk' register, according to the *Birmingham Mail*, and 'suffering slow decay', the church, which boasts a generous allocation of stained glass, did not look to be in danger of collapse any time soon.

Crossing the Coventry Road, I carried on to reach Barn Lane where a large redbrick pub called The Lynond (*NO ALCOHOL TO BE CONSUMED IN THE CAR PARK*) stood with sun-faded Eng-er-land flags curtaining its windows. Finally, after an hour's brisk walking from setting out at Marston Green, I reached the Grand Union Canal at Otley.

The steps at the bridge took me down into a watery world so suddenly still and silent that it was unnerving. Blotch-leaved sycamore branches hung over the canal, its soupy water barely troubled by any sense of flow. Downstream, upstream – there was almost no way of knowing.

Slouching Towards Birmingham (Another Venice)

I set out along the concrete towpath, a steep wooded incline rising up to road level on my right. A signpost – *Gas Street 8km* – pointed in the direction of the centre.

With its continuous strip of waterside vegetation, the canal serves as a conduit for wildlife in what is otherwise an environmental wasteland of concrete and brick. The canal might also be considered as a narrow ribbon of edgeland: an elongated frontier that straddles the boundary between urban and rural. Edgelands are not necessarily always on the urban fringe: they sometimes penetrate the core of the city. Like threads of otherness, canals have always been a means by which the countryside can sneak its way into an urban realm.

In the early decades of the 19th century, when countless navvies laboured to create a network of waterways to connect the newly industrialised cities, canals dramatically changed the face of much of the British landscape. But their dominance was short-lived: the arrival of the railways a few decades later saw to it that much of the newly constructed canal network was soon reduced to the status of a white elephant, although the water it provided would always be valuable for industrial processes. In a city like Birmingham, where the natural supply of water (the less than impressive and non-navigable River Rea) was inadequate, the canals also came in useful in providing a place for dumping factory effluent.

While many of the nation's canals have been cleaned up to encourage leisure traffic in recent years, the well-maintained towpath of the Grand Union Canal that entered Birmingham from Oxford and the south seemed to have few users. Thanks to high-budget projects, like the curvaceous, disc-clad Selfridges building and the newly redeveloped New Street station, Birmingham does seem to be enjoying a minor renaissance but it is unlikely that inner-city areas like Sparkhill and Small Heath will ever make the Sunday papers' travel sections. Consequently,

I had the canal almost to myself as I followed the towpath west towards the city centre. True, I came across the odd cyclist, an optimistic fisherman here and there, but for the most part, I was oddly, unsettlingly, alone. The silence and emptiness of the canal path gave me a vague sense of unease. I was, after all, easy prey for any muggers that might be lurking behind the arches of a bridge – there was neither an easy escape route nor anyone else about who might come to my rescue should the worst happen. Ignorance is sometimes a blessing.

At Olton, the canal was a microcosm of rurality, its green banks bursting with leaf and life, but as I approached the city centre the vestiges of industry drew closer. High factory walls and railway sidings flanked the water at Small Heath, Victorian warehouses at Sparkhill, railway bridges and flyovers at Bordesley. I walked on past bricked-up factories with long-redundant wharves. Making the most of the crumbling trappings of industry, feral nature had seized a foothold wherever it could: buddleia and Canadian goldenrod sprayed out from piles of rubble, and traveller's joy and Russian vine clothed factory walls. Rose hips and blackberries grew plump and abundant in the tangle of shrubby growth beside the towpath.

The few fishermen I came across, spaced well apart from one another and not in the business of being sociable, did not even look up as I walked by. I said nothing either, although no doubt if I had engaged them in chummy angling chat then they would have responded favourably. Either way, there was something noble, almost romantic, about their presence here – the stoicism of their pursuit, the juxtaposition of rod and canal against a gritty backdrop of soot-stained industry. It was, perhaps, something to do with the solace of nature against the odds, the time-honoured tradition of working men making the most of what they had been given. I wondered if they ever caught anything. More importantly, were they at all bothered?

At Sparkbrook, the jade-green dome of Ukim Jamia Masjid rose high above the canal wall. Adjacent to the mosque was a tall clock tower that advertised Tetley Bitter in bold white capitals. Across on the opposite bank, a helmeted worker in orange hi-vis shouted into a mobile phone. On the canal bank a signpost pointed in the direction of London for those boatmen uncertain as to which way they were headed – it was a binary choice, first or second city.

Spanning the canal ahead was a bridge and lock close to a Victorian church. I could make out three figures sitting on the lock gate and as I drew nearer these were revealed to be an Afro-Caribbean, an Asian and a white man. All three were in late middle age and engaged in easy conversation – a reimagined *Last of the Summer Wine* set in the multi-cultural West Midlands.

The church was Bordesley's Holy Trinity, the oldest surviving Gothic revival church in Birmingham, although it no longer serves that function. Like many similar buildings in the inner city it is redundant, its size more a hindrance than help for its repurposing to a new civic role. As with any city, Birmingham has a limited need for large draughty Victorian buildings that have outlived their original purpose.

St Andrew's, Birmingham City FC's ground is nearby. I was never a supporter but always had a soft spot for their battle hymn, Harry Lauder's *Keep Right On to the End of the Road*, which was a walking song full of courage and optimism – an instant earworm whenever I thought of it despite probably not having heard the song since childhood.

The Blues' ground is one of a trio of football focal points in the city: St Andrew's here in Bordesley Green, Villa Park in Aston a little way to the north, and the Hawthorns, West Bromwich's ground in Smethwick, west of the centre. Tribal rivalries are as fierce as you might expect, with team loyalties, firm and unflinching, often handed down from one generation to the next. With a loose sense of geographical allegiance, Birmingham City is the team of choice for many households in the south of the city, although this is by no means universal.

In recent years the club has seen the expiry of a century-long curse, a malediction supposedly inflicted by irate Travellers turfed off the St Andrew's site in 1906 when the ground was built. Such a curse was a convenient excuse for erratic performances and for never having won a trophy over all those years. It was also suspected to be the cause behind the disaster that occurred when the ground's main stand went up in flames during World War II, which resulted in the indignity of the team having to share Aston Villa's ground for many years afterwards. In later years various measures were taken in an attempt to nullify the spell. In the 1980s crucifixes were placed in each corner of the ground, and then, a decade later, manager Barry Fry even went as far as urinating on each corner of the ground – counsel that supposedly came from a Romany source who knew about such matters. But both piety and pissing proved to be ineffective and it looked like the curse was going to run its full term before there would be a change of fortune. True to form, 2006, the curse centenary year, did see a temporary return to the English Premiership, although in truth the club only enjoyed sporadically good form in the years that followed. Ten years later, in 2016, John Baines, a wealthy supporter who was not wholly satisfied that the curse had been lifted, financed new seating for the club and, for good measure, had a priest sprinkle holy water on the blue leatherette upholstery. This seemed to have the desired effect, temporarily at least, with Birmingham winning three of their next four games.

It is interesting to reflect how the notion of a curse, an act of supernatural witchery, lingers on in the popular imagination despite the modern age's propensity to believe in the observable laws of causation. There remains a willingness to believe in an 'other', in a world beyond reason. Scrape away the surface and it is a world that lies beneath the entire English landscape: a couple of centuries of scientific progress underlain by a rich medieval seam of superstition, intrigue and fear that coexisted with an unforgiving monotheistic religiosity so firm in its beliefs that it would punish terribly those it considered to be heretical. A blue plaque next to the Irish Centre in Deritend, barely a mile from here, commemorates the locally born Bible translator John Rogers, who was burned at the stake at Smithfield, London in 1555, the first victim of the Marian persecution waged during the reign of Queen Mary. This, only a few centuries ago, fewer than a score of generations: just a thin layer of cultural sediment beneath the pavements that we now walk upon.

If Birmingham City Football Club had suffered from malicious magic, there had been a broader curse at work in surrounding industrial areas like Sparkbrook, Small Heath and Bordesley Green: wretched poverty and occupational entrapment. The story was universal. In the newly industrialised world of the 19th century, progress came with poverty and pollution, and the wealth created by Victorian industry did not filter down freely to the workers at the base of the manufacturing pyramid, those who did the hardest work in the worst conditions for the least reward. However, for early migrants to the city factories the rewards were, at least, better than those of the countryside where the entrapment cycle was even harder to break free from. It was a familiar story; it was even my own family's story. Time-yellowed birth certificates in my mother's possession tell of great-great grandparents from both sides of the family who had worked in service in the Worcestershire countryside up until the early to mid-19th century: coachmen and maids in rural villages, thereafter, their descendants would have a Birmingham address and a job of some sort in industry.

*

Beyond the lock, the canal curved right beneath a railway bridge. Small Heath is historic *Peaky Blinders* territory. The popular TV series has put the city on the map in a surprisingly positive way considering the manner in which it dishes out violence, sex and occasionally implausible plots to the viewer. Having a handsome Irish actor play the lead character certainly does no harm, nor does its breathless pace and atmospheric film sets – 1920s industrial Birmingham channelling gangster-land Chicago or Mafia-run New York. It is a welcome change from dramas that, as a rule, only ever present a sooty Manchester or dockland Liverpool as a provincial alternate to that of a romanticised London East End underworld.

Perhaps Birmingham is at last beginning to be seen as more than just a provincial wasteland by those not native to its soil. Lauded and mocked in equal measure for some of its shiny new architecture – the hula hoop-decorated ziggurat of the new Library, the melted Dalek of Selfridges in the Bullring – the city with 'more canals than Venice' has gradually earned a little cultural respectability, not that most Brummies care that much for what outsiders think. Growing up in a nearby satellite town, Birmingham for me was always the bright lights, the red glow on the horizon. For a small-town provincial boy, the city had significant gravitational pull: a place to go shopping, hear music, buy records and hang around the Bullring with friends on a Saturday afternoon. A good number of the students at my school came from its outer reaches, bussed in each day from the city's southern suburbs. Birmingham was always a place of otherness, the big city, the only one I had any experience of. It wasn't until I moved away from the Midlands that I started to get an inkling of how others perceived the city and the good-natured mockery that sometimes went along with this. It took a while to adjust.

Birmingham has long been vilified for its lack of glamour, its singular accent, its bolshie car-manufacturing and metal-bashing workforce. Even the quality of its manufactured goods has suffered frequent pejorative abuse: a 'Brummagem screwdriver', meaning a hammer, was once a favourite term to portray the quality of Birmingham workmanship in which the city's craftsmen would carelessly bodge anything they turned out. Until relatively recently, to describe something as 'Brummagem' was to condemn it as cheap, shoddy or poorly made. Such a malign stereotype is wholly incorrect, of course. It is a dig at the perceived laziness and lack of sophistication of the people of England's second city, a flagrant denial that Birmingham was the world's first great manufacturing centre and later would go on to invent such innovative marvels as powdered egg-free custard (Bird's), heavy metal music and the *balti*. There is even a book, *101 Things Birmingham Gave the World*, which, tongue firmly in cheek, pays tribute to the inventiveness of the 'City of a Thousand Trades' and its craftsmen, although some of the claims (gynaecology, The Beatles) veer towards the tenuous. Even the epithet 'more canals than Venice' has long been seen as something of a joke, as if it were mere wishful thinking on the part of Birmingham's citizens. But the claim is correct, even today, although admittedly the city can provide far fewer Renaissance mansions and glittering plazas than its Venetian counterpart.

The canal network was just one aspect of the city to be lauded in a 1981 Harold Baim promotional film narrated by the then highly popular Telly 'Kojak' Savalas. The film, a 'Quota Quickie' short made to satisfy the requirement that British cinemas broadcast a set percentage of home-produced films, was entitled *Telly Savalas Looks at Birmingham*. The American actor did just that – look at projected images of the city as he faithfully read the script in a Soho recording booth, although the conceit that he had first-hand knowledge of the city by using the first person throughout was patently and unashamedly a falsehood. The film begins almost beatifically as Savalas describes 'spectacular cherry blossom time in Birming-ham's Bournville', referencing the pleasant, chocolate-making borough south of the centre that hitherto had never been acknowledged for its resemblance to Kyoto. As the film cuts from baby pink blossom to a high-rise view over the brutalist concrete architecture of the city centre, Savalas waxes even more lyrical: 'This is the view that nearly took my breath away.' Drawing in more breath, the narrative continues, extolling the virtues of the city's flyovers, underpasses and multi-carriage motorways as the camera compresses telephoto shots of Austin Allegros and other future rust buckets of the British Leyland late '70s range. The cars are shown speeding through the city on wide roads that seem half empty by modern standards ('You feel as if you've been projected into the 21st century'). You had to admire the film's audacity – this was early '80s Thatcher-era Birmingham at the nadir of its industrial decline – but even when the action cuts to a discomforting disco-dancing competition for the over-forties in the park, Savalas maintains a straight face and unflinching non-ironic voice-over. The film concludes with a heart-felt declaration from Savalas that 'Birming-ham is my kind of town'. But, although they are not mentioned in the voiceover, so were Portsmouth and Aberdeen, as Telly 'off-the-telly' had also managed to find time to voice warm paeans to both these cities during the same flurry of London recording sessions.

The city did have its genuine admirers. George Borrow, who in the 1860s passed through the city's main railway station on his way west in *Wild Wales*, enthused about the city's thrusting modernity, declaring, 'That station alone is enough to make one proud of being a modern Englishman.' The writer and television filmmaker Jonathan Meades is another aficionado. In one of his entertaining television documentaries, he sums up the city as 'a place that is at once hyperbolically typical of England and hermetic, an ignored void at the heart of the country'. A man able to generate lengthy lists of that which he does *not* like – Blair, God, most modern architecture and city planning – Meades speaks of his genuine affection for the city, and of how it lies just south of what he calls the 'Irony Curtain', north of which people tend to say bluntly what they meant while south of it they shelter behind ironic humour. The Midlands, with its self-deprecating inhabitants is, in his view, equivalent to the North but without the chippy attitude. This rings true, especially the ironic humour aspect, although it complicates things conceptually to add another axis for consideration in any North/South divide debate.

*

I followed a kink in the canal beneath a dual carriageway and continued past new office and residential blocks and a warehouse converted for use as a nightclub. The city centre's familiar high-rise buildings remained surprisingly elusive. A canalised section of Birmingham's unassuming and largely hidden waterway, the River Rea, joined from the right. The Rea is easy to overlook: a half-forgotten and largely hidden river, its presence and influence has long been trumped by the city's much more imposing canal network. As Roy Fisher, one of Birmingham's most celebrated poets, asserts in his poem *Birmingham River*, the river is unequivocally underwhelming – 'Where's Birmingham's river? Sunk. Which river was it? Two. More or less.' The other 'more or less' river is the Tame, which flows through the Black Country before conjoining with the Rea in the shadow of Spaghetti Junction north of the centre. There is also a third river, the Cole, which I had already witnessed flowing unspectacularly through Coleshill and Chemsley Wood, but this hardly counted as it does little more than dampen Birmingham's far eastern suburbs.

A sign-posted canal branch led off from the main channel to Typhoo Basin in Digbeth, where the wharf area around a defunct 1930s tea factory is stoically awaiting regeneration. Production of the eponymous beverage began in 1903 when a

Birmingham grocer started to sell his own blend under a brand name rather than loose over the counter, advertising the brew as a cure for indigestion with the slogan *The tea that doctors recommend*. Digbeth (its name derived from 'dyke path', or possibly 'duck's bath') is also where the Bird's Custard Factory stands, the large Victorian building where the famous egg-free powdered custard was once manufactured, although it has since been turned over to studios, art galleries and a music venue. Digbeth is now up-and-coming in a rundown post-industrial sort of way – a 'creative hub' of artists' workshops, warehouse bars and clubs in a neighbourhood of abandoned Victorian factories and broken windows. Until its recent rebranding the main draw here was its long-distance coach station. Surprisingly perhaps, it was Digbeth that was the historic core of the city: the medieval hamlet ('Beorma's Ham') that eventually became Birmingham grew up here around a ford across the River Rea. Now there is little evidence of the pre-industrial city apart from a solitary wooden-framed inn, The Old Crown, Birmingham's oldest secular building.

At Aston Junction the main canal changed direction to curve south. A branch led off north towards Spaghetti Junction, and the idea of walking a towpath beneath the country's most impressive motorway intersection was not without appeal, but I had neither the time nor the energy so just carried on towards the centre.

Some of the city landmarks finally started to edge into view: the Rotunda, BT Tower, the twin spires of St Chad's Roman Catholic Cathedral. Somewhere near Nechells Green the canal looped sharply south to make its final approach into Gas Street Basin. Both towpath and canal were busier now. I had entered an area of inner city restoration and redevelopment. More barges, more runners and walkers, more canal-side bars: healthy alt-urban living; somewhere that might almost be described as urban revival picturesque.

I arrived at a sort of canal roundabout at Old Turn Junction. Overlooked by walkways and a factory that has been reborn as a waterside pub with outdoor terrace, a three-way sign in the centre of the roundabout points the way to Fazeley (fifteen miles, thirty-eight locks), Wolverhampton (thirteen miles, three locks) and Worcester (30½ miles, thirty-four locks) – the Birmingham canal network's very own Spaghetti Junction. I crossed a foot-bridge to the National Sea Life Centre – a confounding choice of location for such an enterprise in deeply landlocked Birmingham – and followed the path up to the multi-parked moorings at Gas Street Basin. In this reinvented canal zone, where smart new apartments looked out onto the water, the towpath was flanked with pubs and wine bars busy with cheerful customers enjoying respite from city-centre bustle. Chalked menu boards listed daily specials and wine offers: feta, focaccia and hummus were available in ample supply; craft ale and wi-fi on tap – here was bona fide gentrification. Here in this thriving inner city enclave you could lose sight of the fact that modern Birmingham is, by and large, a city where the pedestrian is peasant and the motorcar is king. A case of unconscious onomatopoeia, it is not called Brum for nothing.

Chapter 15

City of Metal

Birmingham to Black Country

They came from Birmingham, which is not a place to promise much, you know...

Jane Austen, *Emma*

Wander across England for long enough and sooner or later you are bound to come across a Gormley. Mine came in the heart of Birmingham, next to the Town Hall and a statue of Queen Victoria that depicts the elderly monarch clutching an orb as if it were an unwanted Christmas pudding. It was here that I found Antony Gormley's *Iron:Man* sloping half-cocked out of the concrete paving of Victoria Square: a twenty-foot high rusting metal figure partly risen from, partly still submerged in the earth. The allusion is obvious enough: Birmingham's manufacturing heritage of steel and heavy industry personified by a proletarian cast in base metal. There is also a Black Sabbath connection to reckon with. The originators of the heavy metal sound, who hailed from Aston just north of the centre, had once written a song of the same name, give or take a colon, although their futuristic metal man was more revengeful sci-fi figure than symbolic foundry worker.

Melding industrial noise with rock, with a collective persona that has been affectionately described as 'brickies on acid', a band like Black Sabbath could only have come from somewhere like Birmingham, where artistic pretentiousness is viewed as a serious criminal offence, although imagination and innovation are not.

Despite their moniker, any suggestion of diabolic tendencies was firmly tongue in cheek and more a nod to the contemporary zeitgeist than anything else (the band's name was actually taken from a Boris Karloff horror movie). Their singer Ozzy Osbourne may have promoted himself as the 'Prince of Darkness' but with a mischievous, if perpetually drug-addled, countenance and unreconstructed Brummie accent it seemed improbable that he might ever embody pure evil despite the self-proclaimed title.

Gormley's *Iron:Man* has been here since 1993 but my memories of the square and the late Georgian, Corinthian-styled Town Hall are of an earlier period, long before the square was tastefully landscaped and rendered pedestrian-friendly. This was a place I used to come to regularly as a teenager to see rock bands perform on the Town Hall stage. Ironically, I never did see Black Sabbath play here – my tastes back then were self-consciously indifferent towards heavy metal – although I recall that the band used to sometimes appear at a pub close to the Bull Ring before their fame spread beyond the city of their birth.

Just off the square, the Birmingham Museum & Art Gallery houses another powerful lump of metal with vaguely sinister overtones. This one is non-ferrous, cast from bronze rather than iron. Jacob Epstein's *The Archangel Lucifer* sculpture stands on display in the museum's round room gallery as if centrepiece to a pedestrian traffic island. In Epstein's *St Michael's Victory over the Devil*, which glowers over the entrance to Coventry Cathedral just twenty miles down the road, the Devil is depicted as a defeated Satan, the personification of evil crushed by the power of good; here, Lucifer is represented as the angel before the fall, the pure embodiment of the sin of pride, or if you prefer, the 'bearer of light', the messenger of the unknowable God in the Gnostic tradition.

A tall, winged figure, fully masculine and yet curiously androgynous, I find the work both beautiful and unsettling, more knowing and corruptible than the naive wooden carvings I have so often seen in the rafters of churches in Norfolk and Suffolk. It makes me think of Walter Benjamin's interpretation of the *Angel of History* – the bewildered figure personified in the Paul Klee monoprint *Angelus Novus*, who, propelled into the future by the storm wind of progress, gazes back on the past, unable to intervene in the catastrophe of history. This, in turn, makes me reflect on another backward-facing figure: the Britannia Monument in Great Yarmouth, where I had first set out on my walk. No angel, but a romanticised (and Romanised) personification of British character; Britannia, her back to the North Sea, is also perhaps gazing back at the past; staring inland to the Norfolk interior, not with horror but with doomed nostalgia; to feudalism, the God-given might of Empire, the halcyon days of a country where everyone knew their place.

The Epstein sculpture seems an appropriate symbol for Birmingham's repeated attempts to reinvent itself. It is a process that involves habitually destroying the evidence of the past, before undertaking a comprehensive rebuild (with each reinvention promoted by means of pithy slogans like 'B in Birmingham', 'Birmingham: Europe's Youngest City' or 'Birmingham, The Global City With The Local Heart'). The city's coat of arms motto simply urges: 'Forward'. But *Lucifer* came into the gallery by the back door, almost as an afterthought. Sculpted in 1944–5 for a major exhibition, the work remained unsold and so Epstein felt obliged to give it away to a good home. Both the V&A and the Tate Gallery rejected the piece, and it was only when the Mayor of Birmingham stepped in that Epstein's fallen angel finally found a permanent resting place. 'Shame to waste all that metal,' the mayor is reported to have said, a response that speaks volumes about Brummie pragmatism.

I came across a similar sort of hard-nosed response in the museum café, where a young couple were talking to the man behind the counter. The conversation turned to football and the barista asked the male customer jokingly, 'You're not a Man U supporter, are you?'

'Nah, mate,' he replied, 'I support Walsall.'

The response was incredulous. 'Walsall? Really? Why?'

'Yeah, I know they're crap,' the customer rejoined. 'But I only go there because they've got the best pies. And it's cheap and there's never any trouble. The games are dead boring, mind, so I just watch the traffic go past on the motorway.'

I left the gallery to return to the square. An Eastern European busker was playing a trumpet, its melancholic ringing notes resonating around the tall stone buildings like a slinking mural.

In a city that might be accused of cultural amnesia, of turning its back on its manufacturing past, Victoria Square redresses the balance to some extent. The city centre beyond the square has been so comprehensively redeveloped that it is hard to find much evidence of what had made Birmingham so important in the first place. The more iconic skyscrapers – the Rotunda and Post Office Tower – give little clue, although a pub, The Mulberry Bush, which once stood in the basement of the former, and one of the ill-fated targets of the Birmingham bombings in November 1974 that killed twenty-one innocent pub-goers, had been the locus for a nightmare jolt in the city's more recent folk memory. Even the aluminium disc-clad Selfridges building in the Bullring (a shopping zone, thought to have once been the site of a Bronze Age henge, which breezily takes its name from the deplorable practice of bull-baiting that used to take place here) resembles more a gleaming blob of mercury than the molten-steel of the cast furnace. Devoid of futuristic architecture, but with a clearer focus on the city's imperial past, at least Victoria Square has monuments to represent the two complementary forces that combined to forge England's second city: Empire (Queen Victoria) and heavy industry (*Iron:Man*).

But perhaps there are other forces at work in this grand but otherwise unremarkable square? With a heavy metal humanoid, a neoclassical temple (the Town Hall) and an androgynous Lucifer nearby, it is possible to believe that Victoria Square represents a focus for occult forces in the city: a concentration of earth energies; at the very least, an intersection of ley lines. London has its London Stone and occult alignment of Hawksmoor churches; Birmingham has this square, ostensibly dedicated to the trappings of Empire but with another, less obvious parallel life. Still considered to be the dead centre of the city, the 19th-century Christ Church once stood here, as did catacombs that contained six hundred interned bodies. As for sacred alignments, the Belinus Line, the so-called 'Spine of Albion' that delineates a North–South axis through England and Scotland to connect numerous ancient sacred sites, is said to bisect the square before going on to pass through St Paul's Church to the north.

Such mystical attributes are well and good but it takes a determined imagination to superimpose these invisible threads of occult power on a Victorian square that oozes quotidian Brumminess. Perhaps only the heft of a powerfully wielded Brummagem screwdriver could shatter its concrete paving to expose the secrets that lie beneath the surface?

*

A mile or so west of Victoria Square stands the inner city borough of Ladywood. It has long been a mythic landscape for me, even before I became aware of any sort of Tolkien connection with the area. It was here that my mother grew up in a terraced house on Rann Street with her parents and aunt. The street has vanished from the map, bulldozed to clear the way for high-rise development in the 1960s – housing that grew unfit for purpose well before its allotted time, much of which later was demolished to make way for housing better suited to the needs of city dwellers. A common-enough sequence: Victorian slums, deterioration and bomb damage, wide-scale clearance, human-scale social housing – episodes that began with buildings invested with new hope only to end up as the architecture of contempt. The city, always a palimpsest, sometimes requires deep archaeology to show its traces. Rann Street has become a place that only exists now on old maps and photographs and in the memory of former residents like my mother.

I have a vague recollection of visiting my Aunt Anne at the Rann Street house when I was a child. I recall a house redolent of cats, a dozen at least, although my mother insists there was only ever a maximum of four. Did memory always have a tendency for hyperbole? Aunt Anne (actually, my great aunt) was eventually re-housed in a modern council flat in King's Heath at the city's southern periphery, while her brother, my grandfather, Frank, went to live with his second wife Mabel in another terrace house nearby at Leslie Road close to Edgbaston Reservoir. This I regularly visited with my parents and sister on Sunday afternoons, a reluctant teenager dragged away from Pink Floyd records and surly introspection in a green belt bedroom.

Ladywood underwent considerable decline in the post-war period and I remember vividly the miasma of urban blight that hung over the area in the late '60s and early '70s: soot-stained brickwork, rubbish blowing through the streets, wan-faced children sitting on doorsteps waiting for parents to return from the pub. Many of the terrace houses had been recently occupied by newly arrived Commonwealth migrants, Pakistanis mostly. These new arrivals, culturally at odds with the long-established white working class community, provided grist to the mill for the anti-immigrant tirades of Enoch 'Rivers of Blood' Powell, who at the time was Conservative MP for Wolverhampton South West, on the fringe of the Black Country just up the road.

Inside the Leslie Road terrace, the front room, as in all decent working class households, was only ever used for special occasions such as family funeral gatherings and the like. The small back room, which faced onto a yard and a galley kitchen, was stuffed with bulky furniture: a three-piece suite bolstered with cushions and antimacassars, a sideboard, stiff-backed chairs and a scuffed leather pouffe that was never used.

Grandad, as I remember him, was a short rotund man with thinning hair Brylcreemed into a barcode across his pate. Like all of his generation, there was no such thing as casual dress. The trousers he wore were not so much high-waisted as halfway up to his armpits and seemed as if they came with some sort of integral cummerbund, defying gravity by means of braces, belt and beer habit. Mabel, his second wife and my step-grandmother, was only ever referred to by her first name. A 'big-boned' woman, Mabel, who resembled a spinster straight out of a 1940s photo-nostalgia book, seemed to be all angles. With sharp corners rather than curves, she was a Picasso *demoiselle* in National Health specs and pinny. Mabel did not tend to say much, but then neither did my grandfather. The only thing that really seemed to animate him was the 'The Club', the social club run by his former employer Lucas, where he went most nights to drink gassy pints of Mitchells & Butlers beer. Another of his interests was to write regular letters of complaint to the *Birmingham Post* regarding the failure of 'the Corporation' (Birmingham City Council) to safely maintain its pavements.

Our relationship as grandchildren was cordial, a little distant perhaps – a throwback to the stern attitudes of the Victorian era whose final days cusped my grandparents' birth. My grandfather would dutifully give my sister and me two half-crown coins each birthday and Christmas and always referred to us as 'the nippers', which, as I recall, started to irritate me by the time I became a know-it-all teenager.

Grandad Frank meant well but it tended to be Aunt Anne, his sister, who provided most of the fun and warmth, telling stories and improvising songs for the pair of us, spinning colourful, if somewhat unlikely, yarns about her own girlhood – a direct link to the gaiety of Edwardian music hall and the carefree years that led up to the Great War. To our young minds it seemed as if Aunt Anne was both ancient and ageless, as if she had always been here, as if they had built Birmingham around her and the button-pressing machine she operated during her long working life in a city factory.

Grandad's employment at Lucas, the Birmingham electrical component company, had conjured a small imagining in my mind: a coincidence of time and place that allowed a fantasy encounter that almost certainly never took place. The end of my grandfather's career at the plant must have coincided with the youthful employment of one of Birmingham's most famous sons, the aforementioned John 'Ozzy' Osbourne. Pre-Sabbath, Osbourne is recorded as having worked at Lucas for a while testing car horns, a job that must have helped prepare his ears for future battering by thunderous heavy metal sound systems. Most probably he would have worked in a different factory – there were several around the city – and more than likely he would have been on a different shop floor, but I liked to imagine the embryonic prince of darkness creeping up behind my soon-to-retire grandfather and blasting him mischievously with a car horn. How would he have reacted? What would he have said? 'Oy, yer little perisher.' Or something more profane, the sort of industrial language that, as children, we would never hear uttered from Grandad's lips. Alas, Grandad's and Ozzy's respective Venn diagrams probably never overlapped in any way other than a brief temporal connection, but this fancy remained my only grip on any potential *Who Do You Think You Are?-style* connection with rock royalty.

Leslie Road has survived and I made my way there from Victoria Square via Broad Street and the recently gentrified trappings of Gas Street Basin, striking west away from the Birmingham Canal Old Line. A sign on the traffic-choked Ladywood Middleway announced the boundary of Ladywood borough and close to this, astride the central reservation of the dual carriageway, was a curious statue of a tightrope walker. The statue, I later discovered, commemorated a French daredevil called Charles Blondin who had visited the borough in 1873 to cross Edgbaston reservoir by tightrope in, an impressive feat only eclipsed by his seventeen previous traverses of Niagara Falls by the same means.

I soon found my way to Reservoir Road where the Victorian waterworks stands, its elegant, almost Italianate, brick tower a contender for the inspiration for J.R.R. Tolkien's *Twin Towers of Gondor* (the other Middle Earth tower is widely thought to be Perrott's Folly on nearby Waterworks Road). While other sources point towards other possibilities – the Faringdon Folly in Berkshire is another strong candidate as the inspiration for Saruman's Tower – Tolkien and Birmingham are inextricably linked. Although born in South Africa, Tolkien grew up in Sarehole village in north Worcestershire, just four miles from the city centre. It was here that the nearby River Cole supposedly made sufficient impression to later provide the setting for the episode in *The Fellowship of the Ring* in which the Riders are swept away by a torrent of raging water at the Ford of Rivendell. Later, aged ten, Tolkien moved with his family to Edgbaston, from where the two Ladywood towers would have been visible every time he left the house.

Such information came to me later in life. Reading *The Lord of the Rings* as a teenager, I was completely unaware of any sort of Birmingham-Middle Earth connection. The city was too close to home for such otherworldly fantasy. All I knew of the author then was that he was an Oxford academic, a habitué of ivory towers, a classical scholar with a lively imagination and dextrous pen. People like that were simply not found in unglamorous places like Ladywood.

Reservoir Road, as its name suggests, leads down towards the water, and just before I reached the reservoir I found Leslie Road on the left. The street looked much as I remembered it, albeit cleaner and less soot-stained, and the old house seemed to be in decent fettle, freshly painted, with a 'To Let' sign on the wall. I allowed myself a brief reverie of teenage memory before heading back to Reservoir Road and down to the water itself. Standing just beyond the reservoir gate is the low-rise edifice of the Tower Ballroom, a venerable institution that had hosted dances for rhythm-happy Brummies intermittently since the 1920s. Closed in 2005 in preparation for bulldozing, the Tower received a last minute reprieve and, revamped by a local businessman, reopened for business in 2008. Less than a year later it was taken over once more to be repurposed as a glitzy Asian wedding venue with a concession for afternoon tea dances and nostalgic 1940s 'Back in Time' events.

I followed the raised east bank of the reservoir. The view across the shimmering water to the left seemed almost pastoral: a solitary fisherman, a church steeple rising above the trees in the distance on the western bank. To the right, peeking, indeed glowing, through the trees was a sight my grandparents would never have imagined witnessing here in Ladywood: an oriental temple, the gilded stupa of Birmingham's Buddhist Vihara. Although he never got to see it in his lifetime, such a sight would not have been quite so alien for my father who no doubt came across similar pagodas during his war service with the RAF in Burma. This glimpse of celestial glimmer soon gave way to something more prosaic: a semi-wasteland of half-demolished factories and industrial yards occupying the area around a varicose kink of the Birmingham Canal Old Line. Beyond, in the distance, towered the grey stacks of high-rises and the beacon of the BT Tower – an avatar of 1960s architectural futurism that no longer reaches for the sky quite as confidently as it once did.

Leaving the reservoir behind, I emerged at Icknield Port Road, where parents were picking up their kids from primary. Passing the gates of Summerfield Park, I arrived at the major thoroughfare of Dudley Road. My father had been born somewhere along here, above a shop that sold takeaway cooked tripe; his early, pre-war life spent separated from my mother by nothing more than a few streets, a reservoir and a four-year age difference (they finally met after the war at a dance on the other side of Birmingham). He never spoke about the tripe shop – he was probably too young to remember it anyway – so I had no idea of its character or whether it resembled the grim place mentioned at the beginning of Orwell's *The Road to Wigan Pier* with its 'great white folds of tripe... and the ghostly translucent feet of pigs, ready boiled'. The shop presumably went long ago, a victim of changing culinary fashion and increasing prosperity, and Dudley Road, once Birmingham's Golden Mile with the densest concentration of ale houses in the city, was transformed to become a parade of curry houses and Asian greengrocers, boiled offal giving way to more international tastes like *biryani* and *brinjal bhaji*.

I crossed Dudley Road to reach Winson Green Road, where I descended steps at a road bridge to join the towpath that ran alongside the canal below. Immediately calm, tucked away from the relentless rumble of traffic on the streets above, with a sudden absence of people, it prompted a sensation of abruptly slipping over an edge to enter a clandestine, greener world.

The name Winson Green comes with a certain amount of baggage, a generous helping of prison-stitched mailbags, for it is the location of the city's main penal institution, HM Prison Birmingham, which is a Victorian Category B establishment more commonly known as simply 'Winson Green' or 'The

Green'. A menacing place even by high-security prison standards, the prison has seen a motley parade of characters pass through its cells over the years, with most of its inmates presenting a far greater threat to the nation than Ozzy Osbourne, who in his youth had been incarcerated here for six weeks as punishment for a bungled burglary. The Birmingham Six were badly beaten in custody here in 1974 before being falsely convicted and handed life sentences for the Birmingham pub bombings of November 21st that year. Other prisoners did not stay as long as they were supposed to: Great Train Robbery gang member Charlie Wilson served just four months of a thirty-year sentence here before escaping in 1964. Some never left at all: a total of thirty-five hangings took place in the prison during the 20th century before capital punishment was outlawed in 1965. In an unwitting adherence to tradition, the serial killer Fred West also hanged himself in his cell here on New Year's Day in 1995.

In more recent years, Winson Green has achieved national notoriety as the location of James Turner Street, a deprived area of inner city housing that was featured in the 2014 Channel Four social documentary series *Benefits Street*. The series did not show the area or its people in a particularly favourable light and unfairly promoted the stereotypical view that many working class inner city dwellers were benefit scroungers or criminals. A certain section of society – made up of those that are always fast to respond on matters of perceived benefit fraud, especially when carried out by ethnic minorities – was aghast, and apoplectic letters were written and even death threats sent on Twitter to the programme's hapless celebrities. The series was also criticised for purveying poverty porn – some of its viewers relishing the Schadenfreude engendered by observing folk both poorer and more criminally inclined (or knowledgable) than themselves. Many of the characters featured in the series later claimed that they had been misled by the programme's producers, and both residents and city councillors were relieved when the programme upped sticks to Stockton-on-Tees for its second series. The damage was already done, though: as a result of just five broadcast episodes, the street had earned itself a tarnished reputation that would be difficult to shake. When I learned from my mother that my paternal great-great grandparents had once run an off-licence on James Turner Street, I could not help but feel a mild glow of ancestral pride.

*

The canal path led me northwest out of central Birmingham into the Black Country, but where the frontier between the two stood never became absolutely clear.

At Smethwick Towing Path Bridge, the canal split into two channels for a short way before converging again. Soon after, I passed beneath the Engine Arm Aqueduct, a handsome piece of ironwork built by Telford in 1825 to carry water from Edgbaston Reservoir above the New Main Line. Walking through Galton Tunnel, I realised that a barge heading the same way as me had started to slowly slip back from view – a steady footing of three and a half miles an hour had been sufficient to outpace it. The towpath led beneath another fine Telford bridge, and then under a railway bridge where I heard disjointed voices that sounded spectral and strange until I realised they were train announcements carrying on the wind from the Tannoy sysytem at Smethwick station above: '... the next train at platform... trains to Kidderminster...'.

Reaching a sign that read *BIRMINGHAM 4½ MILES/ WOLVERHAMPTON 10 MILES*, I began to hear the stifled roar of traffic from the M5 ahead. I passed beneath it soon after; the motorway, elevated on massive concrete pylons high above the canal. For drivers hurtling towards Worcestershire and the West Country, the water that lay beneath was, at most, a momentary distraction. It seemed anomalous, this peculiar juxtaposition of transport systems; one high-speed, modern and brash, the other a slow-moving white elephant that had long outlived its usefulness – a throwback, a ghost of transport past.

But the canal now has another role to play, one that its engineers had not bargained for. A green corridor that funnels wildlife into this crowded, industrialised conurbation, it serves nature in a way that would never have been imagined. Feral life had chiselled opportunist toe-holds in this half-abandoned world. Buddleia sprouted from the cracked concrete and crumbling red-brick walls of redundant factories, its ragged purple blossom luring butterflies with drug-like nectar. Sprouting from a factory wall, a small, snow-white birch tree grew straight out of the brickwork, rooted in the fissures of English Bond, nurtured by little more than mortar, rainwater and air. The canal water brought its own bounty: latter-day cleanliness had encouraged fish to return and these attracted birds to its banks. These avian fishers were less timid than most of their kind: passing a heron poised for a stab at the water, I received no more than a sideways glance as I sloped by. Further on, I saw a kestrel being mobbed by no less than four magpies. Irritated more than intimidated, the falcon reluctantly put on a display of its superior aerobatic skills to leave its assailants hanging ineptly in mid air.

Spon Lane Locks Bridge led me past an industrial estate, and the smells on the air led me to conclude that I must be in the Black Country proper. And I was: Oldbury.

Oldbury is a town of uncertain geography. It originally belonged to the county of Worcestershire but became an exclave of Shropshire after the Norman Conquest, when the land was given by William I to Roger Montgomery, the Earl of Shrewsbury. The town was eventually reincorporated into Worcestershire in the mid-19th century, only to become part of the new metropolitan county of West Midlands in 1974.

Here was the Black Country and now I was walking on sunshine: the sunshine that lay captured in carbon in the earth below. The sunshine trapped by swampy tropical forests of trees and ferns that, over tens of millions of years of compression, had transformed to a solid energy-rich fuel source; the black rock that set the Industrial Revolution in motion around two hundred years ago – a period of time that on the geological scale of things was little more than a blink of an eye.

Thanks to the thirty-foot-thick seam of coal beneath the ground, Oldbury was at the forefront of the Industrial Revolution. Four blast furnaces operated in its vicinity between the 1780s and 1860s but, as the fortunes of coal mining and steel-making declined in the region in the late 19th century, brick-making took over, exploiting the deposits of Etruria marl that were also found in abundance beneath the coal seam. The town's underlying geology was generous to a fault: the clay was perfect for manufacturing Staffordshire blue brick, a hard-wearing, non-porous brick ideal for use in foundations, bridges, steps and tunnels – the essential hardware of Black Country business. Tar distilling, chemical manufacturing and boiler-making industries also took root in the district later on. The inevitable result was a besmirched landscape – a 'black country' – an environment littered with spoil heaps, abandoned quarries, cavernous marl pits and unbridled chemical pollution. In its heyday, the Black Country had been highly productive – a soot-blasted territory of glowing foundries and clanging metal – but now that energy has drained away.

At Dudley Point, I left the main canal behind to follow the Netherton Tunnel Branch that leads south. This soon vanished from sight as it plunged underground at the start of the branch's North Portal. The OS map showed its course continuing as a dotted line that passed beneath the western reaches of Dudley before reappearing at Warren's Hill Country Park south of the town. The last canal tunnel to be built in Britain, and almost two miles in length, Netherton Tunnel had been created to avoid the bottle-neck of the adjacent Dudley Tunnel that went underground on the opposite side of the hill. Unlike Dudley Tunnel, this one possessed a towpath and so did not require boat crews to lie on a plank across the bows and use their feet against the tunnel wall to propel the boat all the way through – an exhausting and highly dangerous pursuit.

Hanging around the tunnel entrance were two teenage boys on their bikes. One of them looked a little anxious and when I said hello his friend told me why.

'He doesn't want to go through there but I keep telling him it's all right.'

We agreed that it was a long way to go through a dark tunnel but I tried to reassure him – 'Oh I'm sure you'll be fine if you go in there with your mate' – although, in all honesty, I did not relish the idea that much myself.

Although there is undeniably something that draws me to opportunities to explore the world beneath my feet, there is also an ill-defined trepidation. What is this fear? Is it an unacknowledged dread of chthonic forces, a fear of the dark, or just straightforward claustrophobia? And the contrary impulse, the urge to delve beneath the ground, is it an atavistic imprint – an echo of distant ancestors who, finding some sort of sanctuary in caves, mouth-sprayed ochre handprints as apotropaic ciphers to mark their trespass in the underworld?

I left the boys deliberating at the tunnel entrance while I tried to find a way up from the towpath to the road, scrambling up a steep slope through dense undergrowth and following a faintly defined desire path that was no doubt created by local youths heading for the canal.

Emerging in a residential area, I headed uphill towards the Dudley suburb of Burnt Tree. And in Burnt Tree, an entreaty for burnt skin: a tanning studio sign by the roadside that boasted of

SCORCHING NEW TUBES FOR THE BEST TAN IN TOWN in an effort to tempt Black Country sun worshippers denied their UV on overcast days like this.

I arrived at a large, five-way roundabout and a dual carriageway, which I followed further uphill towards Dudley Castle, which I could see, noble but not entirely fairytale, flying its flag on top of the hill ahead. The next roundabout held several large, Black Country-themed sculptures: a steel crucible, bronze cannon, heraldic lion and medieval plough. It looked as if Dudley was doing its best to make the most of its industrial heritage. I wanted to take a closer look but was stuck on the wrong side of the dual carriageway with no safe means of crossing. Eventually, I spotted a footbridge ahead that conveniently led me straight to Dudley's bus station at the foot of Castle Hill, an outcrop of the Wenlock Group limestone that had played a significant part in the town's industrial development.

Weary from walking, I spent the long bus journey back into Birmingham in an almost dream-like state, my head propped against the juddering window as the low industrial sprawl of the Black Country slowly morphed into the concrete and glass of commercial, high-rise Brum. At New Street station I caught a local train to Redditch, the Worcestershire town where I had arranged to stay with my friends Tom and Sara. It was a place that ought to be familiar – I spent of most of my childhood here.

Chapter 16

Black over Bill's Mother's

West Midlands, Black Country/North Worcestershire

> *My modern English pride accompanied me all the way to Tipton; for all along the route there were wonderful evidences of English skill and enterprises; in chimneys high as cathedral spires, vomiting forth smoke, furnaces emitting flame and lava, and in the sound of gigantic hammers, wielded by steam, the Englishman's slave.*
>
> George Borrow, *Wild Wales*

Redditch is old territory yet it was strangely unfamiliar, like the appearance of a friend in a dream who behaves out of character. The town had been the stomping ground of my youth, the place where I lived from the age of five until I was nineteen. A medium-sized market town that has been elevated to new-town status to take on more than its fair share of Birmingham's overspill, Redditch's population has almost tripled in size since I left it behind to move east. Such a transformation has imbued the town with something of a schizophrenic character, an uneasy amalgamation of town-country dichotomies. But a degree of schizophrenia was always present even before the cement mixers rolled in to super-size the place. My old school, the town grammar, had been a 50/50 mix of local children and those who were bussed in daily from the southern reaches of Birmingham – green belt kids, village kids, posh detached double-garage kids and kids from the town post-war council estates. The town's relationship with Birmingham was sometimes fractious and thin-skinned – a small town sense of inferiority prickled by big city bumptiousness. Redditch was sufficiently distant from the city to stand firmly on its own, but it was a provincialism that peered over the hedgerows, with one eye on the Worcestershire countryside and the other on the concrete metropolis just to the north.

The plan for the new town was nothing if not ambitious: a convoluted traffic system threads around the town centre as if it is some sort of mini Los Angeles. The roundabouts involved are many and varied, sending traffic spinning off in all directions in pursuit of a far-lying estate or the highway west to Bromsgrove. It is a territory where you could drive for miles, following signs and navigating endless roundabouts, only to arrive back at the same starting point with little idea of where you have just been. A satnav, impervious to the vertigo created by the meandering ring road, may have been of use, but my geographical instincts, instilled in me in simpler times, were no longer viable. Nor was my outdated mental map of the town, which had never been updated to include the thoroughfares and housing estates of the new town.

The town centre, at least, was still recognisable, as was the area around my old secondary school close to where my friends lived. Getting there required a steep climb from the railway station to the green at the town centre before heading downhill once more. The route was drenched in timeworn teenage memory. Named Unicorn Hill, its mythical beast name-check gives the town a welcome touch of intrigue. Halfway up the hill is the building that used to house Redditch's sole cinema, an art deco theatre of dreams known as The Danilo. It was where I used to enjoy Saturday morning children's matinees. Limbo dancing competitions were held on the stage in the break between cliff-hangers, and there would be an obligatory standing for the national anthem played at the end of proceedings – a memory ineradicably linked to the smell of crisps and Kia-Ora orange squash that came in crinkly plastic cartons. I came here as a teenager too, once sneaking in bottles of stolen beer I had bought from an older boy to drink them unobserved and underage in the cinematic dark. Appropriately perhaps, the building has now been given fresh purpose as a branch of Wetherspoons. Further up the hill, the Fisherman's Catch, another former teenage haunt, is also still in place, although now it is a sit-down fish and ship shop rather than the greasy spoon café it used to be. Across the road, The Unicorn, the pub that once stood here, has vanished without trace, as have most of its memories, although I vaguely recall being half-heartedly threatened outside its door by a drunken knife-waving skinhead one long-distant New Year's Eve.

Church Green at the top of the hill was the cultural epicentre of old, market town Redditch: a small park with a bandstand and benches next to St Stephen's, the parish church where we were route-marched as high school students once a year at the end of summer term. Clustered around the green were newsagents, estate agents, solicitors' offices and the public library where I would regularly scour the shelves for travel books on exotic destinations. The books were invariably of 1960s vintage or earlier, an age when much of the world map was still coloured with the pink of Empire. The books, which smelled of mould and the tobacco smoke-filled homes of previous borrowers, had grainy black and white photographs that depicted stiffly posed natives and stern-faced, topee-wearing explorer amidst tropical vegetation. It did not take me long to realise that here was a world that anyone could explore with a few pounds in their pockets and a willingness to rough it a little. It took me far longer to come to the realisation that to write about this wider world it was not necessarily imperative to be public school-educated or have the right accent, even if hitherto this had pretty much been the tradition. It took an unfashionable Irishwoman, Dervla Murphy, to show me these things. Her first book, *Full Tilt*, would inspire my eventual overland trip to India in the late 1970s and instigate an unquenchable wanderlust that still affects me today. But my initiation into becoming a man of letters started, in the more literal sense, in one of the buildings nearby. Next to the library was the side street that held the post sorting depot. It was here that I had worked for a few months after dropping out of a polytechnic, starting work each day at 4am to sort the mail before footslogging round one of the town's housing estates on my delivery round.

Tom and Sara live down a road that leads off from the opposite side of the green, the same road that held the senior entrance to the secondary school we used to attend. I walked down it past a Masonic lodge and a late Victorian building that now serves as a mosque. Across the road stood a Baptist church of about the same period and, alongside it, the outside terrace of a small drinking club. Such an odd juxtaposition guaranteed that at certain times, Fridays in particular, boozers and believers would be locked in a cultural stand-off across the tarmac.

Continuing downhill past the school, the rolling green meadows of north Worcestershire came into view beyond the housing. The sight of the school did not provoke any marked reaction in me other than mild indifference. My schooldays were neither particularly happy nor miserable but more a typical teenage blur of hormones and emotional insecurity. I remember them best in a visceral sense: the winter cold of draughty classrooms and corridors; the lingering narcotic pall of floor polish and teenage pheromones in the main hall; the lunchtime reek of distressed cabbage and thin gravy. Or, in my case, the smell of orange squash and discarded fish paste sandwiches that wafted from the waste bin in the packed lunch room: odours and tastes that were redolent of a time when fishy goodness came in little glass jars – white bread and pink-brown paste, an unexpected madeleine.

For some reason the words of our old school hymn suddenly sprang to mind. How I managed to recall such detail is a mystery; perhaps my memory of this is somehow embedded in the local geography. It was a song that we only ever sang – reluctantly and unenthusiastically as only bored teenagers can – on the annual occasions when we trooped up the hill in our blazers to St Stephens. Most of us would never study Latin but we were routinely told, ignoramuses that we were, that the chorus, the school motto, translated as 'Nothing but the Best'.

Our school is set in a fair scene,
may our lives, too, be fair.
Like Arrow straight, like needle keen,
may we reject the false and mean,
Nil Nisi Optime. Nil Nisi Optime.

This was a hymn of place – 'Arrow straight' refers to the narrow, not straight but gently meandering River Arrow, a tributary of the Avon, which runs through the northern reaches of the town; 'needle keen' is a reference to needle-making, the town's traditional industrial base alongside the manufacture of fishing hooks. (Redditch is reported to have once produced 90% of the world's needles during its manufacturing heyday.) Written well before Redditch acquired flagship new-town status in 1964, the hymn could be forgiven its bold pastoral romanticism and its failure to mention the extensive dual carriageways that would later frame the town and incorporate England's only cloverleaf interchange, nor was it required to include detail of the echoing retail acreage of the vast Kingfisher Shopping Centre that took over the town centre, or the sprawling housing estates that would eventually stretch north of the town in the direction of Birmingham's white-heat industry.

Redditch, my childhood place of residence, was a version of home. I moved there with my parents aged five and left it behind as a young adult. I could have sought out the two different addresses where I used to live with my parents and sister, the first close to the town centre, the second in the green belt on the leafy fringe of the Elgarian Eden that was the north Worcestershire countryside. I could have walked door to door and be done with it – a John Clare-like return from asylum to home, or perhaps from home to a different sort of asylum. A journey in which I found the poetic not 'in the fields', as Clare claimed, but along the footpaths, beside the canal paths, beneath the motorway underpasses. But being neither a bona fide poet, nor mad in either the literal or poetic sense, the metaphor did not quite ring true. Better then to keep heading west and continue to the coast, make a tidy job of it.

*

I took a train back into Birmingham early the next morning. Getting off at Five Ways station, I sought out the stop for the number 26 bus to Dudley. Waiting for the bus to leave I overheard a young Black man speaking to a Japanese couple who had just nearly been mown down while crossing the road. Patiently and courteously, he explained that they really needed to be careful and always look out for traffic from the left. It was a thoughtful gesture and, not for the first time, I was struck by the pride that Brummies took in being ambassadors for their city. It was hard to imagine the same good-humoured tolerance in a more tourist-weary metropolis.

The bus took an hour to reach Dudley, a journey slowed to jogging pace by the bus stopping every few hundred yards as it meandered through Smethwick and Oldbury. Eventually, the glowering silhouette of Dudley Castle came into sight ahead.

It was raining lightly by the time I arrived. The dusty tang of petrichor was rising from the pavements, the sky darkening with the warning of worse weather to come. Thinking it best to delay for a while, I set off in search of coffee. At Cozy Coffee, where most of the tables were already taken up by shopping-trip pensioners and young mums with kids, the cheery woman serving behind the counter managed to call me 'Bab', 'Darling' and 'Angel' within the space of our brief transaction, which was endearing even if she did exactly the same for all of the customers. Enjoying the warmth, human and otherwise, of this cosy sanctuary I took my time over my cappuccino. Outside, the weather did not improve. In the end, I decided that I could delay no longer so headed back out into the rain.

My aim was to rejoin the canal where it emerged from the Netherton Tunnel Branch outside the town. As I headed south, the rain started to fall more heavily so I took shelter for a few minutes in a bus shelter. The destination board in the shelter showed that the next bus to arrive would be going to Stourbridge, where I was headed. The temptation to hop on a warm dry bus was momentarily immense, but I manage to resist and headed back out into the rain before the bus showed up. Reaching the river, I followed a cycle track down to where the canal emerged next to a series of locks. At the waterside, a gaggle of well-nourished Canada geese were roaming the grass in search of for crusts.

I followed the canal path beside the locks beneath Park Head Viaduct. At the Park Head Junction pumphouse, a life-size cut-out figure in Victorian dress informed me that I was beside Dudley No 2 Canal. A sign pointed the way to Delph Locks and the landscape softened for a while – trees and a hedgerow, the spire of a church ahead, a couple of pleasure barges cruising the water.

The towpath shifted over to the left bank, and two men with three dogs passed by, greeting me, yam-yam vowels bouncing like acrobats:

'Oroit, pal. Worrya done to the weather, then? It ay lookin' good.'

True to their word, the clouds were starting to darken once again, threatening more rain. It really did look 'black over Bill's mother's', as they say in these parts.

At Brierley Hill I came across a new waterfront development complex that was named, somewhat unimaginatively, The Waterfront. It still did not seem quite finished and many of the individuals milling round the car park sported hard hats and high-visibility jackets: surveyors, property developers and the like – the storm troopers of real estate. Merry Hill, a little further along the canal, had a large hotel advertising *FAIRYTALE WEDDINGS,* a promotion reinforced by a giant love heart inscribed *WILL YOU MARRY ME?* On the opposite bank was Brewer's Wharf, a Victorian pub complex that looked as if it had been there since the time that navvies had come over from Ireland to dig the canals. Its tall chimney bore the legend *BANKS'S* in bold white lettering. Banks's, the Wolverhampton ale that quenched many a nail-maker's thirst in these parts – it seemed a shame that the secretive Banksy could not be employed to make some sort of joint venture with his own art here: a Banksy Banks's.

The vast Merry Hill shopping centre is probably the Black Country's biggest draw for anyone with a car and a credit card. It has been in business long enough – since the 1980s – for the shopping complex to be as much a fixture on the mental map of those who live in the area as somewhere with deeper historic entitlement, such as Dudley Castle. More like a diurnal new town than a shopping complex, Merry Hill is defiantly self-absorbed – a world unto itself that has little to do with the canal that passes it by or the industrial heritage of the area. Its retail workers know nothing of lung-clogging coal dust or searing hot metal. Their world is one of special offers, stock-taking and refund protocol.

Further along the canal, Nine-Locks Bridge marks the beginning of Delph Locks, a flight of locks – originally nine but eight now – that cascades downhill to the lower country around

Stourbridge, whose sprawl of rooftops could now be seen below. At the bottom was a pub appropriately called The Tenth Lock.

This was prime territory for murder ballads. The dark watery world of the locks was a fine setting for tales of drowning and lovers' trysts gone badly wrong: a Victorian world of smoke and reeking factories, of hard lives; a polluted monochrome world, of choking industrial fogs that played tricks with the vision and mind. The poet Liz Berry, who fervently champions the Black Country and its native dialect – 'vowels ferrous as nails, consonants you could lick the coal from' – has written of these same locks in her poem *The Black Delph Bride,* in which she evokes an unsettling atmosphere of dark imaginings.

Immersed in the slow, easygoing world of canal boat hobbyists, Black Delph Bridge at the bottom of the flight seemed far removed from anything threatening or macabre. Its ghosts appeared to be vanquished, in daylight at least. I sat for a while to watch as the barges made their way down through the locks. It was a slow business: it took me about five minutes to descend by way of the concreted path; for a barge it meant two hours' hard work.

At the base of the locks, I finally left the canal path behind to follow a cycle path through the suburbs of Stourbridge. Walking past neat housing estates separated by expanses of green parkland, the natural domain of an untold number of dog walkers, I passed through the outskirts of the town without so much as a scent of the centre. I soon found myself heading gently uphill again, following minor roads towards the low ridge that rose in the west ahead. Leaving Stourbridge and the metropolitan county of West Midlands behind, I entered the southern finger of the county of Staffordshire.

My final approach to Kinver followed footpaths across meadows, which was easy enough until I reached a sign that pointed across a field of close-planted, waist-high brassicas. Still damp from the earlier rain, my legs became soaked up to thigh height as I ploughed my way across the field, cursing the farmer who had not deigned to leave a pathway through his crop.

I arrived at Whittington, close to Kinver, grumpy and unkempt. Asking directions at a cottage I enquired whether the occupant knew the whereabouts of the bus stop to Stourbridge. His reply was whimsical, which did not suit my mood.

'Well, why not just stop in Kinver instead?' Adding, with the dismissive air of someone who usually went everywhere by car, 'I think that there may be a bus stop or two somewhere on the high street.'

I sloped off ungraciously, irritated by my conspicuously wet legs and concerned that I might miss my bus. I crossed the River Stour by a small bridge and walked uphill into the village. The stop, thronged with teenagers on their way home from school, was easy to find. When the bus arrived, I was offered a seat by a schoolgirl, which I gratefully accepted, although it made me feel old and perhaps a little pitiable. It was a kind act considering that by this stage, sweaty and with wet legs flecked with bits of field crop, I must have looked like the sort of man her parents had warned her about.

At Stourbridge bus station I waited half an hour for a bus to Kidderminster, where I had another wait before the next bus left for Redditch. There was just enough time for a coffee. Sitting at the tables outside Caffè Nero was an elderly man smoking a Sherlock Holmes pipe. The man also wore a deer stalker; disappointingly, he did not sport a cape.

Although I was born in Stourbridge, and my paternal grandparents lived in a bungalow in a village near Halesowen just beyond its south-western fringe, the Black Country did not figure in my early life anywhere near as much as Birmingham and its Worcestershire hinterland. Like Ireland, the region tended to be on the receiving end of jokes, especially if you came from

Birmingham. My father used to come out with Aynuk and Ayli (Enoch and Eli) gags from time to time. The pair were fictional Black Country characters, and the jokes only really worked when spoken in the correct vernacular; in fact, the dialect was usually the crux of the joke:

Aynuk and Ayli are fishing in the canal...
Aynuk: 'Me mate's fell in the cut!'
Ayli: 'Owd it 'appen?'
Aynuk: 'I just took a bite ov me sanwich an' the mate fell out.'

I decided to spend another day in the area before moving on, so I took a train from Birmingham Snow Hill to Tipton to visit the Black Country Living Museum, which is a microcosm of the Black Country of yore. With all the appropriate cultural trimmings, the sprawling site holds an array of nail workshops, engineering works and forges, along with more rolling stock than you could throw a Brummagem screwdriver at. A couple of Victorian streets stand in situ, more or less intact: narrow, soot-blackened brick terraces; a working chip shop (Hobbs & Sons Restaurant); a gentleman's outfitters with *Peaky Blinders*-style clothes and original Edwardian prices; a window display of period motorbikes (with prices ranging from £38 to £55) at A. Hartshill Motorcycles; and a working pub, the Bottle and Glass Inn. A sign on one of the gables reads: *ROLFE STREET BATHS. First Built in Smethwick 1888.* A half-vanished ghost sign promotes Gold Flake tobacco. On the wall of one of the houses is a metal plaque with the legend: *These Cottages were built with a donation from LLOYDS BANK whose inception was in the BLACK COUNTRY.*

The stained brick terraces and cobbled streets reminded me of weekend visits to my grandfather in Ladywood when I was young – the self-contained air of the working class inner city when the West Midlands was still heavily involved in manufacturing. Only the strewn newspapers – which in my memory seemed to blow constantly, almost apocalyptically, around the cobbles like the tumbleweed of a television Western – were absent.

I took a look round the hut that served as the Black Country Rock & Fossil Shop before wandering into a small building where I was greeted by a young woman dressed in Victorian clothes sat next to a coal fire. We exchanged a few words before I made my way to the coal mine building to join one of their tours. Helmeted and jacketed, safety procedures carefully outlined, we were led down into the pit by a tour leader who had once worked in one of the Black Country coal mines. Our guide did his best to convey the existential horror of the awful working conditions as well as the solidarity that miners felt with those engaged in the same filthy, dangerous pursuit of the deep-buried material that fuelled Midlands industry. Almost any industry, in fact: miners, despised and treated little better than animals by the mansion-ensconced mill owners on the surface, were, to coin Orwell's phrase, the 'grimy caryatids' that supported everything which mechanised manufacturing and modern domestic life depended upon – steam power, electricity, heat, light.

Our guide neatly summarised the dangers and inescapable entrapment of the mining life:

'The miners used to go down the shaft in a bucket like this, twelve at a time. As there wasn't room for more than seven or eight in the bucket itself, some of them had to cling on to the chain as it went down. The journey took about fifteen minutes, so quite a few fell off and died. The bosses didn't care that much – in Victorian times, life was cheap. There'd always be others to take their jobs as they'd get sixpence a day for their labour. You see, in the countryside, where most of the workers originally came from, they would only earn four pence a day, so they saw it as worth the risk.'

After the tour I left the museum to head towards Wren's Nest, a leafy suburb that, while appearing altogether different in character, had a strong connection with Tipton. Black Country industrial history was inextricably linked to riches that are hidden beneath the surface, its coal and iron ore. The strata that bears the area's mineral wealth are twisted and bent – a rollercoaster of layered rock that rise to the surface in places to expose thick seams of coal. The local geology can be seen to best effect at Wren's Nest, a northern suburb of Dudley that is now a designated national nature reserve famous for its fossils.

Geology reflects time at its most inscrutable: deep time; four billion-year-old carbon and very recent Anthropocene scarring, the final flicker of an eyelid in the long, dark night of the earth's dreaming. Four hundred million years ago, the Dudley area had been at the bottom of a tropical sea. Warm, multihued coral reefs thrived where Lidl now stood. The respectable hilltop suburb of Wren's Nest was home to a geological site that could claim over seven hundred fossil types to its name, many of which were unique and found nowhere else on Earth.

I had hoped to be able to find something myself but by the time I arrived at the site daylight was starting to fade. So, after only the briefest of looks I was obliged to turn around and make my way back though dimming suburban streets to the station at Tipton. I waited alone on the platform for the train back into Birmingham, a chilly evening breeze and the distant metallic scrape of an industrial grinder banishing any thought of the warm tropical seas that had once lapped gently over the land I stood on, a territory that would be shifted and uplifted over hundreds of millions of years to eventually become what is now called the Black Country.

Chapter 17

All Round the Wrekin

North Worcestershire/South Staffordshire/East Shropshire

(all) round the Wrekin
Midlands English dialect
the long way round
Collins English Dictionary

I woke next morning to one of those noteworthy Indian summer days in which the air seemed almost supernaturally clear. Crystal-bright and sunny, there was just a hint of a coolness to it that augured the soon-to-come autumn. I left Tom and Sara's home early to catch the first bus to Kidderminster from Redditch's concrete bunker bus station.

As is often the case when I revisit rural Worcestershire, I was reminded of the pastoral splendour that graced Birmingham's hinterland. It is easy to overlook, given the motorways and dual carriageways that carve up this unsung countryside, but northeast Worcestershire has been always a place that stands apart from the city. An ancient green landscape rudely dissected by the M5 and M40, it is a land of rolling pasture and timber-boxed farmhouses, of legend-rich woodland filled with gnarled oaks and steep clay gulleys; a protean landscape replete with haunted houses and imagined witches; a fallen Eden soured by its association with the big city. A territory with an embarrassment of ghost stories, its hamlets and villages are a roll-call for eldritch midland England: Clent, Romsley, Hagley – all places that I have some sort of early-life association with through grandparents, aunts and cousins.

The bus went via Bromsgrove, the market town where I lived for the first few years of my life and where I later returned to attend college to study for A-Levels. The cottage that my parents rented on the outskirts of town was tiny, with just a single downstairs room, an outhouse and no bathroom; gas lighting, no electricity nor hot water. An elderly country couple, the Troths, lived next door and one of my earliest memories is of hearing the frenzied squeals of a pig being killed at the bottom of the garden. I also have a vague recollection of fronds of jungle-like vegetation, which, in retrospect, must have been asparagus. I still possess a mental map of the lane, the row of cottages and the school at the bottom of the hill, although I have no idea how accurate it is as it was sketched and committed to memory when I was only five at the most. At the bottom of the lane was a primary school where, according to my mother, I had once slipped her attention to wander down to on my own – a tiny infant towered over in the playground by inquisitive older children. Seemingly, my interest in education began at a young age, although my enthusiasm for school dissipated considerably by the time I reached my teens.

The poet Geoffrey Hill was born in the town, the son of a local policeman. Later in his Oxford poetry professor life he would reference his childhood in *Mercian Hymns*, a series of prose poems that contrasted childhood memory with a history of Offa, the 8th-century Anglo-Saxon ruler of Mercia. Bromsgrove was also the town where the poet Alfred Edward (A.E.) Housman had grown up, a writer who, contrary to reputation, was not a Shropshire lad at all but, like Elgar – another go-to voice for what might be considered quintessentially English – a Worcestershire one. Housman's much-celebrated 'blue remembered hills', already co-opted by Dennis Potter for scene-setting in the Forest of Dean down in Gloucestershire, were part of his *A Shropshire Lad* cycle but could have just as easily applied to those in this county – the Clent Hills, the Lickeys or the Malvern range. Housman was born in 1859 just outside Bromsgrove in a hamlet with the delightful name of Fockbury (only a few miles south of the equally snigger-worthy hamlet of Bell End), and it was here that he lived before going up to Oxford in 1878. Later, he would teach Latin at Trinity College, Cambridge, where, towards the end of his career, one of his students was the future Conservative Member of Parliament for Wolverhampton South West: 'Rivers of Blood' speechmaker Enoch Powell.

*

Kidderminster is a town of ups and downs, a former carpet-weaving hub that has its central commercial zone and bus station down at canal level while its railway station sits high on a ridge above the town. Tall redbrick carpet factories line the Staffordshire & Worcestershire Canal that twist through the town centre, their long-defunct chimneys sprouting buddleia at improbable heights. Some of the factory buildings have been successfully adapted for life in the post-carpet era: one has become a branch of Debenhams and another, a Premier Inn.

Although detached from the West Midlands conurbation by a respectable span of open countryside, the town – 'Kiddy', as we used to know it – still felt as if it belonged, at least in part, to the Black Country; as if it were an industrial exclave connected arterially to the manufacturing heartland by means of the canal and the A456.

A statue of Sir Rowland Hill overlooks the small square outside the town hall. Sir Rowland, an avuncular figure born in the town, was the instigator of the Penny Post service in 1840 and so Kidderminster could quite reasonably claim to be the place where philately was born. This has some resonance for me, as I licked many a stamp hinge in my younger days and the hobby had to some extent promoted an interest in the geography of the wider world. The Penny Black, the first postage stamp ever to be printed, is of course iconic and I was pleased to see that, as a result of some worthy school project, Sir Rowland's stone likeness sported a patchwork robe of Penny Blacks slung around his shoulders.

I caught the nine o'clock bus to Kinver, the sole passenger on board. We followed a convoluted route along narrow country lanes to reach the village, only a couple of other passengers getting on or off during the entire journey.

Closer than the Welsh coast, closer than the Welsh Marches, closer even than Stourport-on-Severn, the poor man's Stratford-upon-Avon, Kinver is the nearest available beauty spot to the western part of the West Midlands conurbation. At one time, a tramway – the Kinver Light Railway, from Stourbridge – terminated here, making the village accessible to even the poorest of Black Country folk. This service was withdrawn several decades ago but the village's appeal lives on in hearts and minds and so Kinver has remained the automatic choice of easy escape for many in the region.

Long before tourism the village prospered as a centre for cloth making, making use of the River Stour for its water supply. Later on, it became an outpost of Black Country industry, with slitting mills producing iron rods for nail-making, but by the time these closed at the beginning of the 20th century the village had already become a centre for day trippers wishing to flee the noise and pollution of Birmingham and the Black Country.

I went for breakfast at a coffee house down one of the passageways that lead off the high street. The first customer of the day, I ordered tea and a bacon and egg sandwich from the proprietor, a Birmingham exile who was teaching her newly hired assistant how to make a cappuccino. The radio was piping out Louis Armstrong's *What a Wonderful World* and the proprietor sang along as she fried the bacon while her assistant struggled with the unruly hissing apparatus of the coffee machine.

Kinver is probably best known for its troglodyte dwellings: a short terrace of underground houses intriguingly burrowed into the soft sandstone of Kinver Edge beyond the village. The houses were occupied as private properties as late as the 1960s but are now in the possession of the National Trust. After finishing my breakfast I walked up to see them on the escarpment that rose above the woodland just west of the village.

With an Iron Age hill fort standing atop it, Kinver Edge has been occupied since before Roman times. The earliest record of domestic rock houses existing here on Holy Austin Rock dates from the late 18th century. By all accounts the rock houses were dry and clean places to live. Sandstone has its advantages: it is relatively easy to work and if any more space was ever needed for a dwelling then a bit of judicious chipping would soon create another room. Eleven families once lived here, according to the 1861 census, and it was by no means any sort of slum. In fact, by World War II all of the houses had electricity and running water. There was no way of installing a sewerage system, however, and it was this deficiency that necessitated their ultimate closure in the late 1950s and early 1960s. Now, under the auspices of the National Trust, the dwellings still looked spick and span and gave the impression of being diligently maintained by house-proud pixies.

From Kinver, I followed twisting country roads to Alveley, crossing the county boundary into Shropshire somewhere along the way. St Mary's, Alveley's chocolate sandstone church, sits in a churchyard filled with lichen-painted, ivy-strewn gravestones of considerable antiquity. The village was quarantined during the Black Death and lost 60% of its population, although it is unlikely that many of the plague victims ever ended up with a proper burial. The village became a centre for coal mining in the early part of the 20th century, sharing a mine with the more elevated village of Highley, west across the River Severn, and where I was heading.

A track from the village led me into the Severn Valley Country Park, a green expanse of reclaimed mine shafts and spoil tips. The transformation has been impressive and there is little clue to the land's former use now that the site has been reclaimed by meadows and woodland.

Obscured from view until the last moment by conifer woodland, the appearance of the River Severn was sudden. A modern footbridge spanned the fast-flowing water. Viewed from the bridge, the Severn was unexpectedly wide and powerful. It was also unquestionably picturesque; the river's banks masked by the sagging branches of the trees that flanked it on both sides, its course twisting furtively out of sight in both directions. So close to the heavily populated West Midlands, the river's apparent isolation seemed a little odd. But so was the noticeable absence of other visitors to the park: I was crossing Britain's longest river entirely on my own. It was a river that I would be meeting again, further upstream in Wales.

Across on the western bank I followed a path through woodland to Country Park Halt, an unmanned stop on the Severn Valley Railway line that runs parallel to the river. From here, a track led uphill to Highley at the top of the ridge. The stop for the bus back to Kidderminster was in the upper part of the village. I had some time to kill and found the Malt Shovel pub, which was empty apart from a couple of farm workers, who shouted out the back to summon the barman. I sipped a half pint at an outside table before visiting the gents to change into cleaner clothes from my backpack. It was a long, convoluted journey back to Norwich and I wanted to be sufficiently fragrant so as to not offend any fellow passengers.

*

In Birmingham I had to change stations, from Snow Hill to New Street. Birmingham New Street has recently undergone a multi-million pound overhaul and reopened to great fanfare. With futuristic cladding on its exterior, an immense central concourse and a plethora of posh shops on its mezzanine walkway, the new building resembles more a gleaming international airport than a train station. The station has been reborn to be the sort of multifunctional non-place where passengers assemble in colour-coded waiting areas; a zone cordoned off from the Birmingham hoi polloi where you can shop for books and nibble sushi whilst waiting for your train. Or even slurp a bowl of fiery Vietnamese *pho*, as I did. George Borrow, visiting the original New Street station back in the 1850s en route to Wales from Norfolk, had been upbeat about what he found, impressed to the point that it stirred his national pride: 'At Birmingham station I became a modern Englishman, enthusiastically proud of modern England's science and energy.' Borrow, were he still alive, might well have also approved of Birmingham New Street 2.0. The unapologetic gentrification that has come with the station's 21st-century reinvention evidently does not please everyone – I had heard one disgruntled Brummie exclaim loudly to no one in particular as he shambled across the concourse, 'It's like bleeding Tokyo here now,' adding, as response to anyone who might doubt his knowledge of such things, 'And I've not been there neither.'

Chapter 18

Quiet under the Sun

Shropshire

In valleys of springs of rivers
By Ony and Teme and Clun
The country for easy livers
The quietest under the sun…
A.E. Housman, *A Shropshire Lad*

Ten days passed before I returned to Highley by way of much the same route. It was now early October. A mild sunny day with light mist over the fields, oak leaves were on the turn but still clinging defiantly, burnished and beautiful, to their branches. From my elevated viewpoint at the top of the village my destination for the day's walk was clear – the keel-shaped swell of Brown Clee Hill that lay shrouded in haze in the distance beyond the gently folded valleys of south Shropshire.

I left the village heading west, dropping down into the valley below. I soon arrived at Bourne Brook, where a few ruined cottages stood with only a fragment of their lower walls remaining. These were New England Cottages – a bold appellation – which, according to the information board, were built to accommodate workers for the mines at Highley and nearby Billingsley. Another board, its glass partly obscured by dirt and algal growth, gave potted histories of the people who had once lived here; semi-illegible words embellished by Victorian-era photographs of tough, moustachioed, pipe-clenching men and prim, stern-faced women with Princess Anne hairdos. A woodland track led to more ruins – a small industrial building with a chimney. I would not have known what it was had it not been for a note pinned to a board by a band of volunteers calling themselves The Weighbridge Protection Group. The group were petitioning for funds to partially restore the building and were seeking to raise £1,500. It seemed a modest sum, all things considered.

I passed through Stottesdon, a small village that has a small Baptist church set in a plot with a couple of gravestones. Then a winding country road, gleaming silver in the late afternoon light, and footpaths across sheep pasture took me on a meandering route to Aston Botterall, a village of lovingly tended gardens filled with hollyhocks and Sweet William. The village was just one of several Astons in this part of the county, a name derived from Old English for 'eastern settlement'. The Boterall element of the name came from a former landowner, Thomas Boterall, who in the 13th century was influential enough to have control over Clun Castle, a place that lay further along my planned route, two or three days west from here.

It was only a short way to Burwarton, the village where I had booked a room for the night. The map showed a footpath that appeared to go in the right direction but I could not find it and so opted instead for a bridleway that led across fields of young cattle. These animals were feistier than the others I had encountered that day and it seemed as if they could sense my nervousness – my close encounter with the aggressive cattle in Leicestershire was still a raw memory. This time I was not so much frightened, as exasperated. Almost nudging my back, the animals followed me resolutely across the field as far as the fence on the other side. Once across, I climbed the gate to escape their attention and, seeing that the way forward was overgrown with nettles and bramble, improvised a route along the edge of fields instead. Eventually I arrived at a lane that lead up to the main road where my B&B was located.

My room for the night was in a converted Victorian school house across the way from the village pub. It was Friday evening and 'steak night'. This had drawn plenty of customers, and the bar was busy with locals who had come to exchange banter and bonhomie with their mates. I sat at a table on my own with my food and beer, the uninvited stranger in their midst. After another pint, I decided to call it a day and left the bar to head back to my lodging for the night. Stepping outside came as a shock. The blackness of the night beyond the door was absolute: no street lights, no silhouetted hills or trees; nothing to see other than the yellow-lit windows of the pub behind me. It had been some time since I had slept anywhere as rurally remote as this and I had forgotten how all-consuming the night could be away from the street lights of towns and cities.

A heavy mist next morning obliterated any possibility of a view of Brown Clee Hill. The visibility was so poor that it was difficult to even make out the pub just across the road. Like the Wrekin, another well-known Shropshire hill that lies north of here, periodic invisibility has always been a characteristic of Brown Clee Hill. An aerial hazard – more warplanes were said to have accidentally crashed here than anywhere else in Britain, and both German and British airmen's lives were lost as a succession of planes –Wellington bombers, Avro Ansons, a Junkers 88 and a Hawker Typhoon – flew into its fatal, mist-shrouded slopes during the course of World War II.

I zigzagged uphill through the murk along the narrow tarmac road that passed through the grounds of Burwarton Park. Unfussed by the temporary sensory deprivation brought by the mist, horses grazed silently in the pasture alongside. Periodically, the silence was shattered with the panicked cry and explosion of flurrying wings of a pheasant lurking in the undergrowth. The white mist that sat like a blanket over everything had drenched the parkland grass and bejewelled the multitude of spiders' webs that hung like lace from the wooden fence at the roadside. The tarmac ended at a path that climbed more steeply up through beech woods. The view uphill, where tall trees melded in a monochromatic blur in the distance, was eerie; part numinous, part ominous, like the cover of a Gothic murder novel. I followed the path up to a gap in the trees at the saddle of Brown Clee's two main peaks. At something like 450 metres above sea level, this was the highest I been so far on my cross-country route.

The mist started to lift a little as I followed a bridleway down the north side of the hill, at first beside thick stands of gorse and then through bracken alongside a stream. Motorcycle tyre ruts were impressed into the half-dried mud but there was no sign of them today and I was thankful to have the hill to myself. Rooks milled and circled in the air, half-seen through the slowly clearing mist, their occasional harsh cries punctuating the stillness. A party of long-tailed tits flittered about in the tangle of an isolated copse of hawthorn, hazel and wild plum. A pair of ravens cawed low in the distance and I could just about discern the engine hum of an unseen plane. Otherwise the silence was uncanny – the *unheimlich* acoustics of a foggy day.

The track descended between coppiced banks and scattered farm buildings to eventually join a road. Soon after, I came to a crossroads where a converted Victorian chapel stood alongside a post and telephone box. An indignant sign attached to a telegraph pole read, somewhat alarmingly: *Neighbours beware! We have a thief about. Fire logs have been stolen.* As I stopped to take a photograph, a silent heron appeared out of the haze to fly close, before vanishing from view in an instant.

A wooden notice board informed me that this was not just any crossroads but *The* Crossroads, Clee St Margaret. The board gave the lowdown on the social gatherings the area had to offer: *Coffee & Cake at Abdon Village Hall, Harvest Supper at Clee St Margaret Village Hall, Abdon Flower Club – Demonstration at Abdon Village Hall, Burwarton + District Gardening Club programme.* There were also parish council meeting notes, a mug-shot of the incumbent Tory MP for the Ludlow constituency and a selection of business cards that advertised music lessons, garden landscaping, joinery and even a ceilidh band for hire. And a plea: *Cash paid for rough shooting land – Land required for 3 responsible, insured shooters (Father and two sons) who are interested in having enjoyable days in pursuit of Game and Vermin (Rabbits, Pigeons etc).*

I followed a lane that ran beneath the earthwork of Nordy Bank, which rose on the scarp to the south, the remaining bank of one of the three Iron Age hill forts that once stood on the slopes of Brown Clee Hill. Coming towards me was a group of teenagers with massive rucksacks wrapped in orange waterproof covers – unmistakeable Duke of Edinburgh Award initiates. Spotting my own rucksack, which was puny in comparison to theirs, they stopped to ask, very politely, where we were. One of them pointed to their map, which flapped uncooperatively in the breeze. An absent supervisor had inked their designated route with bold marker pen, helpfully even marking arrows to show the direction of travel. They were indeed lost, miles off their route. I slipped immediately into geography teacher mode – the habit has not deserted me completely even after years of abstinence – and tried to break the news gently. They looked crestfallen but were at least relieved to have some certainty about the way they should go. I left them retracing their tracks, a collective wobble of bright rucksacks above wearily shuffling boots.

A few miles further on, I came to Heath Chapel. The small 12th-century church (dedication unknown) was locked but a note on the notice board in the graveyard said that the key was behind it. And it was, hanging on a string. I opened the heavy wooden door set in a Norman arch and went inside. The interior was austere, unchanged for centuries and remarkable for having escaped any pious Victorian refit: square wooden stalls of pews, polished by age and countless generations of shuffling bottoms; a coating of dust on the hymnbooks; a flagstone floor and deeply recessed windows. A tattered Bible was open on the pulpit. The plastered walls bore traces of paintings that peered through the whitewash – palimpsests of prayer and scripture study. Any ghosts that haunted the chapel must have been of medieval pedigree.

I sat on a bench outside to eat an apple, which I had taken from the B&B fruit bowl, before donning my rucksack to take a narrow lane downhill to Boulden. The village's centrepiece, the Tally Ho Inn, made no secret of its partiality, having a sign that depicted a red-jacketed equestrian and loyal beagle, their mutual red-furred quarry suggested rather than shown. Further on, at Peaton, I came upon a large farm complex and a sign that told me that it was seven miles to Ludlow and the same distance to Craven Arms, my ultimate destination that day.

The road towards Great Sutton was entirely without traffic, my footsteps the only sound other than complaining rooks in the fields. Suspicious cows, not expecting company, raised their heads to stare at me from the fields as I walked by. Watching the landscape slowly unfold before me, I had a strange sensation that the landscape, in turn, was somehow watching me back.

At Culmington I stopped to attend to the blisters that were starting to grow on my feet – the result of too much road walking and worn-out boots that were no longer waterproof. From here, a green lane bridleway climbed gently to reach a road at Bache House, from where I continued, only to arrive at a barbed wire fence blocking my way. I wondered how a horse was meant to negotiate an obstacle such as this. Climbing awkwardly over the wire, I managed to carry on in the same direction until I reached a road.

A track led up to Norton Camp, a prominent D-shaped feature on the OS map. The hillfort, an Iron Age settlement of ditches and ramparts, occupied the entire hilltop. The fort must have once dominated the landscape, although its western slopes are now heavily afforested.

The designated footpath led around the ramparts but, tired and impatient to make headway, I strode straight across the private enclosure to reach the opposite bank. This proved to be a mistake as, climbing over the fence on the opposite side, I found that I could not continue far because of the impenetrable brambles. Retracing my steps, I tried another exit and climbed the fence again before clambering through head-high nettles to reach a path. This turned out to be just one of many that threaded through the woods on the western side of the fort. I spent a frustrating half hour trying several different options but none seemed to lead down the steep slope to the main road below. Eventually, I came upon a man with a rifle – a Welshman in a camouflage jacket – who eyed me suspiciously until he realised I was just a lost fool with a rucksack and clearly no threat to whatever it was he was up to. We exchanged a few words and he pointed out the best way down the slope.

I zigzagged downhill to eventually reach the main Ludlow to Shrewsbury road from where I slogged footsore along its pavement to arrive at the outskirts of Craven Arms. A sign welcomed me to the 'Gateway to the Marches', and further on an obelisk gave the distance to the places Craven Arms deemed significant – certainly, they were important to me: *Aberystwyth 71 miles, Bishops Castle 11 miles, Clun 8 miles.*

By this time, I had been walking for 7½ hours more or less non-stop. I phoned my friends Chris and Jen, who live in a nearby village and with whom I had arranged to stay. Thankfully, Chris agreed to pick me up in ten minutes' time from outside the supermarket.

*

We all went for a short walk together the next day, following the route I had planned to take west from Craven Arms – the Shropshire Way through Sibdon Carwood, then a steep climb up to Hopesay Common before returning along lanes to our starting point. It was a glorious day for walking: a light warm breeze, the shadows of billowing clouds marching briskly up the slopes of the common. On the top, where horses grazed and sheep munched contentedly, a tractor was mowing bracken. High circling buzzards mewed on the thermals above. A gallery view of Shropshire's iconic hills – the Long Mynd, Caer Caradoc, the Clee Hills – even the dark bulk of The Wrekin could be made out in the far northeast. The weather, the rolling scenery, the convivial company: it all seemed quite idyllic – a Welsh Marches romance, a poetic fantasy from the pen of Housman.

The following morning brought a change in the weather: thick low cloud and intermittent blustery rain. Chris gave me a lift to the foot of Hopesay Common, dropping me off next to the line of hawthorns that marked the path to the top of the hill. Despite my insistence that this was what I wanted, he told me that he felt a little guilty leaving me there in the rain. The top of the common was lost to low cloud; yesterday's sunlit Housman hills were already just a memory, less blue and remembered than grey and best forgotten. I hugged a wall to walk uphill following the wind-bent hawthorns that traced the boundary fence. At the top, there were no horses grazing today, just a few miserable-looking sheep also doing their best to shelter behind a stone wall.

A broad green swathe of a path led downhill into Hopesay, a handsome cluster of stone houses tucked into the cleft of the valley, where I took shelter from the rain for a few minutes at the lynch gate of the village church. This gave me time to read about the church's history on the noticeboard, which suggested that St Mary's unusual wooden 'Montgomeryshire dovecote-style' tower may have served as a place of refuge from Welsh invaders.

Such was the folklore of border regions like this, where the constant threat of invasion permeated the historic fabric.

I joined the Shropshire Way, which took me uphill along a green lane lined with coppiced hazel. A deer barked unseen somewhere below in the valley. Like parts of Norfolk, rural Shropshire seemed to be in thrall to the shooting industry. I passed several pheasant feeding stations and later on, following a track into Kempton, I encountered birds exploding alarmingly from the hedgerows at what seemed like every other step. Rather than fly off, the birds fell into line in front of me and before I knew it I had something like twenty pheasants leading the way, each one warily keeping an even distance from me as I followed up the rear.

From Kempton, the Shropshire Way led gently uphill past isolated farmhouses and scattered oaks in an area of parkland. By now, the rain had almost stopped and the sheep in the fields were starting to look a little more cheerful. Even so, they froze like statues when they saw me approach, waiting for me to pass before they continued with their sheepish itinerary.

The Walcot Estate, whose land this was, had been home to a large deer park in Elizabethan times, which explained the scattering of venerable old oaks among the sloping pasture. Bought by Clive of India in 1763, the estate was later inherited by his son, the Earl of Powys. During his British exile in the late 1930s, Haile Selassie had lived here with a sizeable retinue for a while before opting for the equally unlikely base of Malvern. As a rare souvenir of that stay, a grainy photo in a 1938 edition of *The Courier and Advertiser* depicts the Emperor, King of Kings, in winter coat and hat admiring a pet goose with his host Ronald Stevens. The Ethiopian Emperor had arrived here, as I had, by way of Craven Arms; in his case, stepping off the train with his entourage at the town's railway station in 1936. It was doubtful that Craven Arms had witnessed anything quite so splendid before or since, although it is the Abbey Hotel in Malvern that now has a blue plaque to acknowledge the Lion of Judah's royal presence rather than the small Shropshire town. As with many stately homes that can no longer easily afford their own heating bill, Walcot Hall has since been re-purposed as a wedding venue, although its website makes no mention of the Emperor's previous tenure, a missed opportunity that disregards those of the Rastafarian community who might wish to tie the knot somewhere special.

The path eventually reached a minor road where a track led up to the hilltop fort of Bury Ditches, which was both Iron Age village and hill fort, one of several in the region and the most impressive in terms of size. A single car was parked in the picnic area at the bottom of the hill and I saw no one else throughout my entire time at the site other than a mountain biker who overtook me on the way up.

This whole border region is rich in prehistoric earthworks, some domestic and defensive like this one, but also others that might be considered sacred. A few miles to the north are several sites where stones had been manipulated at great effort for what archaeologists usually termed 'ritual use', for want of a more complete knowledge of their precise function. A tumulus lies just a mile to the north of here at Aston, while hill forts and motte and baileys pepper the landscape in every direction. Prehistoric cairns stand on the slopes of Corndon Hill, which hugs the Welsh border the other side of Bishop's Castle, and close to this is a mysterious Bronze Age stone circle with my name on it – Mitchell's Fold. Was this corner of southwest Shropshire a sacred landscape, a territory celebrated by the stones and sites that lay upon it? Or had it been rendered sacred by the mere erection of such monuments? Which came first: the stones or the sanctity?

Such a question did not need to be asked of Bury Ditches, as it seemed to be focused solely on defence and the domestic.

The site, well preserved in terms of earthworks, belongs to the Forestry Commission and considerable effort has been made to render it visitor-friendly. There is a large car park, a network of well-maintained footpaths and plenty of interpretative material. As embellishment, a tree trunk has been carved in the form of a Celtic warrior raising a spear, and there is also a rather beautiful cast iron plaque covered with Celtic designs swirls and, for full inclusivity, raised Braille dots. Waymarked walking routes – The Druid's Walk, The Chieftan's Walk – circle the site and spaced along these is a sprinkling of information boards. Aimed primarily at a young audience, these introduce a fictitious Celtic boy named Llew, a blacksmith's son who has taken some iron objects from his father's forge to show his friends and subsequently lost them. His father is out hunting but will give him a whipping when he gets back unless Llew can find them.

Can you help? the board asked, glossing over the explicit domestic violence of the scenario. The hilltop where the village once stood is now little more than an expanse of ragwort and thistles marked by a carved wooden sign of a Celtic boy saying, *Welcome to my village*. A *No Metal Detecting* sign completes the picture. At the site's highest point is a toposcope for identifying Shropshire's topological highlights – The Long Mynd, Caer Caradoc, Wenlock Edge, Brown Clee, Nordy Bank – although the pale haze that lingered from the morning's downpour made visibility limited.

I left the site to head downhill through woodland. Stopping to eat the sandwiches Chris had made for me, I yearned for a cup of tea to go with it. I had seen flyers attached to waymark posts that advertised a tearoom in Guilden Down, a village on the way to Clun – it seemed churlish not to stop. The tearoom turned out to be in the conservatory of a private house whose owner had turned her garden over to a small-scale organic smallholding. Revived by a pot of tea and a generous wedge of lemon-drizzle polenta cake, I walked the final mile or so down into Clun.

I had no recollection of ever having been to Clun before. When I mentioned this to my mother, she told me that I had in fact visited the town as a baby when we had driven over to visit a distant cousin of my paternal great-grandmother, Jessie, aka Nanny Morris. 'A real old-fashioned countrywoman,' as my mother described her, 'it was as if she lived in the middle of nowhere.'

Despite what my mother said, Clun is in the middle of somewhere, albeit somewhere pretty small. The largest settlement in this Welsh Marches panhandle, the town is the last stop on the slow road to Wales, the B4368 that connects Craven Arms with Clun and Newcastle and crosses the border to end at Abermule.

Technically a town, although with all the appearance of a village, Clun seemed to have everything that you might wish for if your desire was for an unhurried rural life: a castle, a church, an ancient packhorse bridge, a hostel, a few holiday cottages and B&Bs, not to mention a supermarket and two pubs. Otherwise, it lived up to the promise of the Housman poem.

Clunton and Clunbury,
Clugunford and Clun,
Are the quietest places
Under the sun.

Clun was quiet, unquestionably; the town-village collectively locked in an afternoon snooze by the time I arrived at its high street. The Sun Inn, which had a jolly medieval-looking pub sign swinging above its door, was open and I was tempted to go in for a pint but did not have much time before my bus came. Besides, I wanted to take a look at the castle before I left. Built above a bend of the town's eponymous river shortly after the

Norman Conquest by Picot de Say, a knight loyal to William the Conqueror, the castle, although now ruined, was a game-changer for this quiet historic backwater.

After a brief exploration of the castle ruins I went into the car park public conveniences to wash and change. Sweaty and a little mud-stained by this stage, I wanted to clean myself up for the long journey home. Each of the self-contained, stainless steel units came with a toilet and sink topped by a multi-functional unit that provided water, soap and a drying stream of air. I chose one at random and, having locked the door behind me, a loudspeaker kicked into action to play, at considerable volume, the theme song from Andrew Lloyd Webber's *Phantom of the Opera*. I did my best to ignore the unrequested musical accompaniment as I washed armpits and feet and changed into the clean, if crumpled, clothes that I had in my rucksack. This took a while to complete and it soon dawned on me that the same song was set on repeat. It took three cycles of the West End crowd-pleaser before I was done. I finally emerged cleaner and fresher but reeling from the aural assault to which I had been subjected.

It seemed an odd choice of music – had this been installed to deter drug addicts or rough sleepers from loitering in the facilities? And did the multi-millionaire peer receive royalties for each airing of his song – a penny a pee? Was he aware that his music, used as an accompaniment to the rough and tumble of the lavatory cubicle, was being degraded in such a way? I had heard of cases where classical music was played in public places to deter local youth from hanging around, but this was something else. It brought to mind something I had once seen inscribed on a sundial on the wall of a Suffolk church, which chivvied any would-be dawdlers with the curt injunction, *NOW BE ON YOUR WAY*, as if unnecessary lingering might encourage wickedness. Did Shropshire County Council have misanthropes on their staff... or clandestine Lloyd Webber aficionados?

According to the online timetable my bus was due to leave at 2.20pm but when I reached the bus stop I spotted a pinned-up timetable that said 2.10pm instead. The time was now 2.15 and I was fully aware that there would not be another bus for days – Clun is nothing if not poorly connected. Mercifully, the bus was a few minutes late.

The bus's only other passengers got off at Bishop's Castle, where another man, an engaging septuagenarian whom the driver clearly knew very well, got on. Both were talkative and knowledgeable about their local area so I was rewarded with a running commentary as we headed north through Shropshire's far-western reaches. Every village, every farm that we passed seemed to have a story worth telling. Eventually, the driver dropped off his friend at one of the villages and told me to come up to the front to chat. Recognising that I looked like a walker, he asked where I had been that day. I told him – Craven Arms to Clun – but he did not seem particularly impressed.

The driver drove as he spoke, slowly and carefully, braking repeatedly to avoid hitting manic pheasants that frequently strayed across the road.

'I don't like hitting them, but they don't seem to want to get out of my way. I don't like killing them, mind,' adding, 'I really can't see why they call it a sport – shooting them in hundreds like that. They don't even eat all those that they kill.'

I got off at Pontesbury, where I was told there would be another bus to take me to Shrewsbury in twenty minutes time. The bus arrived on cue and I was the only passenger until we called into the playground of a secondary school just up the road – the bus doubled as a school service for local kids, and the teachers were doing their best to corral the students as they piled on board. Having spent years as a teacher in which a weekly stint of bus duty was part of my job requirement, it felt like an inglorious return to the schoolyard.

We all got off in Shrewsbury, where I found my way to the railway station and waited half an hour for the next train to Birmingham. A crowded rush-hour commuter train, the carriage was standing room only by the time we passed by the looming mass of The Wrekin just before Telford.

Part Four

Wales

Chapter 19

Over the *Ofer*

Shropshire/Powys, Wales

The Britons who were left alive took refuge in these parts when the Saxons first occupied the island, and they have never been completely subdued since, either by the English or the Normans.
Gerald of Wales/Giraldus Cambrensis (c.1146–c.1223)
The Journey Through Wales

A winter passed before I was able to return to Clun. Continuity may have been desirable but it was unrealistic. The end of British Summer Time meant that it became dark by late afternoon, which shortened the hours available for walking. So, instead, I returned to Shropshire the following May, staying once more overnight with Chris and Jen near Craven Arms. The past may well be another country, but then so is Wales.

Jen gave me a lift to Clun in the morning. The day was warm and sunny – perfect walking weather – with swallows, martins and swifts threading the cloud-flecked sky. Perfect walking, but less than perfect feet: my old boots, by now totally non-waterproof and irreparable, had been consigned to the bin and the new ones I had bought to replace them with were already starting to give me blisters. This, along with a longstanding arthritic toe joint problem, was starting to make walking any distance increasingly difficult.

I took the Shropshire Way out of town, along a shady footpath where strands of sheep's wool dangled like bunting from hedgerow branches. Hawthorns were just beginning to bud as the last of the blackthorn blossom lay like confetti across the path. The footpath merged with a green lane hemmed in by elder and coppiced hazel before joining the main road just before the village of Bicton. The road, silent apart from the occasion retort of a distant bird scarer, led me gently uphill to Newcastle, a village just large enough to possess a primary school and a modest stand of new-build houses.

Approaching Anchor, I crossed the Offa's Dyke Path, a weathered signpost with an embossed acorn logo pointing the way in both directions. The long, linear earthwork that constituted the 'dyke' was no longer a border *per se*, although it still marked a frontier of sorts – an overlap of the Celtic fringe where Anglo-Saxon England gave way culturally and linguistically to Wales.

Offa ruled Mercia in the late 8th century and, although it remains uncertain, it was probably this same king who ordered the construction of the dyke and bank intended to separate Powys from English Mercia. The ditch stood to the west, the Welsh side of the earthwork; the raised bank on the English east. Although by no means completely sealing off the troublesome Welsh from the territory that lay beyond, the dyke followed a straightforward north–south delineation that was quite distinct from the modern convoluted border that now encompasses territory that would once have belonged to Wales. At the time of the dyke's construction, the Anglo-Saxon Kingdom of Mercia incorporated almost all of central England, extending as far south as Wessex, north to the River Humber and Northumbria, and east to Anglia at the present-day borders of Norfolk and Suffolk. The assumption that its name derives from its association with the most powerful of the Mercian kings might seem obvious but there are alternative explanations: *Ofer* is an Old English word for border or edge. Similarly, an *ofer-ganga* refers to one who goes over or beyond a border, a traveller. The act of travel always requires crossing one sort of border or another.

Near Anchor, where a lone caravan stood marooned, curtains drawn, in a gorse-filled field next to a brook, I passed a sign that pointed to Rhos Fiddle Nature Reserve in one direction and Badger Moor in the other. Breathy Welsh place names – Bachaethlon, Cymlladron, Dolfawr – were already starting to appear on the map before I came to Bettws y Crwyn, a hamlet that possessed little more than a notice-board and a post box. A sign on railings, carefully framed and proudly displayed, with nothing remotely faded about it despite its relative antiquity, read, *Calor congratulates Bettws y Crwyn WINNER of the Shropshire Calor Village of the Year Competition 2002.*

Anchor seemed to presage warning. Just before the village I came across the black fan of a crow wing lying in the road, the rest of the bird's body hacked to pieces by a raptor with a taste for carrion. A little further on was the bulky corpse of a car-struck badger, perhaps a denizen of the aforementioned moor, indecorously slumped on the grass verge, its yellow teeth bared to the world of the living.

The village pub, the Anchor Inn, looked sad and abandoned, and although a faded handwritten board outside the door advertised opening hours it did not look as if it had welcomed customers for quite some time. In the days when the inn was a port of call for the drovers who brought livestock from Wales along the Kerry Ridgeway, this would have been a thriving, busy place. Now its roof was missing slates, its sign overgrown by a hedge; its whitewashed stone walls, a grubby grey. Even so, a pair of traffic bollards had been placed on the road outside as if to reserve space for imaginary customers.

I made my way along a road that climbed through conifer plantations up to Kerry Pole and the Kerry Hill Ridgeway. Another dead badger lay on the roadside just before the sign that announced my departure from Shropshire and England. The Welsh equivalent seemed to be missing but a little further on I came to a viewpoint sign (*Creoso Ceri* – Welcome to Kerry) that was marked with a dragon and the logo of the Welsh National Assembly. This was Powys. Wales.

At Kerry Pole, a lone cottage stood at the junction with the ridge path, the old droving route marked by a lichen-capped fingerpost inscribed *Kerry Ridgeway/Fford Las Ceri*. Eastwards, the path led along a minor lane towards Bishop's Castle. To the west, it followed a wool-snagged wire fence lined with hawthorns to climb up to the crest of the hill. I followed it to the top of the rise, where I stopped to perch on a rock for a while to drink water and give my feet an airing.

The Kerry Ridgeway that leads fifteen miles from Cider House in Powys to Bishop's Castle in Shropshire is of prehistoric origin, predating even the Iron Age earthworks that cut across its path. Maintaining a height of around four hundred metres above sea level, it provides an elevated foray into Wales. This was the same ancient route that Welsh cattle drovers once used to follow into England, the last high stretch of ridge tracing the border that divided the two countries. The drovers, finally free of their livestock after reaching market in the Midlands, were wont to make the most of their newfound liberty and tended to make their way home at a more leisurely pace, walking in groups of two and three and stopping at pubs along the way. Their dogs, meanwhile, usually corgis, made their own way back and were said to always arrive home first.

The ridgeway path followed a broad track that gave long, hazy views to the west. Docile grazing sheep, still cosy in their winter coats, speckled the hillside every which way. Scattered clumps of late-flowering daffodils (a wholly appropriate flower given the location) bloomed brightly at the wayside. Next to a fence post was a solitary buzzard feather that had fallen to earth.

At Two Tumps (508 metres), the ridge's highest point, a sturdily constructed stone shelter had framed maps marking the hills that could be seen to the east, north and west (the viewpoint's southern aspect was blocked by a slightly higher hill) and indicated the direction of distant towns like Machynlleth. The 'tumps' in question were not natural but manmade earthworks – twin Bronze Age burial cairns that had been weathered over two millennia to become barely distinguishable. Now they were little more than minor undulations in the landscape, but in droving days they would have provided an important sighting landmark – a gathering place for cattle and drovers to assemble before the final push into England.

After following the ridge for several miles, the track eventually sloped down to join a minor road at Cider House Farm. Eastbound Welsh drovers would have quenched their thirst here before tackling the Ridgeway, although now there is no indication of any sort of alcohol being available on the premises. Tired by now, and even more footsore, I followed the road north into Dolfor, where I had booked a bed for the night. I had seen very few cars and absolutely no other walkers all day, and it was only as I approached the village that the traffic start to pick up a little with commuters to and from Newtown, which lies a little way north along the same road.

My B&B was well appointed, and a little grander and pricier than I would normally use. There had been little choice – my route across thinly populated mid-Wales was as much dictated by the availability of places to stay as it was by the lie of the land. The man of the house fancied himself as a gourmet cook and the evening meal shared with a pleasant, rather aristocratic couple was unarguably a cut above standard B&B fare. After Moroccan lamb and a large glass of house red I retired early to my room. Sleep came easily – I had walked around sixteen miles in total since setting off from Clun that morning.

*

Next morning, I meekly claimed the offered 10% reduction on the bill for having arrived on foot. This was granted courteously by the proprietor with just the mildest of winces at my penny-pinching cheek. Strapping on my rucksack, I stepped outside, feeling more enervated than energised from having eaten a full Welsh fry-up for breakfast.

The morning was overcast, with a little light drizzle blurring visibility ahead. This was the Wales I knew well enough, with all the bad weather, green-but-wet tropes neatly in place. Wales or not, I did not hear a Welsh accent until halfway through the morning when I was greeted by a farm worker, a friendly elderly man in boiler suit and wellingtons, who was ambling to work with the slow, painful gait of a chronic arthritis sufferer.

'Lovely day for a bit of walking, isn't it?'

It was, but walking was clearly quite a challenge for him. It was becoming increasingly more problematic for me, too, given the compounded nuisance of blisters and tender toe joints.

With worsening feet, it seemed that my walk was starting become more a penance than a pleasure – a shuffle of suffering. But penance for what purpose? I had never intended my walk to be any sort of act of valour, or even excessive endurance. Unwittingly, I was becoming something more akin to a footsore medieval pilgrim than a modern-day hiker, simply as a result of inherent flat-footedness and inadequate footwear. I was aware that long, difficult journeys on foot might sometimes be carried out as an apotropaic act, a conscious means of averting evil or bad luck by the ritual of walking. But was it necessary – even desirable – to suffer in the process? Of course, there are many – super-devout religious types, in particular – who might think that a degree of suffering is obligatory. There are Tibetan Buddhist pilgrims who insist on making an already gruelling circumambulation of Holy Mount Kailash even tougher by prostrating themselves all the way. Then there are those Irish Catholics who insist on ascending the rocky path to the mountaintop shrine of Croagh Patrick without shoes on their feet. In the medieval period it was common practice to walk the last part of the way to Walsingham shrine in Norfolk barefooted – even Henry VIII performed this rite uncomplainingly in his younger days, before he fell out with the Catholic Church and adopted a more confrontational approach to institutionalised religion. Other practitioners of what might be termed 'extreme walking' are more secular in outlook, although some sort of faith still comes into it. The film director Werner Herzog once walked virtually non-stop from Munich to Paris to visit the sick bed of a fading film-maker, a near spontaneous act of devotion documented in the book *Of Walking in Ice*. It involved considerable hardship as Herzog walked relentlessly in freezing winter conditions, sleeping rough where he could along the way. Others have adopted an extreme approach to walking as a creative act *per se*; like the artist Hamish Fulton, whose work is entirely based on his experience of walks, arguing that walking is an art form in its own right. There is also Richard Long, another artist who walks fast and far, not as a personal response to the landscape but more as a means of providing structure to his walking-based compositions – less an act of ritual, more one of premeditated geometry.

*

The morning, which slowly brightened as the hours dawdled by, took me west through poetically named hamlets that sounded like an Eisteddfod roll-call: Garreg, Garth-Heilyn, Pen-y-brynn, Old Neudal, Llwyn-Madoc, Wergliodd-gam, Penthryn.

Now that I was in Wales, the sensation of walking against the grain of the land was more pronounced than ever. Traversing a succession of folded valleys, approaching them side-on, almost every step now seemed to be either up and down, never on the level. But constant inclines, painful feet and an overcast sky could not detract from the sheer glory of the landscape. The country roads I followed were narrow and curving, framed by raised banks lush with primroses and violets and topped with hedges. These were not the harsh, vertiginous, slate-quarry slopes of Snowdonia, nor the emerald coal-mining valleys of South Wales, but the Welsh Marches: a softer, less-championed landscape of scattered farms and pasture that seemed to be a Celtic-tinged continuation of the bottle green hill-country of Shropshire across the border.

So far, walking across East Anglia and the Midlands, I had been passing through landscapes that, no matter how hard they tried to fool, were unmistakably Anthropocene in character. The hand of man had been everywhere you looked. From the mechanised agriculture on farms to the ever-improved roads that connected the settlements, from the canals and tamed river courses to the regimented light-starved pine plantations, there had been little that could be described as truly pre-industrial, let alone wild. Even that which had resisted human impact was, as a rule, neatly compartmentalised, with boundaries drawn, a fence installed to enclose it, an information board erected to inform of what we were seeing and what had been lost. Here, though, was a distinct sense that I was walking into a landscape that was far more ancient, although I knew that bare-sided, slate-depleted mountain slopes with their scattered grazing sheep were far from natural. What there was instead was a sense of what the poet-musician Richard Skelton has described as the 'lichen memory' of a place. Wales is saturated with lichen memory, its ancient rocks inform the poetic of place as much as its coalmines and sheep pasture.

The Welsh Marches have no map-defined territory, no discrete border. They belong to that category of landscape that might best be described using that term beloved by psycho-geographers: liminal. A landscape that occupies territory on both sides of a frontier, this southeast corner of historic Montgomeryshire is liminal in the sense that it serves as a threshold between worlds that are intrinsically different – an Anglo-Celtic border zone. Already, it was starting to feel more Celtic than Anglo.

Just outside Old Neudal, an indistinct footpath led downhill through a damp tract of woodland. Immediately I found myself in a deeply shaded world of ancient pollards and thick leaf litter. A sour smell of fungal decay prevailed, a velvety carpet of moss coated every surface and fire-coloured lichens clung to exposed fragments of rock. At the valley bottom, where a narrow brook trickled through the tangled roots of trees, I arrived at a copse where a small clump of wood oxalis was delicately perched upon a moss-lined tree stump. It seemed like some sort of living shrine – a microcosm of lost world landscape; an ancient Japanese woodblock brought to life in hidden Wales. In the tree-stilled calm of the wood, such a finding felt like stumbling across an uncharted sacred grove, as if my eyes were the only ones ever to have glanced upon it. Was this one of the 'thin places' of Celtic folklore, where the physical and spiritual worlds coincided? Such places usually possess some sort of visible marker, a church or chapel, or in more ancient, pre-Christian times, an arrangement of stones or wood. Sometimes though, there are no signs other than an atmosphere, a presence, a hard-wired aura of ineffability. Such serendipitous discoveries are rare but I have unwittingly stumbled on similar places from time to time, especially in wild, overgrown woodland like this – clearings that stand out and seem somehow sparkled with fairy dust, quiet places that glow with an unfathomable numinous presence. The indefinable enchantment of such places is hard to explain, impossible to understand using scientific method. Perhaps the clue is in the poet Wendell Berry's line about there being no unsacred places but only sacred places and desecrated places. So much of the landscape now is, without question, desecrated.

If accidental sacred groves such as this are rare then at least they exist, hidden away to await discovery by off-piste hikers. What I had noticed on my cross-country walk so far was a total absence of other, less spiritually nurturing places that used to punctuate the countryside of my younger days: those slapdash woodland dens littered with cigarette butts, beer cans and the torn pages of top-shelf magazines – the secret territory of adolescent boys. I could not remember the last occasion I had chanced upon one of these, although only a few decades earlier I used to stumble across them quite regularly. Such dens were lost to the elements now; no trace of their ever having existed, no archaeological clues. A missing component of the contemporary unofficial countryside, they have been largely driven into disuse by the ready availability of the Internet, a relatively recent innovation that keeps many teenagers indoors in the comfort and privacy of their bedrooms.

The wood and its sacred grove behind me, I followed a narrow winding road uphill to Penthyrn then took an old service road over four hundred-metre-high Bryn Gwyn. On my way up, I skirted a small, disused quarry used as a tip, filled with domestic rubbish and two dead calves, one relatively fresh, the other, decayed and foul-smelling. It was here that I heard a cuckoo. The birds have become noticeably scarcer over the past decade in East Anglia so it was reassuring to hear one again here in upland mid-Wales. Cresting the hill, I followed a narrow valley downhill past Cwmffrwd and the scar of another abandoned quarry to meet a minor road at Cobbler's Gate, just a mile shy of the small town of Llandinam on the River Severn.

At Llandinam, I stopped to rest for a while and took my boots and socks off to air my blistered feet while I ate an apple. Then, lacing my boots as tightly as I could, headed for the bridge that crossed the River Severn. Nearby was a statue of David Davies. This was neither the modern-day Tory politician and one-time

Brexit Secretary, nor the Kinks guitarist, but a Victorian with the same unimaginative moniker: a squat man with chinstrap beard and stern countenance, who was depicted perusing a document in a manner that suggested a lost motorist reading a map. This particular David Davies was a poor tenant farmer's son who went on to become a wealthy industrialist and politician; a proud example of local boy made good, whose greatest achievement was opening the docks at Barry in the Vale of Glamorgan as a cheaper and less congested alternative to those at Cardiff.

I crossed the bridge over to the Severn's west bank and followed a network of footpaths up towards the ridge. I had intended to join the Severn Way, which would take me all the way to Llanidloes but, either incompetent, unlucky or both, I somehow managed to miss the correct path. I ended up climbing over barbed wire and electric fences into an area of dense woodland where young pheasants were held in cages to protect them from predators. Eventually, after much frustrated squandering of time and energy, I managed to find a track that took me up to the designated footpath, which I followed for awhile before abandoning it in favour of a more direct route along a minor road that took me straight into Llanidloes.

Small, charming and uncompromisingly Welsh, Llanidloes – 'Llani', to those who know it – is the archetypical mid-Wales town. According to a Royal Mail survey, the town is amongst the top five desirable postcodes in Wales, and with a half-timbered market hall, a scattering of quirky shops, a couple of old-school ironmongers, at least half a dozen pubs and a generous allocation of chapels, Llanidloes appeared to possess all the necessary ingredients for a comfortable existence in rural, small-town Wales. There was a degree of unselfconscious eccentricity about the place, too. Hanging like a rescued flood victim on a helicopter hoist above the entrance to one of the butchers' was a life-size model ram. Gazing out of the window from within the shop, an anthropomorphised fibreglass pig in a bonnet provided a further clue, if one were needed, as to the goods on sale.

Although still firmly a farmers' town rather than any sort of tourist centre, Llanidloes has an unaffected, old-fashioned charm that makes it worthy of the epithet 'unspoiled'. The town was once well known for its flannel production, which had originated as a low-key cottage industry in which goods were sent to market in Shrewsbury. But such success was short-lived, and the town's trade fell into fast decline when the hand-washing public shifted favour to the cheaper goods produced by factories in the north of England. Such was the original devotion to the industry that a dedicated flannel exchange once stood in Great Oak Street but, by the outbreak of the Great War, flannel-making had already become a thing of the past and all the mills were closed. In connection with this trade, the town was also a focus for Chartist riots in 1839, which resulted partly as a consequence of industrialisation of the weaving process and also as a response to the recent passing of the Corn Laws, which affected the poor throughout the land. Police constables, specially recruited from London, arrested three of the ringleaders and imprisoned them at the town's Trewythen Arms Hotel before an angry mob stormed the hotel to release the detained men. Order was finally restored after 'Five Days of Freedom', when a further thirty-two townspeople were arrested to be either imprisoned or transported to Australia. One of the ringleaders, Thomas Jerman, who managed to escape to America via Liverpool, would later go on to fight for the Union army in the American Civil War.

After the collapse of the flannel trade, local employment came by way of lead mining in the Van Mine a couple of miles to the north, a mine that was sufficiently productive to warrant the construction of a bespoke railway link to Caersws on the main Shrewsbury to Aberystwyth line. For a brief period Van Mine was one of the most productive in Europe but its prosperity was short-lived and, like the flannel industry that had preceded it, the mine fell into decline in the 1890s, to finally close for good in 1921.

I dragged my tired legs around in the drizzle for a little while before settling down for pie, chips and a pint in the lounge bar of the pub where I was staying. Almost too tired to eat, I limped back to my room and fell immediately asleep only to wake at midnight as the dull thud of techno cut through the damp air from a nearby pub – Saturday Night Fever, Llani-style.

*

Next morning, rain was still falling but the weather forecast predicted an improvement later on. I was in no rush to leave as I had planned just a relatively short walk to neighbouring Llangurig that day and so had time to explore a little. But Sundays in pious mid-Wales are invariably quiet and the town museum was closed, which meant that I never got to see the stuffed two-headed lamb that is said to be its star exhibit. At least the Travellers Joy coffee bar was open. Wholesome, wholemeal Llanidloes advertised itself as a Fairtrade town but I soon discovered that hipster coffee culture had yet to make any inroads here and I felt unwittingly metropolitan and not a little pretentious when I sat down at one of the tables and asked for a cappuccino.

'Oh! We don't do that, love. I can make you an instant coffee with milk, mind. Do you want a cup or a mug?'

While I waited for the kettle to boil, an elderly couple came in to peruse the menu before ordering baked potatoes with beans and cheese, as well as 'a nice mug of milky coffee'.

'Not too strong, mind. Lovely and weak and milky – you know how I likes it.'

A couple of minutes later the friendly waitress came back with my mug of coffee. Putting the drink down, she placed a *Reserved* sign on my table.

'Oh, don't worry about that. That's for later on. Take your time, love.'

I did as I was told and lingered awhile before I decided that, now that the rain had stopped, it was probably time to take my leave of lovely, milky Llani.

I headed out of town along Short Bridge Street, which lived up to the promise of its name. Just before the larger River Severn bridge, stood two large chapels, Baptist and Zion Congregational, on either side of the road in denominational face-off, the stirring strains of *Cwm Rhonnda* emanating from the interior of the former. Across the bridge, perhaps tucked away over the water for reasons on unspoken sectarianism, was the more modest village hall-like Catholic Church of Our Lady and St Richard Gwynn.

It was a relatively short hike to Llangurig: five miles or so along a well-defined bridleway but long enough to traverse the Severn-Wye watershed. The bridleway took me across sheep-filled meadows to a footbridge across the River Severn, from where a greenway between gnarled old hedges continued to a field that held bullocks and more sheep. A signpost pointed diagonally across to the field's far corner. It was a now-familiar scenario and not a welcome one, but the bullocks only took a mild interest in my presence and seemed content to tag along behind at a respectable distance. The same path continued along the edge of an oak wood before arriving at a ramshackle farm where the sheds were in various states of collapse and a rusting van lay half-buried beneath old tyres and plastic seed trays. Congruent with this apparent chaos, the area around the farm gates had been transformed to boot-sucking mire by the repeated stomping of cattle. I edged around as best I could. A green lane enclosed by slanting, wind-bent hawthorns led uphill. After a short rest and some essential foot-tending at the top, I followed the ridge between the valleys of the Severn and its tributary, the Afon Dulas.

The way down from the ridge led through a confer plantation that had larches planted so close together that they scratched my arms. A buzzard rose from the path some way ahead before disappearing into the dense foliage. The path turned into a quagmire, the product of overnight rain and the deep ruts of Land Rover tyres, but I soon emerged into the open again. A line of gorse bushes, their cloying coconut scent almost overwhelming in the sunshine, marked the way down to a large private lake where a single rowing boat was tethered at a fishing platform.

A group of lapwings were calling plaintively – *peewit, peewit* – as they wheeled in the air on the other side of the water. Their flamboyant aerial display seemed more an expression of pure joy than anything else – no ethological explanation required; no purpose to it other than to celebrate the possession of deft wings and a voice that could summon bitter-sweet nostalgia. A nostalgia for something half-forgotten, something that went almost unnoticed until it was lost. I remember a conversation I once had with a birder friend, who remarked that if lapwings were less commonplace we would perhaps pay more attention to their exquisite beauty. In those days lapwings were anything but rare, and almost any bit of open farmland seemed to support a flock of them. Now, like many other, once common birds, they are conspicuously scarcer in southern England and Wales. A similar decline applies, even more alarmingly, to butterflies and insects. Not so many years ago, any car journey on a warm summer's night would result in a windscreen coated with a green-brown sludge of impacted insects; now, they are barely noticeable. Wildlife is failing, biological diversity is narrowing; the natural world is slipping away. Tragically, many seem to barely notice the difference, despite the warnings. It is terrifying to imagine a world without insect life, without bees or moths, let alone without lapwings, cuckoos or curlews. An essential part of this or any landscape, these sloping green hills need the birds and bees as much as they do the sun and the rain.

The track wound down to a ruined cottage by an old quarry that had a yellow JCB digger parked next to it. I looked up to see a large bird fly overhead. Red as a fox, long forked tail, narrow crooked wings, silver-flecked head; it was the first red kite I had seen since arriving in Wales. It was something I should have expected: the birds had re-colonised large stretches of central and southern England in recent years but for much of the 20th century their only British refuge had been in the valleys of central Wales. A symbol for Powys, this elegant scavenger was the same bird that would have swooped over the filthy streets of Victorian London, or for that matter, Cardiff. Carrion-eaters rarely receive much credit, perhaps too close to the vultures that are generally considered repulsive in the human imagination, but this species, a forked-tail beauty, has successfully won over the public since it began to be seen in abundance gliding over the commuter villages of the Chilterns in the last decades of the 20th century.

The raptor sighting was prescient. I passed a farm gate where the name Ffynnon Las ('Blue Well') had been painted on to a wooden board cut in the distinctive shape of a red kite. Soon after, following a farm track down into Llangurig, I saw another kite, perhaps even the same one ranging for food.

The village lies at the foot of a steep hill, stretching modestly along a short stretch of the A44 close to the River Wye. With two pubs, a couple of chapels, a church, school and post office, as well as a woollen goods shop and even a small van hire franchise, Llangurig was modest in scale but undoubtedly a centre of sorts. I had booked a room at The Blue Bell Inn. I checked in before heading down to the River Wye for a late afternoon stroll. After this, to kill a little time, I took a look at the church graveyard and the large water trough that stands on the village's single street. An inscription read, *Colonel George Hope Lloyd-Verney gave the first water supply in 1888 to the village of Llangurig.* Chiselled alongside was a biblical quote: *He sendeth the springs into the*

rivers which run among the hills. As far as Wales is concerned, God's bounty is generous when it came to water. On the way back to my room, I spotted another red kite swooping low over the village's single street, its neck twisting side to side in a relentless search for carrion. The bird did not linger but soon flew off in the direction of the river in the hope of better pickings.

That evening I made an abortive attempt to drain one of the blisters on my left foot before abandoning the procedure to go downstairs and eat a joyless meal of micro-waved pie and chips in the bar. Two middle-aged men were sat at the next table deep in conversation. The subject was shooting – a discourse about bore and bullets that sounded highly esoteric, although they seemed to be talking about target shooting rather than game. The whole dialogue seemed to be more lecture than conversation, as neither of the participants veered far from what appeared to be clearly demarcated roles of speaker and listener. As I ate, a few more customers wandered into the bar, greeting the staff as if they were old friends – it was clear that everybody knew everyone else. The exception was me, the lone Englishman in the fleece and walking boots.

Whilst I sipped my beer and dipped chips in an excess of gluey gravy, a mystery born that same afternoon suddenly unravelled in front of me. One of the young women serving behind the bar had ignored me completely when I greeted her on the street earlier. It had seemed rude, as only half an hour earlier she had shown me to my room for the night. Here was the explanation: sat on a stool at the bar, chatting to some of the regulars, was her doppelganger in pub-branded polo shirt – an identical twin. A stranger to the parish, I must have been the only person in the village who did not realise that these indistinguishable sisters came as a pair.

Chapter 20

The Green, Green Grass of Home

Powys/Ceredigion

-Where was it he was born, Ianto? Llanidloes, was it?
-Nah, Llangurig
-Well that area anyway. Inland like. Farms and mountains, fuck all else. That's all there is yer, just farms and mountains.
Niall Griffiths, *Sheepshagger*

ystwyth (Welsh) adjective: supple, flexible, pliable

I woke to a dull overcast morning with rain forecast later. The small hours of the night had been punctuated by vivid and intense dreams that seemed to be mostly concerned with my letting myself down in social situations. All I could recall on waking was one of my dream-friends telling me, enigmatically, 'Well, you've lost some social capital there.'

I left Llangurig after breakfast, crossing over the River Wye to take a bridleway that climbed up to the high ridge that separated the watersheds of the Wye and Ystwyth rivers. The top of the ridge, with its long hazy views to the north and east, was almost bare of vegetation other than stunted, sheep-cropped grass. The bridleway led to a large conifer plantation, where the OS map indicated that the track should continue straight through. Instead, it just petered out in boggy ground someway short of the perimeter fence. There was no gate to be seen so, trying to avoid the worst of the bog, I made my way as best I could towards the trees. I clambered over the fence and squeezed my way through young conifers to reach a woodland ride, which was so waterlogged that it was effectively a river of tannic brown rainwater interspersed with spongy islands of moss. Seen close, it resembled a forested island landscape in miniature, like an aerial view of the swamplands of the West Siberian Plateau.

The plantation itself was disorientating, the trees too close together for anything else to grow other than the moss that carpeted everything. Gloomy and foreboding, with just a hint of the menace that always seems to haunt territory such as this, it seemed devoid of life apart from the buzzard that I glimpsed rising from the ride ahead of me – a brown blur of claw and feather that vanished almost immediately into a dense tangle of branches. It was clear that I would not be finding any sacred groves in this dark place. Already, I wanted to get out of it as soon as possible. I took a breath, tightened my bootlaces and struck out along the soggy overgrown edge of the ride, squelching along in what I took to be the correct general direction. After fifteen minutes or so I emerged back into the light at the plantation's far side. It was a relief to have it behind me.

A steep slope, scattered with outcrops of pale grey rock, led down to the valley below. I found something that approximated a footpath and followed this to emerge at a road. A bridleway sign pointed back the way I had just come but there was no hint of warning that this was really no viable way for equestrians. The single-track road that wound downhill was so quiet that it was several minutes before a car passed.

The fast-flowing mountain stream that ran alongside the road in the cleft of the valley was the Afon Ystwyth, at this point not far downstream from the its source on the lower slopes of Plynlimon. Standing by the roadside a little further on was a large bilingual information board – *KITE COUNTRY: YMDDIRIEDOLAETH ELAN DŴR CYMRU/WELSH WATER ELAN TRUST* – that gave detailed information about the red kites and bog fauna found in the locality. A *You Are Here* arrow pointed to the northern boundary of the Elan Valley catchment area, where the road from the reservoirs of that valley left the catchment to lead down to the upper reaches of the Ystwyth Valley where I now stood.

*

I have long had a relationship with the Elan Valley. Wales was in my water. Growing up in the Midlands, this same valley had hydrated my childhood. These folded hills had provided the water that came out of the taps at home: feather-soft Welsh mountain water for dry West Midland throats. By way of exchange, Wales was provided with a constant supply of second home-owners and Brummie retirees to their coast, along with plenty of day trippers and the occasional retired policeman seeking a quieter life as a pub landlord in Rhyl or Aberystwyth. A barter of surpluses: Wales had water in abundance; the Midlands had people to spare. But the trade-off came with a human cost: drowned grazing land, lost villages, broken communities and the genesis of a long-standing grudge, although thankfully the practice of setting fire to English-owned holiday cottages is now a thing of the past.

Such anti-English sentiment was nothing new. George Borrow, a self-taught Welsh speaker and life-long cambrophile, had once written that 'it was customary for the English to cut off the ears of every Welshman who was found to the east of the Dyke, and for the Welsh to hang every Englishman whom they found to the west of it'. Clearly, even allowing for the politically charged pyromania of the 1960s and '70s, things had calmed down considerably since those days.

My parents never had anything as grand as a holiday cottage but for several years they did own a static caravan that they kept on a site on the Welsh coast, three hours' drive from our home.

In my teenage years we would go there almost every other weekend in the warmer months. For landlocked Midlanders like us, the seaside always had a strong calling, and any place with sand, sea and a decent fish and chip shop was sufficiently exotic to lure us back at periodic intervals. On these regular summer excursions we used to skirt the Elan Valley en route to our caravan at New Quay. Although I was unaware of it then, New Quay in Cardigan Bay was the 'cliff-perched town on the far edge of Wales' where Dylan Thomas had resided for a while during World War II, a stay that provided inspiration for some of the *Under Milk Wood* voices. To me as a child, New Quay was simply a place of cliffs and long sandy beaches – a place to wander freely around the site looking for diversion or, caravan-bound by inclement weather, stare impassively at fat raindrops sliding down the windows. Later, independent of my parents in my late teens, I ended up back in the town whilst hitchhiking around Wales with a school friend. The weather at the coast was characteristically awful and we ended up taking refuge for the night in the toilet block of the same caravan site where I used to stay with my family – the same greasy raindrops abseiling the frosted glass of the block's high windows. With no map, no local knowledge, this was all I knew. At least it was familiar. This is how children think. And, back then, teenager or not, I was still a child.

On our weekend jaunts to the coast it was invariably the town of Rhyader, just west of the Elan Valley, where we stopped to eat fish and chips on the journey out. The town's distinctive marketplace clock tower is registered firmly in my memory – a marker of time's past habits. I remember a small town at a crossroads – chocolate-dark stone buildings, old-fashioned shops, ironmongers, haberdashers; nothing brash, immodest or even vaguely English about the place. Quintessentially Welsh; like Llanidloes to the north, Rhyader was peak Powys, the perfect embodiment of chapel and chip shop mid-Wales.

The Elan Valley dams were constructed in the years 1893–1904, flooding an area of seventy square miles in total. Like Warwickshire's Forest of Arden, long turned to tarmac and housing, this was another wild territory lost during the glory years of industrialisation: a landscape transformed, made liquid by the alchemy of industrial advance. The valley's captured water was gravity-fed along pipes to the thirsty Midlands, flowing at an average speed of around two miles per hour on its long journey east, roughly the same speed I had averaged while walking west towards the valley's headwaters. If the Elan Valley's water and topography were both valuable resources, its geology was not – stone for the dam had to be imported from Glamorganshire to the south, as the local rock was too flaky to be of use. A massive endeavour: special railroads were constructed to bring in building materials, and something in the order of fifty thousand men were employed, directly or otherwise, in the project. More than one hundred of these lost their lives during the construction process, approximately the same number as those valley-dwellers who were moved from their homes to make way for the scheme.

One of the properties lost to the water was the estate of Cwm Elan, a ten thousand-acre tract of rough grazing that had been nurtured and made luxuriant by Thomas Grove, Percy Bysshe Shelley's uncle, who purchased the land in 1792. The young poet came to stay here in 1811, walking all the way from the family estate in Sussex. Impressed by the romantic beauty of the landscape – 'I am more astonished at the grandeur of the scenery than I expected' – the following year he set up home with his new wife Harriet Westbrook at nearby Nantgwyllt House but was unable to successfully purchase the property and so the couple were obliged to move out. Nantgwyllt, a manor house that boasted an even more glorious setting than Cwm Elan, and described by Shelley as 'embosomed in the solitude of mountains, woods and rivers – silent, solitary, and old: far from any town', was also later lost to the Elan dams scheme. Harriet, Shelley's wife, in what might be viewed as a prescient act, was also later lost to water, drowning herself in Hyde Park's Serpentine in 1816, two years after her abandonment by the poet. Shelley himself also met a watery end, drowned while sailing in the Gulf of La Spezia on the northwest coast of Italy in 1822, a poetic irony not lost on the pre-Raphaelite writer William Rossetti, who observed, 'And now a watery doom effaces the scenes of their short-lived lives, Nantgwilt and Cwm Elan. A world of waters, a world of death.'

*

A roadside sign announced the Powys/Ceredigion border. From here on, it was all downhill to the coast, more or less. Eventually, after I had been walking for some time, a second car drove past, its passengers waving at the novelty of a pedestrian on this scenic road to nowhere. But it came as a surprise to see anyone – the road seemed like an intruder in the landscape, an afterthought in an austere expanse of treeless moorland.

I passed a grave in a field next to the roadside – little more than a carved wooden cross stuck into a pile of rocks. Whether the marker belonged to the victim of a car accident or a local faithful to this landscape was unclear, although a road accident seemed improbable given the sparseness of traffic. Further on I came to an isolated farm that seemed to be deserted despite looking well maintained. No cars were parked in its yard, no tractors; no signs of life. Was it a property investment project, a holiday home for someone with a taste for austere landscapes?

The farm was an outlier of the loose sprawl of habitation that was Cwmystwyth, once the epicentre for mining in the valley. Further down the road stood a large fenced-off area that held the skeletal ruins of mine buildings alongside large heaps of shale. Long abandoned and unloved – perhaps never loved – the stark slate structures gave the impression they were dissolving back into the shattered rock of the valley. The sudden unexpected scream of RAF jets flying low overhead completed the impression of a doomed post-apocalyptic landscape.

Entry to the site was discouraged, but an information board provided background on what it referred to as the Central Wales Orefield. Each of the significant ores mined here – galena (for lead), sphalerite (for zinc), chalcopyrite (for copper) – were illustrated and described in detail in English and Welsh. Amid the low cairns of grey slate stood the remains of buildings – now roofless and with broken walls – that would once have provided lodging for the mine workers. Seen from afar, with no awareness of location or even continent, the buildings might have been those of a ruined caravanserai or a desert palace abandoned to the sands of time. Close-up, any such romance quickly evaporated. The bleakness of long days spent toiling in such a hazardous and hostile environment, and cold nights passed in a cheerless dormitory, was all too tangible. And a bleak life it was: as a result of the inevitable lead poisoning that blighted the health of those who worked here, the average life expectancy of Cwmystwyth mine workers in the 18th and 19th century was reputed to be just thirty-two years.

Across the road, a short length of rail track led directly to the river. Water from the Ystwyth was used for washing the mined ore and the degree of pollution was once perilously high. Now the river has largely recovered from centuries of abuse, although recent analysis suggests that continuing seepage was still contributing to high levels of toxic metals in the water.

Cwmystwyth, its ruined mines now designated a scheduled ancient monument, had long been settled by those who coveted the mineral wealth entrapped in the valley's rock strata. The oldest gold artifact ever found in Wales, the Banc Tynndol sun disc, an early Bronze Age object of great beauty, was unearthed in the vicinity in 1992. Romans, too, had mined here for lead. But precious metals and minerals aside, Cwmystwyth was also significant for its geographical location, standing close to what was estimated to be the dead centre of Wales. If this truly is the very heart of Wales, its Celtic centre of gravity, then what better to symbolise the archetypical Welsh spirit than ancient gold, tough miners and the greenest of valleys?

The valley narrowed beyond the mine workings and the scenery began to brighten immediately, its mineral harshness softened by an increasing number of trees. The repeated call of a cuckoo rang out from across the river. I had heard one calling earlier when I crossed over the ridge from Llangurig and now, with another distant call beckoning from further along the valley ahead, this seemed to be an area where cuckoos held contiguous territories, each calling bird marking out its own piratical domain. It was good to know that the birds were thriving here – those haunts where I had been accustomed to hearing them back in Norfolk have fallen silent in recent years. A once familiar sound of summer, like turtle doves also used to be, cuckoos, particularly English ones, look as if they are becoming yet another casualty of climate change and the questionable practices of industrialised agriculture.

Increasingly footsore, I walked on wearily with a steady but lopsided rhythm to my gait – *cuck-oo*, step, step, limp, *cuck-oo*, step, step, limp. Hobbling up to an old stone bridge at Pentre Farm, I crossed the river to follow the signposted Borth to Devil's Bridge to Pontryhydfendigaid Trail.

The trail climbed a little way up the southern side of the valley to skirt lush woodland before taking to farm tracks parallel to the river. The slate-grey gloominess of the valley had lifted by now, and the path followed the contour line through strikingly verdant countryside – alluring terrain that I might have enjoyed more had I not been so tired and sore-footed.

I arrived at a minor road close to the village of Pont-rhyd-y-groes ('The Bridge of the Cross'), where a bridge led over the Ystwyth. George Borrow had crossed this same bridge whilst chronicling *Wild Wales* a century and a half earlier. It had been here that he met with an unfriendly group of locals who mocked his accented Welsh ('A man from the north country, hee, hee.'), and were no more welcoming when he spoke English to them ('Go back, David, to your goats on Anglesey, you are not wanted here.'). But there was no party to greet me, friendly or otherwise, at the bridge, only the dancing water of the Afon Ystwyth gushing seaward beneath its weathered stone arches.

I spent the night at the Miners' Arms pub, an establishment where miners were no longer the main clientele. Jen, the proprietor, was welcoming, and after I had showered and changed she opened up the bar and offered me the menu. I ate microwaved pie with chips and peas for the third night running, and sipped a pint while Jen leaned on the bar, chatting to me with one eye on *EastEnders* on the massive wall-mounted TV screen. Jen came from Hay-on-Wye in the Marches, while her husband, who was away on business, hailed from Wolverhampton. She told me they had originally been looking for a B&B to manage on the coast but the offer of this pub had come up and so they took it. They had also toyed with moving to Rhyl in North Wales but the town, Jen asserted, was not what it once was. 'Social cleansing' (Jen's words) from neighbouring Llandudno had ensured that many of that town's less desirable council tenants had been moved out to slack-trade seafront B&Bs in Rhyl. Llandudno, it would appear, was hot on social responsibility and civic pride.

'If your house needs a tidy-up and a paint job then the council will let you know in no uncertain terms. If you're a council tenant and your place is not up to scratch, they'll just move you out.'

Rhyl was less choosy. It sounded similar to the Great Yarmouth story in many ways: now that some of the more traditional British holiday resorts have gone into decline thanks to cheap package holidays abroad, properties that would once have accommodated holidaying families are now deployed in a new role as make-do social housing.

*

Next morning I left the village by way of a small industrial estate. Still in situ was a large water wheel that had once driven machinery for the village's former mine. The Lisburne Mine took its name from the earls of Lisburne, the Vaughan family who once owned the lead, silver, zinc and copper mines at Pont-rhyd-y-groes. Like the mines at Cwmystwyth, it was an enterprise that embodied incalculable human suffering and ecological harm. An interpretative board next to the wheel related accounts of the terrible conditions that the mine workers had to put up with – *Sometimes they will spit quite black for days after coming from the mine* – and spoke of the environmental damaged wreaked by their toxic leakage: *Lord Lisburne's mines have destroyed the fish as far as the sea.*

I walked out of the village beside beech woods close to the river's south bank. An occasional lumber lorry rattled past on the road. Wayside bluebells scented the damp morning air. The overcast weather of the previous day had now transformed into a light drizzle, which paradoxically seemed to make everything look brighter, the fresh green leaves of the trees glowing almost preternaturally.

Crossing a bridge over to the Ystwyth's north bank, I came upon another disused mine where the workings had been cleaned up to create a nature reserve. As if on cue, a curlew flew low along the water. The river is wide now, but also shallow, its course punctuated by numerous gravel islands that gleamed with mustard yellow gorse. Further along the riverside path stood a scattering of more ruined mine buildings, each with slender branches of blackthorn erupting from tenuous holds in the mortar. With little more than walls of angular grey shale left standing, they put me in mind of rectangular huts I had seen at Machu Picchu in Peru, as if Inca stonework had somehow been mysteriously transported to West Wales. Further along was a roofless cottage with just gable walls and the remains of a fireplace emerging from its overgrown foundations.

A shady forest track led me away from the river towards Llanafan. Black slugs, as large and as wrinkled as prunes, crossed the track in front of me as they pursued some primitive gastropod urge to explore pastures new. Hidden away in the trees, a great spotted woodpecker drummed. Then, from somewhere deep in the woods below, the strains of a saw mill filtered eerily through the pines. The sound was strangely musical: a metallic whine that resembled electric violins playing variations around a drone – something that might almost be a lost recording of John Cale at his most experimental. Serendipitous harmonics supplied high-pitched counterpoint, and the periodic crash of a sawed-through trunk falling onto a metal base added a percussive element. Further melodic detail was provided by birdsong in the trees – the local blackbirds seemed quite at home with this strange aural backdrop and piped defiantly above it in the same way that songbirds close to a busy road always seem to rise to the challenge and sing louder. I wondered: if a tree falling in a forest requires ears, human or otherwise, to register the noise it makes, does it take human ears to detect music – melody, harmony, rhythm – in any random source of sound?

Llanafan turned out to be little more than a crossroads: a tight cluster of church, village hall and cottages. Next to St Afan's, in a graveyard sprinkled with dandelions and bluebells, were tombstones embossed with unequivocally Welsh names like Evan Evans.

Leaving Llanafan, I was obliged to follow the murderously busy B4340 Aberystwyth road for a while. Lorries and white vans thundered past too close for comfort as I hugged the road edge and periodically mounted the narrow verge to keep out of their way. It came as a relief to reach Trawsgoed, where a bridge crossed back over the river and I joined the route of the Ystwyth Trail, a walking and cycle path that traced the track-bed of the former Great Western Railway route for most of the way between Tregaron and Aberystwyth.

The final miles into Aberystwyth were a soothing amble through dappled green light – the track partially shaded by the overhanging branches of limes and oaks, the gravelly river close enough to be an audible murmur through the trees. At the village of Llanilar, a raised brick bank ghosted where a railway platform once stood, its passengers now long replaced by silver birches. Station Wood, the surrounding patch of greenery that had grown up since the line had been abandoned, was a hat-tilt to the memory of what had once stood here. An EU-sponsored metal plaque with a Welsh poem and English translation paid tribute to the Ystwyth Valley's mining tradition and to the port that would develop downriver at Aberystwyth as a result.

*

The closer to the coast I got, the greener it became. Or so it seemed. The all-encompassing verdancy and Welshness of it all made me think of the cover of the Tom Jones LP my mother had once prized, one of just a handful to go in the record rack besides *South Pacific* and Matt Munro: *Green, Green Grass of Home*, its title track an early hit for Jones the Voice. The cover depicted the singer bundled in an overcoat gazing wistfully over a South Wales valley – tough mining country but also soothingly emerald green, not so very different scenically or culturally from this place; the song, a mawkish Country and Western number about a condemned prisoner dreaming of his birthplace, who on waking remembers that he will only be going home in a coffin. It was a song that adapted readily to a more general Welsh sense of *hiraeth*.

Hiraeth: that singularly Welsh word that speaks of homesickness, yearning, spiritual sickness; a mourning for that which is lost, perhaps even lost youth. Do the Welsh, the Celtic peoples in general, have a monopoly on the free expression of such hard-to-define emotions? Probably not, but they have the language for it and a sympathetic poetic tradition. *Hiraeth* belongs to the lexicon of exile and banishment rather than that of victory and colonisation; the spiritual hurt felt by the land-grabbed not the grabber. It signifies genetic nostalgia, an intangible sense of loss, a longing for 'home' in the deepest sense of the word; a longing for the place where you feel that you most belong, where you will always return to; the place that you think of when times are hard and the outlook is bleak.

I am not quite comfortable with the term 'home' myself. Certainly, I am 'at home' in Norwich; that is, after all, where I live although I could never quite identify it as 'home' in any sense of geographical belonging. I still feel an outsider in some ways, even after decades of living there. I do not really feel that the Midlands are any sort of proper home for me now either, although that is where I came from. It is quite possible that I have unwittingly nurtured my outsider status, not as artifice but as a means of seeing the world at large as the place I belong to. Years of foreign travel have enabled me to feel 'at home' in all sorts of odd places. I am at home in the world; it is the smaller places that I sometimes have trouble with.

The Czech geologist and writer Václav Cílek, in an essay entitled *Bees of the Invisible: Awakening of a Place*, has developed something that he calls 'The Rule of Home'. In this he states:

> *A person is at home in a landscape, some people can encompass two or three landscapes but no more. A small landmark of where we feel at home is more important than a more significant landmark or a different landscape. But despite that, we*

need to travel abroad – for comparison, for the recognition of the smallness of home, and the realisation of where we belong.

This rings true. I have long recognised 'the smallness of home', although the belonging part is sometimes problematic. Even more apposite in this respect is another of Cílek's 'rules', 'The Rule of Resonance', which declares, 'A smaller place with which we resonate is more important than a great pilgrimage, where one is only a visitor.' Modern pilgrimage has many facets, and we are all in search of something, but somewhere familiar that holds personal resonance, surely this is what we all desire?

If *hiraeth* was a yearning linked with sense of place, then another Welsh word, *cynefin*, best describes that place which is yearned for. Untranslatable with any meaningful accuracy, *cynefin* corresponds roughly to the notion of habitat or an individual's homeland. The word's origins were agricultural and connected with the territories of sheep pasture but in modern Welsh parlance it refers to places where deep memory resides, places of resonance where to return to is always a joy and a homecoming. A personal heartland, a spiritual and poetic connection with place, it is somewhere that engenders a strong sense of *hiraeth* if one is forcibly exiled from it. It is home in the broadest sense, but it is more than this. *Cynefin*, for most of us, means less a specific location but more a time-hazed place in the memory where youth and locality coexist. This is one place that we can never return to.

Perhaps it is not so much about home and roots but, rather, home and *routes*? Those routes we put down around the places where we live, work, love and grow old. The desire paths we forge when we step out from our homes. These, to me, seem to have as much – perhaps more – significance than the place itself. Routes, not roots – the regular trails we tread in our everyday lives as we make our own inconsequential but familiar journeys on foot.

These personal routes – desire paths in the broadest sense: the country lanes around my greenbelt childhood home; the roads and alleyways around my old school and the town centre of my youth; the short journey to a friend's house; the lanes and woodland rides of the Norfolk countryside, the coastal paths of East Anglia; almost all the streets of central Norwich; the dirt paths that crisscross my allotment; familiar walks alongside water, around lakes and broads, next to rivers. There are even foreign cities that have exerted a grip on me for a while and whose streets I know better than my own capital, where I always feel like a tourist – places where I will forever be an outsider but which I feel sufficiently comfortable with to have some sense of being at home. And then there are the forgotten routes, like those lost from memory in Coventry. These paths are *my* routes. For Australia's indigenous people, a familiar walk is a memory-cache; a walkabout is a re-engagement with the land to make its acquaintance anew. Is this not the same for everyone in some way, even those – perhaps especially those – who are alienated by life in a city? Home is the stepping-off point: the walk to work, to the pub, to the shops, to a loved one's house; the routine drive to the station or airport. Home is the place to unpack the groceries, to feather the nest. Home is fluid; new paths can always be forged, given time and the will to do so. But the deepest paths are the oldest: those of youth, with its attendant promise and optimism – it is these that we long for the most.

To walk from my house in Norwich to the local supermarket it is necessary to walk up the street to a junction, turn left and then right to circumvent a small area of grass before crossing a larger road into the supermarket car park. I, like many others, often used to take a short cut across the grass and, as a consequence, a visible path soon became etched into it – a 'desire path', an unofficial route created democratically by collective footfall. This remained in place for years before a woodchip path was superimposed upon it to afford it some degree of recognised status. Later on, the path was paved and a bench and a litterbin erected halfway along it. It had been officially sanctioned; what had once been a desire path, a shortcut for lazy feet, was now part of the authorised landscape, a fixture on the map. This, I thought, was similar to what becomes of those cherished paths we create on our customary walks through life – those routes scored by relentless and regular footfall eventually become part of the personal map of deep topography that we all carry internally.

*

Aberystwyth announced its proximity with the sight of a steep hill that had what appeared to be a tall chimney perched on top of it. The hill was Pen Dinas; the towering monument on top – built to resemble an upended canon rather than a chimney – is a memorial to the Duke of Wellington erected in the 1850s. Built by public subscription, local rumour suggested that the plan had originally been to place an equestrian statue of Wellington on top of the column but the project had run out of money, or enthusiasm, or both. Close to the coast now, here is a parallel to the Britannia Monument whose staircase I had ascended before setting out on the other side of the country in Great Yarmouth. Two long-revered British heroes: Nelson overlooking the North Sea; Wellington (in spirit, at least), the Irish. Like the Britannia Monument, the memorial gazes over both coast and a confluence of rivers. As with its Yarmouth counterpart, it was a monument erected in Victorian times to celebrate British military endeavour. More than a century and a half later, it continues to pay tribute to our colonial past by association with one of a pick 'n' mix band of approved national heroes: Wellington, Nelson, Churchill – the familiar tropes of the lamented age of Empire.

The hill itself, located on a spur between the Rheidol and Ystwyth rivers and overlooking Cardigan Bay, long served as a strategic defensive location and a Celtic Iron Age fort once topped its summit. Like the upper Ystwyth valley, with its continuum of active mine working, history runs deep and multi-layered here: a continuity of settlement that spans millennia – the valley's cultural capital is as rich as its ore deposits.

Although Cardigan Bay was not so very far ahead, the sea refused to reveal itself until the very last minute. There had been clues, though. As impatient backseat children driving to Wales with our parents, my sister and I had always anticipated the arrival at the coast. It was a fun game to be first to catch a glimpse of the sea in the distance, but there was more to it than that. There was also the frisson of excitement that came from entering a world so tangibly different from the landlocked Midlands. Unwittingly, we learned to identify the signs that heralded the arrival of the coast – a subtle alteration of light, a perceptible sparkle in the blue of the sky, the gentlest whiff of iodine on the breeze, the tangible presence of a threshold to be crossed.

Almost abruptly, the path became busier – runners and dog-walkers, grandparents patiently shepherding children that wobbled on scooters. Sight unseen, I had fallen into Aberystwyth's orbit. A glimpse of silhouetted figures walking the sea wall next to Tanybwlch Beach ahead in the distance confirmed this. Despite the proximity of the sea, the Ystwyth refused to play the estuary game and merely wound around the base of Pen Dinas before merging with the waters of the Rheidol in Aberystwyth harbour. Two very different rivers: the Ystwyth with its bare slate, mines and ghosts of industry; the Rheidol with its forestry, tourism and Devil's Bridge railway line. The combined Ystwyth-Rheidol that I saw flowing out of the harbour into the Irish Sea was no more than a few metres long; confluence and river mouth separated by no more than the throw of a pebble.

Chapter 21

Land of the West

Aberystwyth, Ceredigion

The estuaries of rivers appeal strongly to an adventurous imagination.
Joseph Conrad, *The Mirror of the Sea*

Traveller, there is no road; only a ship's wake on the sea.
Antonio Machado

There is a widespread belief held in many cultures that the west, the land of the sunset, is also the land of the dead. The old Celtic tribes considered Galicia in the far northwest of Spain to be the place where souls gathered to follow the sun across the sea. Those unworthy of making the journey remained on the land, haunting the paths and byways that connected the villages. Similarly, ancient Egyptians believed the east bank of the Nile to be the land of the living, and the west, the land of the dead. It was not by chance that it was the west bank of that river that was chosen to construct the remarkable funerary monuments of the Giza Pyramids and the Valley of Kings near Luxor. The belief was that, once over the horizon, as the living world slept in darkness, the sun illuminated and warmed the realm of those who had died. Sunsets, anywhere and at anytime, are a reminder that some ancient beliefs still hold sway in the modern world. To watch the sun set was always to rehearse for a death that was inevitable. On this journey, Aberystwyth was my own land of the sunset. At least death was delayed a little while here: five degrees west of Norwich, England's most easterly city, sunset took place an average of twenty-two minutes later here on the Welsh coast.

In the Celtic tradition, the last corporal journey of the deceased would be along the coffin road that connected the place of their death with that of their birthplace. Such roads were not uncommon in Wales, the north of England and especially, Scotland, where many clans had a mother church and favoured burial site, although they were also located in rocky terrain where graves could not so easily be dug. Perhaps we should all try to walk our own personal coffin road in later life? Such an experience is wasted on corpses.

*

Aberystwyth harbour is tucked away from the rest of the town as if it is some sort of guilty secret. But even from this low vantage point, I could make out the town landmarks poking above the roofline to the north: the castle, the brownstone buildings of the university, the winged war memorial. The tide was out and a line of small fishing boats leaned against the harbour wall, their keels sunk into the mud. Down at the shoreline, a group of women were donning life jackets in preparation for a boat trip. A few solitary figures were promenading along the sea wall, strolling out to the harbour mouth to take in the view before ambling back.

I left the harbour to cross the Trefechan Bridge and climb up to the castle mound from where the town stretches out below – a pattern of rooftops, slate and terracotta. Below the mound stands the brownstone turreted buildings of Old College, and beyond this a long terrace of fine Victorian guesthouses, tastefully rendered in pastel shades, that curve around a beachside promenade pinched by a pier and the rocky bluff of Constitution Hill to the north. The modest, supple river that gave the town its name was already lost from view.

Lacking any estuary to speak of, Aberystwyth is no mirror image, but there are some parallels with Great Yarmouth, the port-resort I had set out from. Both towns possess a beach, a pier, a promenade and a parade of boarding houses, but even from a perfunctory inspection Aberystwyth looked to be distinctly more prosperous. In Yarmouth, the glory days of fishing, holidays and North Sea Oil are now a faded memory, but in the ancient market town of Aberystwyth, the sea has always only been of secondary importance. With a well-established university that could claim an, admittedly brief, royal patronage, the town has developed and maintained a role as Welsh language cultural centre in recent years, and the pier here seems to be more afterthought and ornament than a totem of better times.

Although fishing and seafaring were never a major concern, Aberystwyth did come into its own as a resort ('the Biarritz of Wales') in the mid-Victorian era when the arrival of the railway encouraged a tourism boom. Prior to this, Aberystwyth had been an important commercial centre for the farming and sheep-raising country that was central Wales. A drovers' bank, Banc-y-Ddafad, was established in the town in 1762 and had issued its own bank notes until the end of the 19th century. The notes were coded for illiterate drovers: a single sheep to represent a one pound note, two sheep for two pounds and five for five; the ten-shilling note had a black lamb. The pictorial connection of sheep = wealth = currency was an obvious one to anyone who laboured to despatch the animals to market.

With a generous endowment of Victorian elegance along its seafront, Aberystwyth might be said to resemble Cromer, another Norfolk seaside resort, more than it does Yarmouth, but there is another tenuous connection with the Norfolk littoral. Beneath the waves and offshore wind farms at Yarmouth is Doggerland, the former land-bridge that once connected Britain to the Eurasian landmass. Here off the coast of Aberystwyth, lost beneath the waves of Cardigan Bay, is Cantre'r Gwaelod, or The Lowland Hundred. It is a drowned tract of land that some believe to have once been a legendary sunken kingdom. Unlike Doggerland, which is a topographic certainty, there is limited physical evidence to prove the existence of this 'Welsh Atlantis' other than the traces of submerged forests and petrified tree stumps that have been discovered in the mouth of the Borth estuary, a little way to the north. More recently, the discovery of large areas of peat with post holes, fossilised animal and human footprints and the Mesolithic remains of wattled walkways has reinforced the theory that an occupied offshore territory once stood here. To support this conjecture, the existing evidence of changing sea levels before the retreat of the glaciers that heralded the current Holocene period suggests that the island of Ireland was connected to the main British landmass (and, at that time, the rest of Europe) around 16,000BC.

The mythology is less hesitant. Tales of Cantre'r Gwaelod feature strongly in Welsh song and poetry. In legend, Cantre'r Gwaelod occupied a large fertile tract of land that extended twenty miles west of the current coastline between Bardsey Island and Cardigan. In the 13th-century *Black Book of Carmarthen*, the land, known here as Maes Gwyddno, was said to be lost to floods because of an overflowing well neglected by a fairy princess. Later 17th-century legends, which described it as a low-lying territory protected from the sea by a dyke, claimed that at sometime around the 6th century, as a result of drunken negligence, the water gates were left open one stormy night, resulting in the land flooding and over sixteen villages being submerged. The legend of floodgates being left open is a universal one found in many cultures. The moral twist of the story is familiar, too: sunken lost cities destroyed because of the careless or wicked ways of their inhabitants – Noah's Flood, the destruction of Sodom and Gomorrah, and latterly, environmental disaster that is down to hubris – manmade climate change and fundamentalist denial in the face of glaring scientific evidence. The voices still cry out loud and clear; the same unwavering voices continue to be ignored.

*

I checked into my B&B and went out in search of more plasters for my blisters. After patching up my feet as best I could, I tottered out in search of food and ended up in a deserted Indian restaurant next door to the railway station. The newly recruited waiter started to lay four places at my table until a quiet word from the manager let him know that I was dining alone. It was a mistake that amplified the discomfort I often feel when eating out on my own – always the worst part of the day for the self-conscious lone traveller. As I ate my *bhuna*, the saccharine high-register saxophone of Kenny G serenaded me from the speaker system, the blandness of which – the *muzak*, not the food – made me feel as if I were in a lift or on an airplane waiting for take-off. I felt no inclination to linger.

After a deep, exhausted sleep in my cramped single room I ventured out for a stroll around the seafront next morning. My recollection of Aberystwyth was hazy: a small town of narrow streets that twisted inland from the seafront, it was somewhere that I thought I knew better than I did until I realised that the last time I had visited the place I was only eighteen years old. I had been touring Wales with three school friends, one of whom had recently passed his driving test and bought a clapped-out Mini. It must have been a Sunday when we arrived here as all the pubs were closed – Aberystwyth was a dry, chapel-going town in those days. We managed to find a working men's club where we were cheerily signed in by a couple of members on the door. Stairs led up to a large, boozy hall – a loud, echoing microcosm of good cheer. With beery Welsh voices lifted in convivial conversation all around us, the atmosphere was far removed from anything that resembled a dour Methodist Sunday. We stayed for hours, enjoying our temporary status as Welsh working men, and even more the cheap drinks and cheerful ambiance that this cosy haven offered. I could not recall where we slept that night but can only imagine that it was spent slumped, cramped and uncomfortable, in the Mini, parked up on the seafront somewhere.

The seafront still seemed vaguely familiar but my memory was of weather that was grey and drizzly, of somewhere that had the dispiriting atmosphere of a British seaside resort seen through rain-spattered glasses. Today, after all these years, it was sunny.

The voices on the street were an amalgam of *Cymraeg* and lilting, Welsh-accented English peppered with occasional Brummie grace notes – the resorts of Cardigan Bay are popular with retirees from the Midlands. The streets of the town centre were busy enough but down at the seafront it was almost deserted. The Royal Pier (had Prince Charles in his student days ever taken a break from Welsh language study to play the slots here?) was still closed for business, its facilities – Amusements (*Fully Airconditioned*), Pier Pressure (*Best in Category – Club 2009, Overall Winner 2011, 2012*), Delish Doughnuts – untroubled by punters at this early hour.

Just along from the pier, a dark-haired young woman was sat on one of the seafront benches staring out to sea. She remained motionless, lost in thought for a while before she stood up to go and join a tough-looking man who was loading something into the boot of a car. The two of them looked as if they were about to make a long journey somewhere. The young woman appeared wistful but fully resigned to whatever it was she had to do. Had things perhaps not worked out as planned? Had she been thinking about another sea, another home? Sometimes it can be hard to read a face. Was it regret or longing that troubled her, or a hankering for an old country, a sense of *hiraeth*? Was she going home? Had she been 'at home' here in Aberystwyth?

To stare out to sea is always a reminder of that which is lost. Despite the 'nothing to see here' frivolity of the waves, the vast heaving skin of grey water puts us in mind of losses and absences. We grow accustomed to absences – it is, perhaps, the definitive modern condition – but some are so personal and deeply rooted that we convince ourselves that they no longer matter. For my part, I still ache from absences that are decades old. To focus too much on that which is lost is to engender a melancholia that is hard to shift. What is incontrovertible is that the more we learn, the more we realise how much is missing. Absences of friends, of family, of nature; of geography lost from the map, lost from daily life. Unchartered history: lost territory, lost villages, lost species, lost causes; lost faith; the ever-approaching spectre of extinction.

I climbed down the steps to the shore and, retrieving the pebble I had carried with me from the Norfolk coast, placed it among the others on the beach. An alien rock on a foreign shore; a case of fraudulent geology, of human-powered western drift, it may have been an interloper but it was clearly in good company. Turning my gaze away and then turning back again, I could no longer identify the stone secreted among the others.

I took a last look out to sea, Dylan Thomas's same 'sloeblack, slow black, crowblack, fishingboat bobbing' Irish Sea. West, across to where Ireland lay beyond the horizon and the ghosts of Cantre'r Gwaelod swam beneath the waves. In my mind I traced the route of how I had arrived here: a slow progression along rivers and valleys, across countless fields, through grain and stubble, along canal towpaths and bridleways, city streets and farm tracks. It was an unfolding map upon which was marked my own desire path across Norfolk and the Fens, alongside the ghosted valley of Rutland Water and through the rolling cattle country of the East Midlands before the canals and city streets of the West Midlands led me into pastoral, evergreen Shropshire. Then... the dark hills of the Welsh Marches; finally, Wales itself – Celtic, emerald green, a surfeit of *hiraeth*. It was a line made by walking: a trajectory framed by tramlines of longitude that meandered between fifty-two and fifty-three degrees north, a wavering line drawn between two rivers. Two rivers, two estuaries – Yare and Ystwyth, my own Tigris and Euphrates – framed by the land, my personal Babylon, which lies between: a stage-set for a life.

Given what had led me here, the voluptuous concavity of the coast that I surveyed would have been all too easy to fall in love with. There was a resonance, a sense of harmony, a promising union of landscapes. The gentle sweep of Cardigan Bay, curving out to sea to the north and south, would accommodate the swell of the east Norfolk coast that bulges gibbous into the North Sea: a moon to its sun, a topographic coming together. Did the lapping waves sound any different here than there?

It was time to leave, time to collect my bag from the guest-house and make my way to the station to catch the Birmingham train. Seven hours later I would be walking through the door of my house on the other side of this odd, occasionally bewildering island. Coast to coast, sea to sea; against the grain as ever: I was going home.

Select Bibliography and Sources

Aldersey-Williams, Hugh, *The Adventures of Sir Thomas Browne in the 21st Century*, Granta, 2015

Ayers, Brian, *Norwich: Archaeology of a Fine City*, Amberley, 2009

Ballard, J.G., *Concrete Island*, Fourth Estate, 2011

Benjamin, Walter, *Illuminations*, Pimlico, 1999

Berry, Liz, *Black Country*, Chatto & Windus, 2014

Berry, Wendell, *The Peace of Wild Things*, Penguin, 2018

Blackburn, Julia, *Time Song: Searching for Doggerland*, Jonathan Cape, 2019

Borrow, George, *Wild Wales*, Collins, 1972 (first published 1862)

Cílek, Václav, *To Breathe with Birds: A Book of Landscapes*, University of Pennsylvania Press, 2015

Clare, John, *Major Works*, Oxford University Press, 2008

Cocker, Mark, *Crow Country*, Vintage, 2008

Conrad, Joseph, *The Rover*, J.M. Dent & Sons, 1950 (first published 1923)

Coverly, Merlin, *The Art of Wandering*, Oldcastle Books, 2012

Defoe, Daniel, *Tour through the Eastern Counties of England*, East Anglia Magazine, 1984 (first published 1722)

Dickens, Charles, *David Copperfield*, Penguin Classics, 2004 (first published 1849)

Dutt, William A., *Highways and Byways in East Anglia*, Macmillan & Co, 1923

Ellis, E.A., *The Broads*, Collins, 1965

Farley, Paul, and Roberts, Michael Symmons, *Edgelands*, Vintage, 2012

Fisher, Mark, *Ghosts of My Life*, Zero Books, 2014

Fisher, Roy, *The Long and the Short of It*, Bloodaxe, 2012

Griffiths, Niall, *Sheepshagger*, Vintage, *2002*

Hamilton, Craig, Bounds, Jon, Hickman, Jon et al, *101 Things Birmingham Gave the World*, Paradise Circus, 2014

Hanley, Lynsey, *Estates: An Intimate History*, Granta, 2007

Herzog, Werner, *Of Walking in Ice*, Vintage, 2014

Hill, Geoffrey, *Selected Poems*, Penguin, 2006
Hollis, Matthew, *Now All Roads Lead to France*, Faber & Faber, 2011
Hoskins, W.G., *The Making of the English Landscape*, Penguin, 1985
Housman, A.E., *A Shropshire Lad and Other Poems*, Penguin Classics, 2010
Kingsnorth, Paul, *The Wake*, Unbound, 2015
Lopez, Barry, *Arctic Dreams*, Macmillan, 1986
Mabey, Richard, *Nature Cure*, Chatto & Windus, 2005
Mabey, Richard, *The Unofficial Countryside*, Little Toller, 2010
Macfarlane, Robert, *The Old Ways*, Hamish Hamilton, 2012
McCarthy, Michael, *The Moth Snowstorm*, John Murray, 2016
Meades, Jonathan, *Museum without Walls*, Unbound, 2013
Mee, Arthur, *The King's England: Leicestershire and Rutland*, Hodder & Stoughton, 1966
Mee, Arthur, *The King's England: Warwickshire*, Hodder & Stoughton, 1966
Mitchell, Laurence, *Slow Travel Norfolk*, Bradt, 2018
Moore, Alan, *Jerusalem*, Knockabout, 2016
Moran, Joe, *On Roads: a Hidden History*, Profile Books, 2009
Morton, H.V., *In Search of England*, Methuen, 2000 (first published 1927)
Parker, Mike, *Real Powys*, Seren, 2011
Pevsner, Nikolaus, *North-East Norfolk and Norwich*, Penguin, 1962
Pevsner, Nikolaus, *North-West and South Norfolk*, Penguin, 1962
Orwell, George, *The Road to Wigan Pier*, Penguin, 2001 (first published 1937)
Oosthuizen, Susan, *The Anglo-Saxon Fenland*, Windgather Press, 2017
Rackham, Oliver, *The History of the Countryside*, J.M. Dent & Sons, 1987
Rose, E.M., *The Murder of William of Norwich: The Origins of the Blood Libel in Medieval Europe*, Oxford University Press, 2017
Sebald. W.G., *The Rings of Saturn*, The Harvill Press, 1998
Seymour, John, *The Companion Guide to East Anglia*, Collins, 1970

Sinclair, Iain, *Edge of the Orison*, Hamish Hamilton, 2005
Skelton, Richard, *Landings*, Corbel Stone Press, 2015
Solnit, Rebecca, *A Field Guide To Getting Lost*, Canongate, 2006
Solnit, Rebecca, *Wanderlust: A History of Walking*, Verso, 2001
Thomas, Dylan, *Under Milk Wood*, W&N, 2014 (first broadcast 1954)
Thomas, Edward, *The South Country*, Little Toller, 2009, (first published 1909)
Thomas, R.S., *Selected Poems*, Everyman's Poetry, 1996
Tolkien, J.R.R., *The Lord of the Rings*, Allen & Unwin, 1968
Toulson, Shirley and Godwin, Fay, *The Drovers' Roads of Wales*, Wildwood House, 1977

Other sources

Chapter 2

...a sediment layer on the beach...exposed fossilised hominid footprints
https://www.theguardian.com/science/2014/feb/07/oldest-human-footprints-happisburgh-norfolk

Chapter 4

Queen Kapi'olani, who was touring England...
https://www.edp24.co.uk/news/hawaiian-queen-s-1887-whistlestop-tour-around-norfolk-recreated-by-professor-1-4556441

...the site of Arminghall woodhenge, another timepiece of sorts...
http://www.heritage.norfolk.gov.uk/record-details?MNF6100-Arminghall-Henge

...the domain of Black Anna, aka Antoinette Hannant...
https://norfolkwomeninhistory.com/1900-1950/antoinette-hannent-black-anna/

'From Barford Bridge I danced into Norwich...'
The full text of *Kemps Nine Daies Wonder: Performed in a Daunce from London to Norwich* (1660) is available online at:

http://www.gutenberg.org/files/21984/21984-h/21984-h.htm

...the entire text of Thomas More's Utopia...
https://www.culture24.org.uk/places-to-go/east-of-england/norwich/art38387

Chapter 5

...'faerie fayre' reincarnation of the well-attended Barsham Fayres...
http://fairsarchive.org/the-fairs

...a handful of DMVs (deserted medieval villages)...
For further suggestions on the causes of desertion *see:*

http://www.literarynorfolk.co.uk/Norfolk%20Deserted%20Villages/Causes%20of%20Desertion.html

Chapter 6

The Goob (2015) Director: Guy Muyhill
For interview with Liam Walpole, the film's star, *see*

https://www.theguardian.com/film/2015/may/28/the-goob-liam-walpole-norfolk-noir

Chapter 7

...Martin had lived as an isolated bachelor in a rundown farmhouse...
https://www.theguardian.com/uk/2000/apr/20/tonymartin.ukcrime2

Chapter 9

'One of the most impressive ancient sites in the region.'
https://peterboroughharchaeology.org/borough-fen-iron-age-fort/

Chapter 10

...a dedicated website that monitors sightings of little owls in England...
http://littleowlproject.uk

Chapter 12

...according to Danny Dorling Professor of Geography...
http://news.bbc.co.uk/1/hi/england/7724573.stm

... the territory of the Danelaw...
https://www.historic-uk.com/HistoryUK/HistoryofEngland/

The-Five-Boroughs-Of-Danelaw/

Energy in Northampton, a big production pop ditty by Linda Jardim... https://www.youtube.com/watch?v=CpRRPU3rrPo

...the Tile Hill painter George Shaw... https://www.theguardian.com/artanddesign/gallery/2011/feb/13/art-george-shaw-in-pictures

Chapter 13

...even given the subterranean presence of 2½ million remaindered Mills & Boon novels...
http://news.bbc.co.uk/1/hi/england/west_midlands/3330245.stm

... one Coleshill resident reported seeing twenty soldiers walking waist-deep...
https://www.theguardian.com/uk/2006/oct/31/britishidentity.martinwainwright

Chapter 14

...the expiry of a century-long curse...
https://www.birminghammail.co.uk/sport/football/football-news/birmingham-citys-gypsy-curse-st-11926781

Telly Savalas Looks at Birmingham: 1981 promotional film by Harold Baim https://www.youtube.com/watch?v=GxZ1xn2ml10

Jonathan Meades: Birmingham on YouTube
https://www.youtube.com/watch?v=esM41oWNW6Y

Chapter 15

...Tolkien and Birmingham are inextricably linked.
For more on Tolkien's Birmingham connections *see* https://www.birmingham.gov.uk/info/50166/j_r_r_tolkien/1589/tolkien_videos

Oldbury is a town of uncertain geography...
http://www.historyofoldbury.co.uk/2story.htm

Chapter 19

The Kerry Ridgeway that leads fifteen miles from...
http://www.shropshiresgreatoutdoors.co.uk/route/kerry-ridgeway-2/

the artist Hamish Fulton, whose work is entirely based on his experience of walks...
http://www.hamish-fulton.com/

There was also Richard Long...
http://www.richardlong.org/

...the town was also a focus for Chartist riots in 1839...
http://history.powys.org.uk/history/llani/chart1.html

Chapter 20

The Elan Valley dams were constructed...
https://www.elanvalley.org.uk/discover/reservoirs-dams/building-dams

The young poet came to stay here in 1811...
http://history.powys.org.uk/history/rhayader/shelley1.html

...Cwmystwyth, once the epicentre for mining in the valley.
http://www.cambrianmines.co.uk/Cwmystwyth.htm

Chapter 21

Tales of Cantre'r Gwaelod feature strongly...
https://www.ancient-origins.net/myths-legends-europe/cantrer-gwaelod-mythical-sunken-kingdom-wales-003023 *also* http://www.bbc.co.uk/legacies/myths_legends/wales/w_mid/article_1.shtml

Acknowledgements

A few passages from this book have appeared online in an earlier form – either on my East of Elveden blog (eastofelveden.wordpress.com), or as a themed post for Burning House Press webzine (burninghousepress.com) courtesy of guest editors C.C. O'Hanlan and Rachael de Moravia.

Thanks, first and foremost, go to Sara Hunt at Saraband, who took an immediate interest in my proposal and had the resolve to see the book through to publication during what was a very difficult time for the publishing industry. My gratitude also goes to Craig Hillsley, who took this on at short notice and edited so scrupulously and efficiently in equally difficult circumstances.

I owe much to the following fellow writers and bloggers, who gave encouragement along the way: Alex Cochrane, Paul Dobraszczyk, Murdo Eason, Anne Guy, Paul Harley, Thom Hickey, Julian Hoffman, Brian Lavelle, Alan Nance, Clare Pooley, Nigel Roberts, Mark Rowe, Hanne Siebers, Duncan J.D. Smith and Klausbernd Vollmar.

Thanks, too, go to all those pals in Norwich and beyond who lent an ear while I was trying to make sense of what I was writing. I am also grateful to my Berlin friends, Nicky Gardner and Susanne Kries, who have long supported my work and who gave much valuable advice.

Special thanks go to those friends who provided beds, food and friendship while I was walking the route: Haydn Mathews and his son Jake in Northampton, Tom and Sara Phelan in Redditch, and Chris and Jenny Cordwell in Shropshire. I am also much indebted to Martin Daly and Clare Brennan, who loaned me their East Lothian home as an Arctic-themed writer's refuge during the 'Beast from the East' of 2018.

Finally, and most importantly, I must thank my wife, Jackie, who provided love, lifts and unstinting support, and my mother, Joyce, who filled in some of the memory gaps and set me off on the road in the first instance.

The Author

Laurence Mitchell is a travel writer with a strong interest in walking, wildlife, landscape and local history. As well as a number of travel guidebooks and walking guides he has also written features for magazines like *Geographical*, *Walk* and *Discover Britain*, and is a regular guest writer for the Berlin-based magazine *Hidden Europe*.

The pier, Aberystwyth